War Stories: An Enlisted Marine In Vietnam

By

Stephen G. MacDonald

CARLO
    BEST WISHES.
 I HOPE YOU ENJOY THE BOOK

    Steve MacDonald

War Stories: An Enlisted Marine In Vietnam

By

Stephen G. MacDonald

ISBN-13   978-1466464445

ISBN-10   1466464445

Dedication

To Red.

The world would have been better if he had lived longer.
He gave his life for his country.

Acknowledgments

I'd like to thank my wife Monica for granting me the time to write this. She could see my need to get it all down on paper, and went along with that for all these years, even though some of the early results must have seemed like such a waste of time to her.

I'd also like to thank her for helping me find most of the errors in this book. She found many that I missed. Those that remain I own, because it is my decision that it's time to put it out there. Good enough will just have to do.

I'd also like to thank the contributors to and sponsors of the OpenOffice.org software suite, which I've used for free for several years now. If I'd had to put up the few hundred dollars here and the few hundred dollars there that it would have taken to buy software to prepare my documents for electronic submission, it might have been a showstopper for me.

Preface

This book is narrative non-fiction. It is the best representation of my time in the Marine Corps that I have been able to come up with, but there are limits to memory. Although all the events happened, some of the details such as conversations are not verbatim replicas of the conversations that occurred, but more like guesses at what the conversations were like. I can remember having the conversation, and what it was about, and what it meant to me at the time, but the exact words are gone. Because I've been working on this memoir off and on, mostly off, for over forty years, many of these memories, but not all, were still fresh at the time they were first committed to paper. Those that were two or three decades old when first written down were still documented well before the time when I began to doubt my ability to remember well.

All the names, except my own and my brothers', have been changed so that I can say what I really thought, but please remember that I am expressing my opinion, an assessment based on partial information, and sometimes misinformation.

This is a recounting of my personal experiences, what it was like for me. There is almost no higher level perspective here, because I understood almost nothing of the big picture. I don't know if that is typical for low level grunts, but it's the way it was for me. Still, this book should give you a good idea of what being an enlisted Marine in an infantry battalion at the DMZ during the Vietnam War was like. Those things that seem unbelievable are absolutely true. Where I've had to resort to narrative art has been in dealing with the mundane, not the extraordinary, which is permanently etched in my mind.

The fact that an incident is included here doesn't necessarily mean that I am proud of what I did. The fact that an opinion is included here doesn't necessarily mean that I still hold that opinion. I think my story has the most value if I just tell it as it was.

Please try to ignore any typos, misspellings, grammar errors, misplaced commas, etc. Because this book is being self published, it has not been subjected to the multiple readings by various professional editors that is typical of a book presented by a major publisher. I have rewritten and reread this book many times, and I can no longer see any errors, but I know there are still mistakes here. I hope they will not detract too greatly from your reading experience.

Stephen G. MacDonald, October 2011

War Stories: An Enlisted Marine In Vietnam

Enlistment

It was early November of 1965, and I was a few weeks shy of my nineteenth birthday. I mention my youth so that you won't judge me too harshly when I tell you that I had expected that I could work a full time job all night, attend classes at Tufts all morning and part of the afternoon, spend nearly three hours commuting on public transit between home, job, and school, and still find time to do homework, eat and get enough sleep. It seems like a simple math calculation to see that the hours per day added up to way more than twenty four, but apparently I didn't do the math. Sleep deprived, flunking, defeated, and on the verge of a nervous breakdown, I was walking up the granite steps from the lower campus, "off hill", to the upper campus, "on hill". Between the flights were landings, and embedded there were memorials to the men from Tufts who had fought in every American war since the school was founded. Although my purpose that day should have caused me to pause at those memorials, I walked over them as careless of their meaning as I had on each day since matriculation.

Perhaps because I had just arrived on campus after my night's work, and it was early, or perhaps because the Dean's secretary could see my desperation and decided to squeeze me in before the Dean's first appointment, I got to see him right away. He motioned me to a seat in front of his desk. "What can I do for you Mr. MacDonald?"

"Well, sir, I'm actually here to quit school. Not for good. I just need to take a break for a couple of years."

He paused for a moment. "What will that accomplish?"

"I'm not sure sir, but I'm awfully tired. I have to help support my family because my father can't work and my mother can't stand him, so she moved out of state. So I work all night at Metropolitan State Hospital, and then I come here to school full time, and I'm just so tired that I can't do it any more."

"I see. Why don't you just cut down to part time work?"

"If I do, I can't make enough money to help support my family, because nobody pays part time workers squat. If I cut down to part time school, I'll get drafted."

"But you'll get drafted anyway."

"Yes, sir, but the difference is that if I quit school now, I can work two jobs for a couple of months before they get around to drafting me. Then, just before they would draft me, I can join the Marine Corps, because they'll let me defer active duty for ninety days. My older brother just joined, and they let him wait before starting."

"So your brother's in the Marine Corps?"

"Yes, sir. I've got cousins and uncles who've been Marines too. Plus I'm from Somerville. A lot of people from Somerville join the Marine Corps."

"I see."

"Anyway, I should end up with five or six months to work two jobs and build up a nest egg. That, plus the small amount of money I can send while I'm in the Corps, plus what my brother sends, plus what my mother sends, should be enough to get my father and two younger brothers through until my older brother gets out."

"Sounds like you've thought this out a little bit. I wonder if you could at least wait until the end of the semester before leaving. It seems like such a waste to quit in the middle of a semester. You're already beyond the point where you can get a tuition reimbursement."

"Yes, sir, I know, but I'm mostly on scholarship anyway, so I wouldn't

3

have gotten that much back. I mean I know it would make a lot more sense to stay, but I can't do it. I just feel too awful right now. It's like when your body aches with a bad cold, only I'm not sick, so it's not going to get better in a couple of days. My bones are aching while I sit here talking to you. I'm so tired that most days I can't stay awake in class. One day last week I was sleeping so soundly that the professor had to wake me up, because my snoring was interfering with her lecture. I'm not even going to start the second job until next week, because I can't do it until I rest first. I just need to know if I can come back after I get out. I'll have the GI Bill to help then, so I'll only have to work part time. And if that's too much, I can even slow the pace at school and take an extra year to graduate, because I won't have to worry about the draft anymore."

"Yes, you can come back. Instead of quitting outright, just write me a letter requesting an indefinite leave of absence, effective immediately. I'll grant it. But before you write it, think about this. The Vietnam War is escalating, even as we speak. What if you get sent there? What if you don't come back? What if you come back maimed, or insane."

"I wouldn't mind going there. What an experience. I'll just have to take my chances on coming back in one piece."

"You just can't imagine that you won't come back whole. I'm asking you to try to imagine that, before you make your decision."

"I've already decided. I just can't do this anymore, or I will go crazy. I'm sure of that."

He got up and extended his hand to me. "Good luck, Mr. MacDonald. I hope your plan works for you."

"Thank you, sir."

I was so relieved to have it done that I felt giddy. I took the stairs "off hill" two at a time, racing over the landings and their memorials to the war dead as carelessly as I had on my way up the hill.

My next stop was off campus, across Powder House Boulevard, to grounds that had once housed a Revolutionary War powder house. The Somerville, Massachusetts offices of the draft board were in a squat stone building that was decrepit enough that I mistakenly believed it was the barracks for the soldiers of the original powder house. I felt patriotic as I opened the heavy door to the building, as if registering for the draft somehow connected me with the patriots who had built the powder house to protect the ammunition they used to free themselves from the British. The feeling didn't make sense, because I wouldn't have been there if it weren't for the draft laws, but it's what I felt.

I walked up to the counter and waited until the lady at the first desk looked up from her piles of paperwork. "Can I help you?"

"Yes, I'm here to give up my student deferment."

She moved to a file cabinet to get a form and brought it to the counter. I filled it out and then waited until she looked up from here work again. She read through the form and then stared at me, right in the eyes, perhaps trying to see a lie there. "You put today's date down as the day when you left school."

"Yes, I just quit."

"Do you have any proof that you quit today? Because, you know, you have only ten days to report a change in status to us."

"If you mean like a letter or something, I don't have one. I had a meeting with the dean, and he did say that he would like me to put it in writing, but I haven't done it yet."

"When was the meeting?"

"Just before I came here. You can call up there, right up the hill to the dean's office at Tufts. I mean I didn't have an appointment ahead of time, so maybe I'm not in the appointment book, but it's less than half an hour since I left. The dean is bound to remember."

She looked at me for several seconds, perhaps deciding that my story was too easy to check for it to be a lie, then broke eye contact to reach under the counter for her stamp. She held it over the form then looked at me again. "When was the last time you attended class?"

"Yesterday."

"All right," she stamped the form, and gave me a copy. "You'll be hearing from us."

I was sure she was right about that. In Somerville nineteen year olds without a deferment got drafted quickly.

As I walked out of the draft board office, I didn't feel patriotic any more. The draft board lady had taken that out of me, leaving the fatigue that was always in the background now.

I walked back up the hill to say goodbye to my school friends, who were obviously saddened by my leaving. I tried to lighten the mood, joking that I was just glad that I wasn't Japanese, because if I was, and I quit school, I would probably feel like I should commit suicide. They didn't laugh very hard. I didn't stay very long. Before noontime I was home in bed, sleeping soundly.

About a month later I went for my draft physical (part of the classification process now that I had lost my student deferment) at the old army base in South Boston. The physical was designed to make the best use of the doctor's time, without much concern for the potential draftee's privacy or inhibitions, just more proof that the system had total control over us.

They sent us in groups from station to station where we assumed various states of undress, depending on the test to be performed. For tests like the eye exam we were fully clothed. The group waited outside a dimly lit room while each individual went in and read the eye charts or described the shapes on the color blindness test pictures. For tests like range of motion, we stood barefoot and in our skivvies, all making the prescribed arm and leg movements together. For tests like the check for hemorrhoids, we stood naked in a long line. The doctor ordered us to bend over and spread our cheeks, and then he advanced down the line behind us, examining each anus as we spread our cheeks with our hands. Once he'd checked you, you could let go of your ass, stand up, and put on your skivvies.

At the end of all the testing came the review of the medical history. The doctor went down the form I'd filled out on arrival, and everything was normal until he got to the question about bleeding problems. Although I'd wanted to just check off the "No" answer, the small print about perjury had intimidated me, so I'd left the question unanswered.

When he saw the omission he asked, "Do you have a bleeding disorder?"

I said, "Well, I have slow blood clotting times. My mother calls it hemophilia, but I don't. I've always bruised easily, and once when I was small I had an incident where I bled from my bowel, but they never did figure out why that happened."

"Why does she think you have hemophilia?"

"After the bleeding incident she took me to Children's hospital, but, like I said, they couldn't find anything wrong. So she took me over to Saint Elizabeth's, and they did a lot of clotting time testing there in the hematology lab, over a period of a year. I was in some kind of a study there. One time I remember sitting out in the parking lot eating as many peanut butter sandwiches as I could stomach before going in for a whole afternoon of clotting tests. From all of that, she claims that I have some kind of pseudo-hemophilia, whatever that is. I think I'm fine."

"Is all of this documented?"

"I guess so, although the doctor who did the study has gone to Chicago. I don't know if the records would be with him or at St. Elizabeth's."

The doctor paused for a moment, then said, "OK, let me ask you this. Do you want to go into the service?"

I'm pretty sure that if I'd said that I didn't want to I would have gotten a medical deferment. But I had my plan pretty well fixed in my mind by then, and I didn't want to be a sick person, and I didn't want other people going to Vietnam in my place, and I wanted to know what it was like to go to war. I said, "Yes, I'm going to join the Marine Corps."

"OK, you got it," he said. He put a check mark on "No" for the bleeding question, reviewed the rest of the questions, and told me that I would be classified medically fit for service.

I remember going to see the recruiter at the Marine Corps recruiting station in the basement of the Post Office in Union Square, Somerville, but the only other thing about the enlistment process that I remember is that it took several days longer than I had thought it would, because my name was misspelled on my birth certificate. I had to get several people who had known me for years to sign affidavits saying that I always used the spelling that I had used on my enlistment papers. It's clear to me now that they like to close every possible loophole before you get to boot camp, but at the time I couldn't understand what all the fuss was about.

The swearing in ceremony was at the old Customs House in Boston, near the waterfront. There the group from the Somerville Marine Corps recruiting office joined about fifty people from other recruiting offices, including those from other branches of the service. Even though we were a rag tag group, each in whatever clothes we'd worn to the recruiting offices that day, mostly jeans, the officer who ran the ceremony made it clear to us that we were about to take a solemn oath, and that we should think about the words as we repeated them after him. And so I meant it when I swore to defend the Constitution of the United States of America, and to obey the orders of the President of the United States and our officers. I wondered if it would always be possible to live by that oath.

One night during the time between my enlistment and the start of my active duty, a period during which I was technically in the Marine Corps Reserve, I was riding the trackless trolley to Waverly Center in Belmont, where I was to meet several coworkers to carpool the last few miles to Metropolitan State Hospital in Waltham. I was sitting on the long bench seat at the back of the bus when a drunk got on. He sat down about a third of the way back, and began swearing loudly, with no apparent meaning to his words, just pure obscenity.

The driver yelled back for him to keep it down, but the drunk kept swearing. Finally the driver pulled the trolley over to the curb, came down the aisle, and stood over him. "I'm telling you right now. Any more filthy language and I'm throwing you off the bus."

The drunk shut up, and the trolley driver went back to his seat. As soon as the driver wasn't standing directly over him, the drunk started muttering under his breath, but apparently he was quiet enough to satisfy the driver that the other passengers wouldn't be disturbed.

After a couple of miles, the drunk hauled himself up using the pole beside his seat, and pulled the cord to signal that he wanted to get off at the next stop. He staggered to the front and steadied himself using the fare box, but he never dropped his money in.

The driver passed the stop.

The drunk started yelling, "Hey, that's my stop. Stop the fucking bus."

The driver said, "I'm not stopping this trolley until you put your fare in the box." Then he sped up.

The drunk started another stream of vulgarity.

The driver kept driving.

Finally the drunk let his fare drop into the fare box. "Okay, asshole. There's my money. Now stop the bus."

Maybe it was because the bus was between stops at that moment, or maybe the driver was angry at being call an asshole, but the trackless trolley didn't slow down from its unusually fast pace.

The drunk went crazy, yelling incoherently, not even swearing now, just emitting a loud growl. He stepped past the fare box and grabbed the driver by the throat with both hands, shaking him back and forth. As the driver's head and upper body rocked from side to side, the trolley began swerving from lane to lane, turned by the driver's hands still clutching the steering wheel.

I sat in my seat, looking down the length of the bus, waiting for someone to get up and grab the drunk. No one moved. After several seconds I realized that no one was going to move. It was up to me, the guy at the back of the bus, to get the drunk off the driver at the front of the bus.

I stood up and started down the aisle, but I had taken only two steps when we sideswiped the first of the parked cars that we would demolish. I started to go down, but managed to grab the handhold on one of the empty seats, pulling as hard as I could to keep my face from crashing onto the filthy floor. I hung on, pulling myself up, getting my feet back under me. From there I used my arms to pull myself forward seat by seat, while using my leg strength to counter the sudden lurches that shook the trolley each time we hit another parked car.

When I was about halfway to the driver, the bus turned more toward the center of the street and we stopped hitting cars. The ride got smoother. Fortunately, I didn't let go of the seat handles as I moved quickly toward the front, because there was one more jolt when the trolley came off its wires and lost power. Now we were coasting across the street with no headlights, the only light in the trolley coming from the streetlights outside.

Fortunately there was no oncoming traffic, but straight ahead of us were the gasoline pumps of the Mount Auburn Street Gulf Station. I looked down at the driver, now slumped over the steering wheel, unaware of our direction of travel, limp in the hands of the drunk.

I took the last two steps to get behind the drunk and wrapped my right arm around his neck in a choke hold, with my left hand holding my right and my left forearm pushing in against his back, applying enough pressure that he couldn't move out of my grasp. I almost fell down again, because I was expecting resistance, but instead the drunk let go right away and stepped backwards with me as I pulled him from the driver. His body was relaxed, totally acquiescent. It almost seemed as if he was relieved that someone was stopping him from doing any more damage.

As soon as the drunk let go of the driver's neck, the driver started to revive. Fortunately, even in his groggy state, his instinct was to take his foot off the dead accelerator and move it to the brake pedal. Apparently the brakes weren't electric, because they worked, even with the trolley off the wires. We stopped, straddling the oncoming lanes of Mount Auburn Street, with about 15 feet to spare before we would have demolished the first gasoline pump and saturated the trolley and gas station parking lot with gasoline. The odds that no spark would have ignited us in a ball of flame seemed small.

The driver opened both doors, and all the immobilized passengers found their legs and evacuated. Even the driver got off. I found myself standing in the middle of the aisle of the darkened trolley, my arm still loosely around the drunk's neck. I guided him to the nearest seat, and stood over him until the police arrived and took him into custody. The first police officer to board looked up at me as he leaped up the trolley stairs, and then spotted the drunk where he sat. I'm not sure how he knew who was who, because he never said a word to either of us. Fortunately for me, he guessed right, because the next thing he did was to smack the drunk in the head with a heavy metal flashlight, and drag him off the bus and into the back seat of a squad car, fighting all the way. My guess is that if the cop hadn't hit the drunk, the drunk would have gone quietly.

I got off the bus, gave another police officer my name and took the next trolley to Waverly, late for my carpool, but with a good excuse.

Boot Camp

On March 29, 1966, I began my active duty in the Marine Corps. Several of us took the train from South Station and we picked up other recruits along the way to South Carolina. With layovers and a bus ride at the end, we arrived at the front gate of Parris Island at about 3:00 A.M. on March 31, a typical arrival time for a batch of new recruits. I was awake, excited, and wondering how I would do on Parris Island. I wanted to make PFC at the end of the training, and I thought I had a good chance to do it. Only about ten percent of the recruits in a platoon get promoted, but my brother had given me so much information about what to expect that I thought I had an inside track.

When the bus stopped at the guard shack, a Marine boarded and began screaming instructions. I couldn't see him very well because the bus's interior lights were out as we drove the short distance to the receiving barracks, but I could easily hear him over the bus's diesel. When we arrived, the lights came on and the Marine began moving down the aisle, stopping at each row of seats, yelling at each pair of recruits, first the pair on the left and then the pair on the right.

When he got to me, I wasn't prepared, even though I had just seen him shout obscenities at seven rows of people in front of me. It was different when he leaned down, his face filling my whole field of vision, the bill of his hat less than an inch from the top of my forehead, directing the volume of his scream into my ears. I breathed his breath as he yelled, "Get your slimy maggot ass, and everything you own, off my bus, and put your smelly feet

12

directly on two yellow feet painted on the deck. Now."

I was afraid. It had never occurred to me that I would be, but my shallow breath, pounding heart, and churning bowels could not be denied. It seemed like he really thought I was a maggot, perhaps deserving to be crushed. I reminded myself that he hadn't actually touched anyone in all the rows in front of me, even the few who had managed to actually sleep on the bus ride, and who had woken to particularly caustic doses of obscenity. I screamed, "Yes, sir."

He stepped aside. I sprang out of the seat, and ran down the aisle, filled with dread after only three minutes on Parris Island. What had I gotten myself into?

Once everyone was off the bus, it was driven away, along with the Marine who had boarded at the gate. The receiving drill instructor marched us inside where they had six tables arranged in a U shape, with just enough room between the tables and the walls for us to stand.

The DI moved to the middle of the U, dragging a metal trash can behind him. "OK, ladies, empty your pockets and your ditty bags onto the table. Anything I find on the table could have come from anywhere, maybe from your sorry ass, maybe from the fuckup beside you. Since I don't know where it came from, all I'm going to do is put it in this GI can and take it away.

"Once you leave this room, if we find you with any contraband, we will take it away and we'll take you away – to the brig. Trust me, you don't want to spend time in a Marine Corps brig. I was once a brig guard, but I was too nice, so they made me a DI instead."

A couple of us started to laugh.

The DI stepped in front of one of the other recruits who'd laughed. "Are you laughing at me?"

"No, sir"

"That's good because I didn't say anything funny. So you were just laughing at nothing. Is that right?"

"Yes, sir."

"So what, are you some kind of a crazy fuck? Why are you laughing when there's nothing funny?"

"I don't know, sir."

"You don't know. Do you know how to do a jumping jack?"

"Yes, sir."

"Do jumping jacks. Don't stop until I tell you. You just lost your chance to get rid of contraband. You better not have any."

"Yes, sir." The recruit started doing the calisthenics.

The DI watched the first couple, to make sure he was doing them right, then he began to make his way around the room, removing most of what people were putting on the table and putting it into the GI can.

When he got to me, he returned my comb, wallet and handkerchief, but he picked up my book, "Black Like Me" by John Howard Griffin. "Is this your book, asshole?"

"Yes, sir."

He looked it over, read a couple of the blurbs from the back. Since it wasn't pornographic, I expected him to return it to me, but instead he threw it into the bucket. My shock that he would throw away a good book must have shown on my face, because he stopped going through the rest of my stuff and sneered, "What are you, some kind of college pansy?"

It felt like an accusation. Since when was going to college a bad thing? But I didn't want to make him angry so I played it down. "Yes, sir. I was in my second year when I quit to join the Marine Corps."

"Oh, so you're a fucking quitter."

I wanted to object, but he was right, in a way. I answered, "Yes, sir."

"Well don't think you can just up and quit here, asshole. This island is surrounded by swamps filled with quicksand and hungry alligators. There's only two ways off this island. You can graduate, or you can leave in a body bag. What's it going to be for you?"

"I'm going to graduate, sir"

"I guess we'll see about that," he said, and went back to sorting through people's personal property.

At the end of it he went back to the recruit who was doing jumping jacks. "OK, maggot. Now put your ditty bag on the table and empty your pockets."

The recruit did as he was told and then stood at attention. The DI checked through his stuff, threw a few things out, and returned the rest to the recruit. "I guess this is your lucky day, asshole."

"Yes, sir"

The DI scanned the room and said, "You will exit the door behind me and turn to the right. Down the corridor you will see a line of recruits who arrived before you, and who still have hair on their heads. You will line up behind them and wait your turn for a haircut. This haircut is not optional, and will include the removal of all beards and mustaches. As will be the case for each weekly haircut that you will receive on Parris Island, you will be charged $1.00, which will be deducted from your pay."

I was astonished that they were going to take money back out of the ninety-seven dollars a month that we were to be paid. But when the DI's glance scanned past me, I made no attempt to get his attention in order to register my disapproval.

The DI continued, "Once you have received your haircut, you may choose any empty bed you can find in the rooms beyond the barber shop, and go to sleep. Now, move."

We ran down the corridor and got in line. Every minute or so a recruit would come out of the room, with no hair on his head, and someone else would enter. There were three barbers in the room, each with clippers that were set to zero height so that, after the haircut, no hair was left. Except for people with very dark hair who still showed a five o'clock shadow on the tops of their heads, the best way to guess someone's former hair color was by looking at his eyebrows. Several recruits had blood trickling where the clippers had nicked their scalps.

When my turn came, the clippers lopped off all my hair, and the top of an old scar I'd gotten as a kid when I'd fallen off a fence. Head wounds bleed a lot, and I think I bled almost as much that night as I had when I was originally cut. I was amazed at how much more we all looked alike once they took off our hair.

Once shorn, I entered one of the bunk rooms, which contained a few dozen bare bunk beds, and nothing else. Bare meant no sheets, no blankets, no pillows, and no mattresses, just the frames and metal bed springs. But by now it was 4:30 A.M. and I was tired. I crawled onto the bare springs, sitting up for a few minutes, waiting for my head to stop bleeding. Once I was pretty sure I wouldn't bleed anymore, I laid down. It wasn't exactly comfortable, but it wasn't as bad as I thought it would be. Of course I had the advantage of a heavy coat to lie on, having come from Massachusetts. Some of the more thinly dressed southerners might have felt the metal springs more than I did. I think I actually managed to fall asleep for a few minutes before a new day began.

A drill instructor began rattling his swagger stick in a GI can. "Get up, Get up, Get up. Get your sorry asses out to the parking lot, and get your feet lined up on a pair of yellow feet."

Once we were assembled in the parking lot he yelled, "A-ten-hut. This here is Staff Sergeant Hickox. He's your drill instructor for your eight weeks here on Parris Island." Hickox and the reception DI each took a head count, then Hickox marched us to the mess hall.

When we got to the whitewashed mess hall, we stood in formation until it was our turn. While we waited, Hickox told us how to eat. "OK ladies, this is how you eat on Parris Island. You will enter the chow line from the right. You will take a tray and silverware, and move to the left down the chow line. You will take everything that is put on your tray, whether you like it or not. The Marine Corps knows what you need to eat. You will exit the chow line on the left, make a beverage selection, and proceed to a table with other recruits from your platoon. You will not sit at a table with recruits from any other platoon. You will not talk. You may leave the table only to refill your beverage mug. You will eat all the food on your tray as quickly as you can, and when you are done you will wait for my signal to leave. On my signal you will place your empty tray at the dishwasher and exit, reforming in the exact places where you are standing now. Do you understand?"

"Yes, sir," we yelled in unison.

"I can't hear you."

"Yes, sir," we screamed as loudly as we could.

He marched the platoon to the entrance and then commanded us into the cafeteria one row of the formation at a time.

After breakfast, Hickox marched us back to the barracks where the other DI's were waiting for us. It would take me a few days to peg them, but three of them seemed to fall pretty well into the roles my brother had told me about. Hickox, the senior DI, was a father figure, although with a little too much emphasis on sternness, but still, someone who you could expect to take care of you. Sergeant Brady was a bit softer, almost friendly, but still in authority, sort of like a mother, although I would never have been stupid enough to say such a thing to his face. Sergeant Saunders seemed downright mean, and maybe a little bit crazy, certainly unpredictable. Our fourth DI, Sergeant Phillips, didn't seem to play a single role like the others. I decided that the training was based on three drill instructors, and three roles – that's what they actually had in First and Second Battalion where the barracks were smaller. But with the buildup for the Vietnam war, we had over a hundred recruits per platoon in the larger barracks of Third Battalion, so they needed a fourth person just to keep an eye on us all. Bottom line, sometimes Phillips was fatherly, sometimes motherly, and sometimes unpredictable, whichever seemed appropriate at the time.

The squad bay itself was a long room, with twenty-eight two-tier bunks on each side. In each row the beds were only about three feet apart so that if two recruits were making their beds and needed to pass each other they would both have to turn sideways. Near the head of each bunk was a metal locker, with two compartments, one for each bed, and under the lower rack were two wooden footlockers. The occupant of each bed stowed all his belongings in his compartment of the metal locker and in his footlocker.

Cement columns, the supports for the building, stood near the foot of some of the bunk beds, and between the two rows of columns was open space, except for a chalkboard and a desk at one end. When classes were held in the squad bay - these were usually less formal classes that didn't require any equipment other than the chalkboard - the drill instructor would sit at the desk and the recruits would sit on the cement floor, forming several semi-circles in front of the desk.

Beyond the squad bay on the left was the duty drill instructor's office/bedroom, which he usually referred to as his "house." Opposite the DI's house was the toilet with half a dozen urinals and half a dozen toilet stalls without doors. Ten or twelve sinks with mirrors for shaving filled the area of the room in front of the toilets. A separate shower room off the toilet entrance held eight or ten shower nozzles distributed evenly around the perimeter of the tiled room.

On that first day we needed to learn how to go to the bathroom. Normally you would expect the average eighteen or nineteen year old to know how to go to the bathroom, but there were some special considerations at Parris Island because they didn't allot very much bathroom time in the training. One hundred and ten of us all needed to do our business in just ten or fifteen minutes, depending on the whim of the drill instructor.

To use a urinal, you would unbutton your utility trousers while you waited in line. The person in front of you urinated, flushed, and moved to the right and back. While he was still buttoning up, you would step up on the left, center yourself on the urinal and start doing your business.

To use the commode, it was similar, but with the obvious adjustments. While waiting in line at a stall, you'd unbutton your trousers and pull your trousers and skivvies part way down, all the while trying to look somewhere else than at the person sitting in front of you on the commode. He would prepare his toilet paper while grunting, and as soon as he was finished, he'd wipe himself, flush, and rotate off the seat to your right. He would proceed out of the stall with his pants still down while you rotated onto the still warm seat from the left, while pulling your pants the rest of the way down. While you prepared your toilet paper and did your business, your predecessor would button up and leave while your successor unbuttoned. If you couldn't go within a minute or so, you had to get off the toilet and leave without finishing. Pretty efficient, but not exactly relaxing.

There was no relaxation at Parris Island. I'm not sure if it was because they'd condensed the twelve weeks of training down to eight weeks, in order to build up for Vietnam, or if the pace had always been so unrelenting. For example, even when you had a few minutes between training exercises you didn't just sit around and put your feet up. You would stand at the end of your bunk in the at ease position, which, although easier than being braced at attention, is not exactly a totally relaxed position. In your hand you held up at eye level a little red pocket manual of military facts to be memorized. You were allowed to change hands if the "break" was long enough that your arm got tired. There would be a test.

For those of us who smoked, several times a day they would announce, "The smoking lamp is lit. Smoke 'em if you got 'em." In civilian life, smoking was an activity that I had always associated with relaxation, but at Parris Island, it was just a way of meeting an addictive need. When the announcement came, we smokers would rush out the door, rain or shine, and quickly form a circle around a bucket full of water. We would all light up at once, on command, and proceed to smoke as quickly as we could, because, in about half the time that it takes to smoke a cigarette in civilian life, the command would come to put out the cigarettes. We would immediately file past the bucket and each of us would throw his cigarette into the water, without one last puff, or hesitation of any sort. To do otherwise would cause the withdrawal of your smoking privilege. If too many people hesitated, the whole platoon could loose its smoking privilege.

"Free time" was in the evening, usually between the last class which ended at about 7:00 P.M. and lights out at about 9:00 P.M., but it wasn't free in any real sense. Before you could do anything else, you had to polish your shoes and boots and brass, and then you had to clean your rifle. That done, you could strip down to your skivvies, which also served as your pajamas, wash up for bed, and sit on your wooden footlocker to write letters in whatever time remained, which was usually less than 30 minutes.

I found that it was risky to be one of the first people to break out the letter writing paper, because that usually invited scrutiny from the duty DI. So even if I had everything polished to my own satisfaction, I would continue to shine my equipment until a few of the people who were squared away to the drill instructor's satisfaction started to write their letters.

The only other free time was on Sunday morning, when you had almost two hours to maintain your gear and write letters while people of different religions than yours went to church. Since your gear was essentially unused since the night before, it usually didn't take long to get to the letter writing.

Everyone had a religion. Hickox told us, "There are no atheist Marines, and I know there are no fucking atheist maggots in this platoon. If we had an atheist here, we'd have to come up with some very special duties to keep the slimeball occupied while all you God fearing worms went to church. We've got Protestant services at 0900, Catholic services at 1000, and nondenominational services at 1100. Are there any of you ladies who can't find a religious service to go to this morning?" He scanned the room. No one raised his hand.

The training at Parris Island was a form of brainwashing. The first weeks were devoted to taking away all your individuality, tearing you down, making you unimportant, just a part of the "green machine." The physical transition was quick. By halfway through the first day we had no hair on our head or faces and we wore identical olive green utility uniforms. We had already packaged up and shipped all our civilian clothes and any effects that might have served to individualize us. Except for the names we'd stenciled over the left breast pocket of our uniforms, we looked nearly identical.

The mental transition to being just part of the machine took longer, but it was clearly an objective of the training. One activity that emphasized this was marching in formation. It didn't matter if someone had longer legs or a walking pace that was naturally a bit faster, or a tendency to swing his arms a little more. In formation it only mattered that you could march with the same stride as everyone else, swing your arms to the same height, start on the same foot, and execute the commands at the exact same moment. Marching in formation looked good only if everyone overcame their natural differences and did it in precisely the same way. If one person did it differently, we all marched until there were no differences.

Another technique they used to make us more important as part of a group than as individuals was the method of determining when a group task was completed. For example, they would break up platoon activities like cleaning the barracks into individual activities like sweeping the floor, washing the sinks, etc. The key here was that nobody in the platoon was done until everyone in the platoon was done. If you were the floor sweeper, you weren't done once the floor was swept, unless everything else was done as well. Once the whole barracks was spotless, then each individual was done.

An effect of this was to play off the individual against the group. If the floor sweeper saw the sink washer just standing around, he would be tempted to say something to get the sink washer back to work. The end result was that during work periods you had dozens of bosses making sure you did your work quickly and well, not a pleasant way to work. The pressure was further increased because, if a DI decided that there was an attitude problem in the platoon, a PT party could ensue.

PT is physical training, calisthenics. We had PT classes nearly every day, administered by physical trainers, and the point of the PT classes was to gradually build up our bodies over the course of our time at Parris Island. A PT party was something different. Typically all the DI's were on hand and suddenly Hickox would get himself all worked up, usually, it seemed, over nothing. The tirade would always end with something like, "I can see that this platoon has attitude problems. You maggots just aren't trying to get with the program. If you're not going to care about your work, and give it your best effort, then I'll give you something to care about. Everybody get down and give me two hundred bends and thrusts."

We'd count out the bends and thrusts then he'd say, "Everybody give me two hundred jumping jacks."

We'd do the jumping jacks then he'd say, "Everybody give me two hundred pushups."

We'd all get down on the squad bay floor and try to do two hundred pushups, but nobody could do that many, which was the point. Some recruits could do thirty or forty pushups, and a few could do seventy or eighty, but nobody could do two hundred. If somebody could have done two hundred they would have told us to do four hundred. The point was to cause us the pain of working our muscles beyond their capability. The way to avoid the pain in the future was to always give the appearance of caring and trying your hardest so there wouldn't be another PT party. Study harder, polish brighter, run further, obey more quickly.

One valuable lesson I learned at a PT party came when my muscles were exhausted and I just couldn't grind out another pushup. I saw Hickox coming over to me and I gave it all I had and I got about halfway up, but that was all there was. I couldn't finish the pushup.

Hickox got down on his hands and knees next to me and began yelling in my ear, "Is that all, you fucking maggot. This is what I'm training you for, so you can just quit when you feel like it? You better start doing some more pushups, mother fucker, or we're going into my house to have a little talk."

I said, "Aye Aye, sir," and to my own amazement I started doing more pushups. I had believed that there was nothing left, but a little fear, adrenalin, whatever it was, and I was doing more. The muscles that I thought were done, still had usable energy in them, and I was accessing it to do more pushups. The thought occurred to me then that there really was no upper limit. If I wanted to do more pushups, wanted to do them badly enough, I could do them. Even when Hickox walked away and I ran out of gas again, I still believed that I could do more if I just wanted to badly enough.

Fear was an important tool, necessary to make the recruits go along with the dehumanization. One of our greatest fears was the fear of being sent to STB, the Special Training Battalion, also known as Motivation. This was reserved for people who weren't getting with the program. Either they refused to submit to normal discipline, or they didn't seem to try hard enough, or they didn't seem to take the training seriously. The threat was that you would be sent to Motivation for a week or two, and therefore would miss graduating with the platoon. We were told that if you then joined another platoon part way through its training you would be treated specially for the rest of your time on Parris Island, not a happy thought in a place where all the attention you got was negative and the best way to avoid trouble seemed to be to try to be invisible.

Aside from the delayed graduation threat, Motivation Battalion itself was not a nice place to be. All of the activities were designed to exhaust you, to bring you beyond the breaking point. For example you might go on a fifteen mile run with an overloaded pack on a hot day. You might fill a hole full of dirt by digging another hole, then refill the new hole with the dirt from a third location. You could move a pile of sand from place, to place, to place. You could make little rocks out of big rocks. Bottom line, Motivation was designed to help you get with the program by motivating you to never return to Motivation.

About four weeks into the training several people from our platoon went there for just a day, a Saturday so they wouldn't miss any of the important classes. The threat was that if they didn't get squared away in a single day, they would stay there for a week, or as long as it took, and they would be dropped from the platoon. All four returned to us that Saturday night subdued. Not that we weren't all subdued by that point in the training, grim faced, hunkering down, just trying to make it through. But those four each had a stillness of the body born of muscles too tired for unnecessary movement. Even more frightening, though, was an immobility of the face that prevented any expression from shining through. Days later, even when their muscles had recovered, they remained subdued. Not one of them was sent back to Motivation. Not one of us who saw them when they returned was ever sent to Motivation.

Another fear we had was fear of physical abuse. Although it was illegal in the Marine Corps, our drill instructors both threatened and used corporal punishment to enforce discipline. Because of the official position taken by the Marine Corps, serious physical punishment was usually administered in the DI's house. I never wanted to be invited to the DI's house. Nobody looked happy going into the DI's office, and almost everyone appeared to be in some kind of pain when he came out.

Minor punishment, typically consisting of a single blow, would sometimes be administered in public. My one personal experience with this came one evening during the third week of training while we waited in formation at the mess hall. I swatted and killed a sand flea that was taking a particularly long time to make a meal out of my neck. Sand fleas are numerous in coastal South Carolina in April and May, and can often be seen flying in huge swarms. No formation of recruits has ever been moved or diverted by even a fraction of an inch in order to avoid a sand flea cloud. In spite of their numbers, they are a protected species on Parris Island.

Unfortunately, Sergeant Phillips happened to turn my way at the moment when I murdered the sand flea on my neck. He sauntered over. "MacDonald, did you just kill a sand flea?"

I came to attention when he addressed me. I hesitated for a moment, trying to think of some way out, but there was none. Any kind of flip answer, or indication that I didn't take the situation seriously could only make the retribution worse. Even just a smile could cause the situation to escalate. So would lying. There was only one way to defuse the situation and that was to take my punishment and hope it wasn't so harsh that I couldn't stand it. I answered, "Yes, sir."

"You know that you're not allowed to swat the sand fleas here on Parris Island, right?"

"Yes, sir."

"And we just had a class about avoiding detection yesterday, about how you have to hold perfectly still in order to be invisible to the enemy, didn't we?"

"Yes, sir."

"And they told you that even if a bug was biting you, you would still have to hold still, didn't they?"

"Yes, sir."

As he talked he began to take aim at my stomach, pulling his arm back and then thrusting it forward, stopping with his fist just touching my stomach. I stood perfectly at attention, my arms at my sides, my thumbs at the seams of my utility trousers, my stomach totally unprotected. I didn't even dare tighten my stomach muscles too much, because if he felt me tightening up he might hit me harder. If I tried to block the blow, or to flinch, or to take any action other than total submission, it would only increase the punishment.

"So here we are, just a day later, and you get an opportunity to show you can do it, and instead you give in, just because a sand flea was bothering you. And if this was combat you'd be dead now. And some of these other pussies next to you would probably be dead too."

As I started to answer, "Yes, sir." he let loose with the real punch. I could tell it probably wasn't the hardest punch he could have thrown, that would have been for if I'd tightened up too much, but it was still a pretty good punch. Fortunately he'd measured carefully, and it landed solidly in the central abdominal muscles, not a few inches higher in the solar plexus where the muscles are weaker. I was still able to stand up almost straight and to breath. I forced myself back to attention, even though it hurt.

Then came a further torrent of verbal abuse. "You fucking no balls pussy asshole mother fucker maggot. You can't take a little pain? You'd rather kill a sand flea than save your platoon? Give me two hundred bends and thrusts. Begin."

"Aye aye, sir," I answered, and I began my bends and thrusts, a study in submission and perfect obedience.

I'm not surprised that the recruiting posters don't tell you that being a Marine is all about learning obedience, because that's not a highly prized virtue in our society. Somehow the catch phrase "The few, the proud, the obedient, the Marines" doesn't seem like a strong seller. But to obey orders at all cost is the real bottom line for an enlisted Marine. If you end up with a huge welt on your neck where the sand flea keeps eating, so be it. Just do what you're told.

After fear, the next most powerful weapon they used to break us down was exhaustion. One way they exhausted us was with running. There were rules about not running on the hottest days, and they were carefully observed, at least by our DIs, but that only kept us from running on two particularly hot days. It seemed like they were only observing the letter of the law though, because on the days we did run, the rule seemed to be that we would run until the weakest recruit began to stumble or fell down. It just took a little longer for that to happen on a ninety two degree day, than it would have on a ninety five degree day.

Just in case somebody got the idea that they could end the run early by faking fatigue, Hickox told us, "You will run at double time until I tell you to halt. Any pussy that stops before then better fall down. And any maggot that falls down better end up with his nose caked with dust and blood, because if you have enough energy left to stick your hands out in front of you to break your fall, you should be using it to keep running. I guarantee you that if you fall down and you haven't passed out, I will make your life so miserable that you will look back on the run when you gave up as having been an easy time."

During some of those runs I had to keep reminding myself that the Marine Corps would not let these DIs injure recruits on a regular basis. I just trusted that they knew what they were doing and weren't pushing us too far, even though I felt overheated and exhausted.

Another exhausting exercise we had didn't involve the hot weather at all; it was in the swimming pool. Drown proofing is a technique that every Marine has to learn. It's a way to stay afloat in the water indefinitely, even with no life preserver. They also taught us how to use our clothing to make a temporary floatation aid, but the real meat of the training was the drown proofing which we did in bathing suits. Given that Marines often serve on Navy ships or on amphibious craft in warm water, and could conceivably end up in the water with no life preserver, drown proofing was a potentially life saving skill. Still, until I got the hang of it, the training sessions at the pool were grueling, one more source of total fatigue.

If the key to the PT parties and the long runs was to learn how to push myself harder, the key to drown proofing was to learn to not push at all. At the first class the instructor explained that swimming, or even just treading water, is such an energy intensive activity that even a well conditioned person who needs to do it for an indefinite period of time will eventually get a buildup of lactic acid in the muscles causing cramping, and, eventually, death by drowning. The only way to survive in the water for a period of many hours or even days is to learn how to breathe while expending a minimal amount of energy.

To do this we learned to float face down in the water, totally relaxed, slowly exhaling into the water. Near the end of the exhalation, you give a single breast stroke with both arms and a single scissors kick with both legs, while lifting your head out of the water. Then you take a single quick, deep breath, and gently bring your head back into the water and begin the next slow exhalation. This sounds easy, and it is once you get the hang of it, but because the breathing is not in most people's natural rhythm, we had to learn it. Most people had an experience similar to mine.

I tried the technique for a few minutes, but I didn't seem to be able to get enough breath. I became so short of breath that I needed to gasp for air, and eventually I decided to tread water for a minute to catch my breath. Of course this exertion only increased my need for air so that when I tried the technique again, I felt even more breathless, unable to slow down my breathing enough so that I could stay in the relaxed exhalation part of the cycle for more than a few seconds. I treaded water again, this time for a couple of minutes, until Sergeant Hickox screamed at me to stop. I tried the technique once again, but since I was even more out of breath by then it seemed impossible. I was getting too tired to even tread water effectively, and my head was so low that I was starting to draw small quantities of water into my mouth with each breath, almost to the point where one of my next inhalations would bring water into my lungs. Finally, totally exhausted, I swam over to the side and hung on to the edge of the pool.

When the drown proofing instructor spotted me holding on, he waited about thirty seconds to see if I would let go on my own. When I didn't, he came over and screamed, "Let go of the fucking wall, asshole." Once I let go his manner softened. He was almost nice when he yelled, "Breath slower. Exhale for as long as you can, even to where not much air is coming out anymore." Then he pushed the pool hook, which was supposed to be for pulling people out of the water, into my side and forced me back out to the middle of the pool.

Fortunately the thirty seconds of rest at the rim of the pool had allowed me to get my breath back, at least partially, and I was able to start taking longer breaths, using my muscles less.

Making a point of breathing out longer did seem to help. Somehow, even though I really wanted to breath in more, breathing out longer somehow convinced my panicking brain that I would be breathing in soon, slightly reducing the tremendous desire to breath in, allowing me to hang there in the water for a few extra seconds before doing my stroke and kick. Once or twice during the remainder of the session I felt like I was beginning to get it, but then something would throw my rhythm off and I would start to struggle for air again.

A week later we had our second drown proofing session, and it was still difficult, although this time I was careful not to get myself tired at the start. As soon as I was in the water, I began breathing with the drown proofing technique rather than by treading water. It took a while for the breathing pattern to begin to feel natural, and several times I lost the rhythm and treaded water for a few strokes. But each time I quickly forced myself to stop, relax completely, hang in the water, and exhale fully with my head under water. I tried to breath out a little longer then I wanted to on each cycle, even though my body was telling me to breath in. Each time the rhythm came back after a few cycles and I was able to stop struggling for air. I was getting it.

The following week was the test. We were supposed to stay in the water drown proofing for a full hour, but most of us were out of the pool within twenty minutes. Once they saw that we were able to maintain the rhythm consistently and relax in the water, they passed us on the test, and let us leave the pool. I knew as I pulled myself out of the water that if I could get the rhythm down in pool water, I really could float indefinitely in the greater buoyancy of ocean water.

One of the formal training modules we had was a movie about the partition of Vietnam into North and South in 1954. Even though I recognized it as a propaganda movie that told the story only from the perspective of South Vietnam, I was still affected by its contents. The pictures of some of the million refugees who fled south, many of them Catholics wishing to avoid persecution by the communists, were persuasive. I still remember one scene showing a line of Vietnamese on foot, carrying all their belongings in rickety carts or in massive bundles balanced on sticks on their shoulders, crossing what the movie called the Freedom Bridge at the seventeenth parallel that separated North Vietnam from South Vietnam. These people had a choice to stay in the Communist north or to move south, and the movie showed them enduring great hardship to move south.

Of course this was not surprising to me. Having received a Catholic education for 10 of my K thru 12 years, I had heard many stories of religious persecution against Catholics by Communist regimes. The fact that so many North Vietnamese would flee south to avoid persecution fit well into my understanding of the world. Although I was no longer a Catholic and was attending Catholic services under duress myself - it's ironic that Marines forgo many of their own rights in order to defend the constitutional rights of the nation - I believed that people should have the right to choose their religion and to freely practice their religion of choice without government interference. Many of the Vietnamese who were fleeing south were probably economic refugees, more interested in being able to seek and own capital than in going to church, but it was really the religious argument that persuaded me most. It made Vietnam a holy war.

A few days after the movie, we were having an informal class given by Sergeant Saunders, the crazy DI. I can't remember what the class was about, but at some point he said, "I'm looking for volunteers to go to Vietnam. If you're interested, raise your right hand."

I was a little concerned about the word volunteer, because everyone had always told me 'Don't volunteer for anything', but I wanted to find out what combat was like, and I was afraid if I didn't volunteer that I might not get the chance. I put up my hand, and one other guy did too, but everybody else kept their hands at their sides.

Saunders scanned back and forth across the squad bay, looking for hands. When no hands beyond the two went up, he started yelling, "Two hands. One hundred and ten swinging dicks in this squad bay and I see only two hands to go to Vietnam. What the fuck are the rest of you here for?"

Red faced, with the veins popping in his neck, he started walking around the perimeter of the group, leaning down over the heads of the recruits who sat frozen as he passed behind them screaming into their ears. "So you want to be a Marine. Why do you want to be a Marine? So you can go home and put on dress blues and make Patty Pussy cream for you?"

When he got to the part about Patty he was at the side of the group, next to one of the steel bunk beds. He took three quick steps to move behind the rack, grabbed it by the bottom, and flipped it end over end towards us, sending several recruits scurrying to avoid being hit by the heavy steel bed frame. It was a wonder that they got out of the way in time, since they were

31

all supposed to be facing front. Somebody must have been risking eye contact by looking, and once one started to scramble, they all did.

He continued screaming, even as the bed came crashing down. "Well, you can forget that. When you're in Vietnam, Patty will be putting out for someone else. All you'll have left of Patty will be the perfume on her 'Dear John' letter."

He picked up one of the footlockers that had been under the bed and lifted it over his head. By now nobody was trying to give the appearance of eyes to the front of the room. I thought that he had totally lost it, and I wasn't sure what he would do next. It was clear that he didn't necessarily have our best interest at heart right then. That thought scared me, because the way I often got through the more difficult parts of the training was by reminding myself that it was just training, and that they were making us stronger, and that they wouldn't push us too far because that would get them in trouble. But at that moment I felt like anything could happen, a scary thought.

He heaved the footlocker up in the air, and it came crashing down in the middle of us, but because he'd thrown it up rather than down on us, the guys in the middle had a chance to scramble out of the way. He picked up the other footlocker and threw that too, but it landed on top of one of the mattresses from the bunk, not really that close to anyone. He came charging in through us and jumped up on the first footlocker. "So why do you pussies want to be Marines. You want to tell all your asshole friends how tough you are? You want to go pick fights in bars and scare the shit out of the guy you're fighting when you tell him you're a Marine? It don't work that way. If you get hit beside the head with a beer bottle, you're going down just as fast as anyone else. There's only one thing being a Marine is good for and that's combat with other Marines at your side. If you scumbags don't want combat, you don't want to be a Marine, and if you don't want to be a Marine tell me right now."

He scanned the squad bay. Nobody told him they didn't want to be a

Marine, and that seemed to calm him somewhat. He jumped down off the footlocker and waded through the recruits in the direction of his office. "I'm going into my house now. I'll be back out in five minutes. If you assholes don't have this place ship shape by then, we're going to do us some extra physical training, until your muscles are as limp as your sorry dicks."

That night Sergeant Brady, the mother DI, gave the informal last class of the day, as he often did. He began by running through the chain of command a couple of times with us. Marines are required to know by heart the names and ranks of every person in their chain of command. After he wrote down the names on the black board and ran through them twice, he said, "Notice that the people above the Commandant of the Marine Corps are not Marines. The Commandant takes commands from the Secretary of the Navy, who takes commands from the Secretary of Defense, who takes commands from the President of the United States, the Commander in Chief, who is elected by the people of the United States.

"In other words the Marine Corps is under civilian command, and, when we swear to uphold the Constitution of the United States, we are swearing to submit to civilian authority. We go into combat if and only if the civilians in our chain of command tell us to. They decide when we should fight, we don't. That's important.

"The world is full of assholes and a few of them are running countries. There are a lot of different mechanisms available to our civilian leaders for dealing with other countries whose interest might not align with ours in every way. Some are carrots and some are sticks. Our job as Marines is to be a very big stick. We need to be strong so that our country can be strong, and negotiate from a position of strength. We need to be strong so that the leaders of other countries who are assholes don't think that they can push the United States around, because some of them will take advantage of us or even kill us if it suits them and if they think there will be no consequences.

"Every day we should pray for our leaders, that they will have the wisdom to use our strength wisely, but it's not our job to decide if that prayer has been answered. We have no way to know. Whether a war is fully supported by the civilian population doesn't provide an answer. Marines have died in popular wars and in unpopular wars. Even World War II was an unpopular war until the day the Japanese bombed Pearl Harbor.

"It's not our job to decide where or when. It's our job to be trained and ready and willing when the orders come down from our civilian leaders."

A few days later we had our training in the Code of Conduct. This was a set of guidelines that was developed after the Korean War, so that members of all the armed forces would know what their country expected of them. The bottom line, at least as it was interpreted in our training at Parris Island, was that my life as an individual didn't mean much. For example, if I were confronted by a superior force, even one that was sure to be able to kill me or capture me, I wouldn't be allowed to surrender until I had used up every bit of my ammunition. Of course, if I got killed while firing those last few meaningless rounds at the superior enemy, that was just tough.

In a similar vein, if I were captured and tortured, I wouldn't be allowed to give out any information voluntarily. Now the reality is that if I was being tortured, I would end up giving out information. I know this for sure from when I was a child being beaten with a strap. Always I would tell myself that this time I wasn't going to cry, and each time I would end up crying, and in pretty short order. If the rules are, you will be beaten several strokes beyond the point when you cry, then you will cry. If the rules are you will be tortured until you answer the questions, you will answer the questions. Even the Code of Conduct recognizes that you will eventually answer.

If the enemy had no way to check the information, I might be able to get away with lying for a little while, but I would give out some kind of information. And if the enemy had control of me for long enough to be able to check what I told him against the information other prisoners told him, I would for sure end up giving that enemy true information.

I couldn't understand why our country would expect us to endure either death when the battle could not be won, or unnecessary torture when in the hands of the enemy. It seemed to me that it would make a lot more sense to recognize the situation you were in and respond to it. Wasn't that what I had to do every day at Parris Island, give in to superior force?

Of course I kept this opinion to myself. The training lectures in the Marine Corps were truly lectures. The trainers did not seek the opinion of the recruits.

Classification day, when we took all our written tests to determine our MOS, military occupational specialty, began with a ream of paper work and a brief interview with a clerk who was responsible for seeing that all the documents were completely filled in. When he reviewed my questionnaire he came to the part about a criminal record and asked, "How come did you leave it blank where it asks for your criminal record?"

I wasn't sure if I was supposed to call him sir or not. He wasn't a DI or an officer, just some PFC clerk with a lousy duty station. I decided to play it safe. "I don't have a criminal record, sir."

"What do you mean, you don't have a criminal record? Not even a juvenile record?"

"No, sir. No juvie record either, sir."

"Not just convictions. It's asking for your arrest record."

"I've never been arrested, either adult or juvenile, sir."

"Wow. You are a miss goody two shoes. Take two number two pencils, sharpen them on the way in, and take any empty seat at a long table."

Aside from his sarcasm, he had seemed incredulous. I knew that most of the kids I grew up with had some kind of record, but I just figured that was because a few of the Somerville cops, especially the ones assigned to juvenile affairs, seemed to hate teenagers. It had never occurred to me that having an arrest record could be the norm for Marine recruits. I'd certainly heard stories about recruits who'd been involved in the court system and been given a choice between volunteering for the Marine Corps and going to jail, but who knew how often that actually happened. All I really knew was that the clerk had made me feel like not having a criminal record made me some kind of a freak in the Marine Corps.

One night at one of the informal classes, Sergeant Brady began telling us about combat. "Soon some of you will be going to Vietnam. You'll be Marines then, not maggots like now. You'll be highly trained, in combat with other Marines, men you can depend on. It will be good to know then that you are fighting with the best. If you remember everything that we teach you, it will help to insure your survival, and the survival of the others in your unit.

"But still, because we are so disciplined, Marines are often sent to fight in difficult situations. We've already told you about many of the places where we've fought. In the Pacific, places like Guadalcanal, Tarawa, where the water was red with the blood of Marines, Iwo Jima, Okinawa, the last island before Japan itself, where the resistance was so complete that even now, twenty years later, they occasionally find a Japanese soldier who doesn't know that World War II is over. In Korea, at the frozen Chosin Reservoir, when the hoards of Red Chinese invaded from the north in the dead of winter. In Tripoli when the Barbary pirates wanted to take what wasn't theirs. In a dozen different places in Latin America. The list of places Marines have fought and died began when the United States was founded as a country, and has been growing ever since. Now we can add Vietnam to that list.

"A year from now some of you will be in Vietnam. Some of you will die there, some of you will be wounded. That's a fact. The monsoons are over and Marines are being killed and wounded there nearly every day now."

He scanned the squad bay to see how everyone was taking this. I for one didn't doubt that some of these recruits would die there, but I didn't really see myself as one of the ones who would be killed.

He continued, "I can't promise you that you won't die, or that you won't be wounded, but I promise you this. Once you are a Marine, if you die in combat, you don't have to worry about the enemy finding your dead body and mutilating it. Your head won't be carried around on a stick as a trophy. We'll bring your body back and bury you with full military honors, the respect due to a Marine who has died fighting his country's battles. If you're seriously wounded and can't get back on your own, we won't leave you out there. We'll pull you back and get you evacuated and fixed up. That's how we do things in the Marine Corps."

Since I didn't think I was going to be killed or seriously wounded, I'm not sure why it was such a consolation to know that they would fight for my body, but it was.

One of the things they had to do at Parris Island was to desensitize us to the idea of killing other people. One way they did that was to depersonalize the enemy, always referring to them with derogatory names like gooks or slope heads, much as they dehumanized us by never referring to us as anything human, except when calling us by female names like ladies or pussies.

Another way they got us used to the idea was by incorporating it into the physical training. For example, during the bayonet practice it was common to yell, "Kill. Kill. Kill." as we made thrusts with the bayonets fixed to our rifles. Fortunately, just a few days before the first bayonet practice, I received a letter from my brother, John, that included the advice 'Don't let them make an animal out of you.', so I screamed with the others during those exercises, but I always held something back, never committing myself fully to the idea that killing was desirable.

Another way of desensitizing us to killing was by making it clear that it was a question of self defense, kill or be killed. In bayonet training they did this by pitting two recruits against each other, getting us used to the idea of going for the kill against another human being. Since they couldn't have recruits actually killing each other with bayonets, they used a device called a pugil stick, which was a bar with the length and heft of a rifle, but with both ends covered by foam pads, a smaller piece wrapped around the bayonet end, and a larger piece wrapped around the butt end.

Two recruits would face off in a circle formed by the other recruits, and go at it with the pugil sticks. The tactics were the same as with a real rifle and bayonet where the objective was to either stick the "bayonet" into the other recruit or bludgeon him with the "butt."

When my turn came, they matched me against another recruit about my size, and each of us tied on an exterior groin protector cup that was worn during the matches. We took up our pugil sticks and moved to the center of the circle. When the DI blew his whistle, we began to fight.

It lasted only a few seconds. I ducked a bayonet swipe to my face. This left my opponent with his bayonet off to the side, and I used the opportunity to attempt to stick him in the face with my bayonet end. He recovered enough to force the tip of my pugil stick up past his head with the center of his stick, but that left him with his stick overhead, his body totally exposed. I used a move that they'd taught us that day, where his stick, and all the force he was applying on it to parry my face thrust, became a fulcrum pushing against the bayonet end of my stick. I quickly rotated the butt end of my stick into his groin. He went down on one knee, and I drew back my stick, quickly rotating the bayonet end back, getting ready to smash the butt end into his face as hard as I could. Before I could deliver the killing blow to the already disabled recruit, the DI blew his whistle. The fight was over.

I immediately stepped back. As I watched my opponent fall to his hands and knees, I immediately felt guilty, wondering if he was alright. I remembered the feeling I had as I drew back the pugil stick, to be able to smash his face more powerfully, and I wondered if, in spite of my efforts to distance my mind from the training, I was becoming an animal. In the movies, the good guys never hit a man once he's disabled, and my opponent was definitely disabled, if only temporarily. Either he hadn't put the cup on correctly, or the force of the blow was so great – because of the fulcrum effect, it had the strength of both of us behind it – that it had moved the whole cup, pinching one of his testicles between the edge of the cup and his body. The DI helped him get back to his feet, and made sure that he was going to be OK, then he declared me the winner of the fight.

I think that my aggressiveness in that fight may have been one of the first things that led to my being considered for a promotion to PFC. There were others, one of which occurred the next night.

Each night a list of recruits to be on fire watch was posted. The job was just to walk around the inside of the barracks and make sure that everything was all right while everyone else slept. Although it was called fire watch, I think it was primarily a theft deterrent, since there were no open flames allowed in the barracks, but it was also useful for teaching us things that applied to standing watch in general, rules like "I will quit my post only when properly relieved."

Each watch lasted only an hour, and on the night in question I was fortunate to have the first watch, so my sleep wasn't even going to be interrupted. Just before lights out I put on my cartridge belt and helmet liner, and got my flashlight out of my footlocker. When the lights went out I began to make my rounds. It took a few minutes in the dimness before I could actually see much, but, once I had my night vision, there was enough light coming from the bathroom area and the exit lights to illuminate the squad bay.

The first fifteen minutes or so were uneventful, the one unusual thing being a guy crying himself to sleep, but I chose to ignore that, rather than embarrass the guy by asking what was wrong. Especially since I already knew what was wrong. Parris Island was not a nice place to be.

Then as I neared my own bunk on one of my rounds, I saw movement in the bottom bed two down from mine, a kid named Phillipston. I turned on my flashlight just in time to see him covering himself with his blanket. Instead of wearing only his skivvies to bed, like the rest of us, he had put his utilities back on.

I shone the flashlight on his face and whispered, "Phillipston, what the fuck are you doing?"

He whipped back the covers and got out of bed. He whispered back, "I'm getting the fuck out of here. I just can't take it anymore."

"What are you, crazy? You'll never make it off the island. They already told you about the alligators and quicksand. I think they'll never even find your body, and it won't be because you've left the island."

"Turn off the flashlight. You're ruining my night vision." When I turned it off he repeated, "I just can't take this place anymore."

I said, "Look, you don't have any choice. If you run away, you'll either die or get caught. If they catch you, they'll probably send you to Motivation, or even to the brig. Either way, when you're done, you'll have to come right back here and finish. There's no choice."

"But I just can't do it," he said again.

"Sure you can do it. Look you're half way through, and you're getting in better physical shape every day. Week after next is mess week, no real training there. Then it's the rifle range, most people don't mind that too much, except for the snapping in. Then it's just one more training week and then graduation. You've already made it through the worst of it. You can do it. Just keep trying."

He thought about it for a few seconds, then he said, "OK, I'll hang in. Maybe I can do it." He took off his utilities and got back in bed.

Looking back on it now, I wonder if I did the right thing to talk him into staying. He did make it through to graduation, but I don't know if he made it through the Vietnam War. I truly believed that there was no choice, and, perhaps because of the buildup for the war, that was true at the time. But now I know that, at least in normal times, something like ten to fifteen percent of recruits do not graduate from Parris Island. Still, it wasn't whether he would eventually participate in the war that was his problem that night. It was the difficulty of Parris Island itself that had psyched him out. I helped him over that hurdle, and I know that, if he survived, he was probably a lot better off in his own head for having graduated.

I continued on my rounds. Although all my other fire watches at Parris Island were uneventful, there was a second incident on this same watch. It took about ten minutes for my eyes to get fully acclimated to the darkness again, so it must have been about fifteen minutes later that I noticed Wilson was playing with his bayonet. This is not a euphemism for another activity. He was lying in the top bunk, slowly, gracefully turning his bayonet in front of his eyes while passing it from hand to hand, totally mesmerized by it. He didn't even know that I was watching him. The only other time that I'd seen anyone so enthralled by his own hand motions was when I had worked at the state mental hospital.

I was afraid to confront him, unsure if Parris Island had driven him crazy. Would he attack me if I spoke to him?

I backtracked on my rounds and went to the DI's house. The normal procedure would have been to pound loudly on the door with the flat of my hand, but instead I knocked softly. I was afraid of disturbing Wilson, of triggering him. Sergeant Brady, the nice guy DI, was on duty that night, so maybe there wouldn't be a big deal about knocking rather than pounding. I heard a muffled, "Enter," through the door, and I opened it and stepped inside. It was dark. Brady had been sleeping.

I wanted to report as quickly as possible, so I broke protocol again by not asking permission to speak, but I still used the formal manner required when talking to a drill instructor, except that I talked softly instead of screaming. "Sir, Private Wilson is playing with his bayonet in his bunk, sir."

"Is it in the sheath?"

"Sir, no sir. The bayonet is out of the sheath. I don't know if he's going to kill himself with it or what, sir."

"Alright, MacDonald, continue on your rounds. Do not speak to Wilson when you pass his bunk."

"Aye, Aye, Sir." I did the mandatory about face and left the office. I continued on my rounds, passing silently past Wilson who was still manipulating his bayonet, oblivious to everything else. When I got to Phillipston's bunk I checked to see if he needed a warning that the DI was probably going to be coming into the squad bay, but Phillipston was already asleep. That was fortunate because just then the DI came out of his office. He was wearing his tee shirt, trousers and shoes, but no shirt. It was the only time I ever saw a DI not starched and creased to perfection.

By the time I got to Wilson's bunk, the bayonet was back in its sheath on the cartridge belt at the end of the bunk. Brady was talking to Wilson, but in a voice so low that I couldn't make out the words. The tone was not pleasant.

The next time around, Brady was gone. Wilson saw me and said, "What'd you go and report me to the DI for."

"I saw you with the bayonet, and I didn't know what you were doing. I thought maybe you were going to commit suicide or something."

"Jesus, no. I just like my bayonet, that's all. I hope I'm not in some kind of deep shit now."

"Sorry, man, I wasn't finking on you. I really thought you were gonzo. I thought maybe I was saving your life or something."

His only response was a disgusted, "Shit."

That fourth week was probably the peak of the pressure. The following week was just as difficult, but knowing we had mess duty, which would be a kind of break, coming up for the sixth week made the fifth week go by more easily. I suppose that was the bright side of having to do only eight weeks at Parris Island. Most Marine recruits had to do about a dozen weeks, but, because of the buildup for the Vietnam War, which peaked at Parris Island in March 1966, the month I started there, the training had been compressed into eight. Grueling, yes, but once we got half way there, we were actually most of the way there.

At any other duty station, mess duty is not something to look forward to. It involves doing all the scut work in the mess hall, jobs like serving the food or scrubbing the constantly replenished piles of dirty pots and pans. But at Parris Island, mess week was the best duty a recruit would get. For one thing the regular kitchen personnel just wanted help, and although they didn't lavish kindness upon us at every opportunity, they didn't go out of their way to harass us either.

Another benefit was that we could smoke anytime. We still had to grab a bucket and pretend to be in a circle centered on the bucket, even if only two of us were there, but we could do it anytime we wanted that didn't interfere with the work. It was almost like having a regular job.

The one downside that I encountered was that I got assigned to be a DI waiter, the poor soul who had to serve all the drill instructors their food. Most of the work for a DI waiter wasn't that bad, sweeping and mopping floors, cleaning tables, and making the mess hall presentable. It was only during the meal service itself that the job was awful, because then I had to deal with two tables full of drill instructors.

The key of course was total subservience; the DI is always right, just like everywhere else on Parris Island. By that I don't mean groveling, just instant obedience. Whatever they wanted they could have, and right away. They were on tight schedules. I think they considered the meal as a break period, an opportunity to talk to someone else as a person, not some dumb recruit in need of training. Perhaps they just didn't want to take the time to hassle me right then, being too busy giving each other examples of just how inept a recruit could be. Whatever their reasons, they pretty much left me alone, except for their demands for food or beverage refills.

The one problem I had was near the end of the week, and it was of my own doing. Hickox sat at my table for supper that night, and part way through the meal he said, "Hey, asshole, we need more gravy over here."

I whisked the gravy bowl off the table and hustled to the kitchen and refilled it. I returned to the table and leaned over to place the gravy bowl down, but I had barely straightened up again, when I saw Hickox leap to his feet, just inches from me. He yelled, "What the fuck are you doing, asshole."

I could see that he was angry. I stood at attention because he had addressed me, but I didn't know how to answer him because I didn't know what had happened.

Finally he said, "What do you think that's funny? Get over there." He motioned to an area near the door, apparently not wanting to disturb his friends while he handled this discipline problem. I marched, literally, to the place that he had pointed to and returned to standing at attention.

His face only inches from mine, he yelled, "Look what you did to my trousers."

Still at attention, I allowed my eyes to roll down until I could see a small dark stain about a third of the way down his pant leg. I must have dripped some gravy on him when I brought it to the table. The drill instructors were all meticulous about their uniforms, and I immediately understood why he was so angry. When he had asked if I thought it was funny, he meant that he thought I had done it on purpose. Now I was really scared. I had no idea what he would do next.

Fortunately my fear must have shown on my face, and perhaps it convinced him that it had truly been an accident, because he changed tack, yelling, "You clumsy cock sucker. Who's going to pay to have these cleaned? Speak."

"Sir, the private will pay to have the drill instructor's trousers cleaned, sir."

"That's a gravy stain. What if they can't get it out?"

"Sir, if the trousers can't be cleaned, the private will pay for a new pair of trousers, sir.

"You bet your ass you will. Now get back to work."

"Aye, aye, sir."

I returned to work, and Hickox left to change his trousers. He couldn't be seen wearing trousers in that condition. I think he must have gotten over it after he calmed down, because he never did take the dry cleaning money from my account. Maybe the whole thing had been staged as entertainment for the other drill instructors. I didn't think of it at the time, but later, in Vietnam, I heard two stories of other DI waiters who had spilled gravy on their drill instructor, and it made me wonder if maybe the dark stain I'd seen was really just water, not a wiped off gravy stain. It could also be that it really was gravy, but he let it pass because of the incident at the rifle range.

The week after mess duty we went to the rifle range for a week. This was where we would learn to shoot our M-14 rifles with both speed and accuracy. The secret to being able to do both was a process called snapping in, where I would learn to tightly wrap the rifle sling around my arm in a manner that ensured that I would always be looking down the rifle sights in exactly the same way.

The problem with snapping in is that it involves getting your body into an unnatural pose. You lie on your stomach facing the target with your left side touching the ground and your right side slightly raised. Your right hand grips the rifle stock near the trigger and pulls the rifle butt into your shoulder. You press your cheek bone into your thumb between the two joints. This positions your head exactly in relation to the rear sight. The rifle barrel is resting on your left hand while your upper body weight is resting on your left arm. To do this in a way that doesn't allow the front of the rifle and its sight to shift position in relation to your eye, you need to wrap the sling very tightly around your arm with your elbow nearly centered under your body. This is a position that you can't even get your body into on the first day on the rifle range because it requires that you stretch certain tendons in your left shoulder.

Once you learn to do it though, you can aim at a target, and fire very rapidly at it, because each time the recoil lifts the front of the rifle, and your arm with it, you will immediately fall back into a position very close to where you were just before you fired. A minor adjustment of the front of the rifle and a squeeze of the trigger and the next round goes to nearly the same place that the previous one did. Rapid fire with accuracy.

The second day on the rifle range, I had a very sore left arm. I'd done the stretching aggressively the day before, and my left arm had tightened up overnight. Because of the inflammation, when I started snapping in, I couldn't get my arm under me as far as I had the previous afternoon.

As I was trying to position it, Hickox stood over me and yelled, "Come on you fucking pussy. Get that left arm underneath you more."

I reached down with my right hand and pulled my left elbow under me as far as it would go.

Hickox apparently thought I could go further because he kicked me in the left elbow. Sure enough, it moved to the proper position, but when it did I felt like my left shoulder was tearing apart. Apparently the pain must have shown on my face, because Hickox seemed to examine it closely, perhaps wondering if he had overdone it. I don't think that he had intended to kick me that hard.

I think he might have been caught off guard by the pain he had caused because he said, "That's better." That might not sound like much of an admission of guilt, but a drill instructor never says anything civil to a recruit. A drill instructor giving a recruit an actual complement is unheard of.

For my part, I hadn't been given permission to speak, and so I said nothing. After a few seconds the severity of the pain lessened, and I was able to slowly release my breath, which I had been holding to keep myself from screaming. My arm was in the proper position for cradling the rifle while supporting my weight, so I didn't have to stretch it any further, and the rest of snapping in actually became easier.

Fortunately no permanent damage was done to my arm when Hickox stretched it in a moment to a place that it wasn't supposed to get to for another whole day. I think my stoicism during the pain, contributed to my making PFC at Parris Island. It might also be why he took it so easy on me on qualification day.

The last day at the rifle range was qualification day. Depending on how well I shot, I would either be unqualified (in which case I would have to requalify later, since every Marine has to have a minimum proficiency with a rifle) or I would be awarded a medal as a marksman, a sharpshooter, or an expert. Since shooting was considered to be one of the most important skills for a Marine, it was impossible to make PFC at Parris Island if you didn't qualify on the rifle range. Also, the better you did, the more it would enhance your chances of promotion.

Although I had never been trained to shoot until that week, I had learned well, and thought that I might shoot expert. I had a chance right up until my scores came back from the last event, the 500 yard slow fire. I was two points shy of an expert score. I was still feeling disappointed when I reported my scores to Hickox. It seems incredible when I look back on it, but I walked up to him and without asking to speak, or even properly addressing him I said, "I only got a 218."

He looked up from his clipboard and said, "What are we friends now. You going to come here and tell me your troubles, like I should give a fuck if you're unhappy? Get over there and give me a hundred jumping jacks."

I snapped out of my despondency immediately and answered in a military

47

fashion, "Aye, aye, sir." Then I went and did my jumping jacks, the whole time wondering why he'd let me off so easy for such a serious breach of protocol. The only thing I could come up with was the incident a few days before when he'd kicked me.

When we returned from the rifle range we went to have our pictures taken for the graduation yearbook. I was surprised to learn that we would not be issued dress blue uniforms. Nearly every recruiting poster I'd ever seen had shown a young marine in dress blues, and I had always just assumed that they were standard issue. On picture day I found out that only Marines who are assigned to duty where the dress blues are a requirement, for example embassy duty or duty in the Marine Corps Band, are issued the uniforms at government cost. Many other Marines will buy the blues at their own cost, but that wasn't an option at Parris Island. For me, it was never an option because I never had enough money to pay for them.

Since the Corps was not going to issue dress blues, the powers that be didn't want to go to the expense of tailoring a set for each recruit, just for the graduation picture. What they did instead was to have several sizes of the dress covers - the white hat with the gleaming eagle, globe, and anchor on the front and the highly polished black leather brim - available, along with several of the dress blue blouses. To make the blouses look like a perfect fit on camera, they were slit up the back, with the two sides held together by several elastic straps that could be adjusted to give a tight fit at the neck and trunk. Since the pictures would be taken from the chest up, there was no need for dress trousers at all. We just had on the blue tunic covering the top of our green utility trousers.

So on picture day I stood in line, and waited my turn to find the best fitting cover and to strap into the dress top. When it was nearly my turn and I saw the two recruits in front of me, with the backs of their blues held together by elastic, I kept thinking that this must be what happens when the new widow brings her deceased husband's suit to the funeral director, but the suit is too small to fit the corpse. I felt ripped off.

The last week at Parris Island we were scheduled for a field trip to learn how to use all the equipment we would need for living outdoors. The first two days we lived in the barracks while learning field related skills like how to put together a full field pack, how to assemble the pup tent from two shelter halves, and how to cook field rations. On the third day we would march to the field with all our gear and stay overnight.

We were cleaning the barracks, getting it ready for our departure to the field, and at the same time we were preparing our field packs for the trip. I finished my cleaning assignment, sweeping the barracks floor, and then I assembled my pack in the exact way that they had taught us. Just as I was finishing, Stanski, who was having trouble making his pack look right, asked me for help. His main problem was that he hadn't rolled his shelter half properly, so it didn't fold neatly around the pack. It looked sloppy.

I got down on my hand and knees and began showing him how to pack it properly, using the weight of my upper body to make a tight, even roll, when Paulson, the platoon guide, the lead recruit for the whole platoon, came over. Perhaps he was miffed that Stanski had asked me for help instead of him, or maybe the cleaning was behind in the head. Whatever his reasons, he said, "Hey, MacDonald, what the fuck are you doing? Get in the head and help them clean the showers."

I was angry at his attitude, since I had already finished my own job and, rather than just looking busy pushing the broom around – which surely would have avoided any additional work – I was helping another recruit. I let my holier-than-thou anger get the best of me. Without checking to see who else was around, I looked back over my shoulder at him and said, "Fuck you, Paulson. I'm showing Stanski how to make up his pack."

Rather than the expected response from Paulson, the next thing I heard was Sergeant Brady saying, "MacDonald, get your ass into my house. Now." I knew I was in deep trouble.

Brady preceded me to his office, opened the door and stood there, waiting for me to enter first. Since he owed me no courtesy, I thought maybe he intended to hit me as I passed by. It was all I could do to keep from flinching as I moved within inches of him. I took three steps into the office, then halted and stood at attention.

Brady walked around me and then turned to stand directly in front of me. "What the fuck was that all about? Speak."

"Sir, I was finished with my job sweeping the deck so I made my pack, and then Stanski saw it looked pretty good so he asked me to help with his, so I did, sir."

"I'm talking about with Paulson."

"Sir, as I was helping Stanski, Paulson came over and told me to help in the head, and I told him I was busy helping Stanski, sir."

"I heard 'Fuck you.'"

I was afraid of what was going to happen next, and frustrated that I was being made out the bad guy, especially at a time when I was going out of my way to make myself useful. As I spoke the pitch of my voice rose. "Yes, sir. I was sort of pissed because Paulson sort of implied that I was fucking off. But I wasn't, sir." The last four words barely made it out in a tiny screech.

"Paulson is the platoon guide. That means he has authority over you and every other recruit in the platoon. It doesn't matter what he implies or how you feel about it. He doesn't have to be nice about it. If he says to do something, you will do it.

"When you are given a direct order by anyone in your chain of command, you will obey it, immediately and without question. If you think an order is unlawful, you will still follow that order, and discuss it later with a superior officer."

That last statement bothered me. I remembered from the movie

"Judgment at Nuremberg" that a lot of Nazis had gotten in trouble for blindly following orders. It seemed incredible to me that after what had happened in World War II, the Marine Corps was giving the highest precedence to obedience, but there was no mistaking the message.

"That's the way it has to be. Marines are sent on difficult missions. When you get the order to take the hill, you don't stand around and discuss it. You take the hill. You learn that by cleaning the head when you're told to clean the head, no matter what you think about it. Now get your sorry ass out there and clean the head, like Paulson said to. And when you're done, start doing bends and thrusts, and don't stop until it's time to get into formation to go to the field."

Fortunately the monologue had gone on long enough that I had my voice under control again. I shouted, "Aye, aye, sir," did an about face and left the office. When I got to the head, nobody was there; the cleanup was finished. I went to the front of the squad bay and began counting out my bends and thrusts. Fortunately my pack was already put together for the field march.

We actually marched for the first mile or so. One of the things the DIs emphasized throughout the eight weeks was that the platoon needed to learn to march together as a unit, perfectly aligned in rows and columns, executing the marching orders in synchronization, one more subjugation of the individual to the group.

We had it down pat now, but Hickox wasn't going to pass up this opportunity for extra practice before graduation at the end of the week. Finally, once he was satisfied that our marching would make him look good on graduation day, he ordered us into a single file, and then ordered, "Route step, march." This freed us up to walk at the speed of the platoon, but no longer in step. The file lengthened as we allowed more distance between ourselves until we had a typical combat distance of about fifteen feet between one recruit and the next.

I had just begun to enjoy the walk at what was an easy pace for me when Hickox came up beside me and said, "I heard you fucked up bad today."

I trained my eyes on the back of the head of the man in front of me, wondering how bad this was going to get. I said, "Yes, Sir."

"Sergeant Brady told me about it. Disobeying a direct order." He paused but I knew better than to say anything without first being given permission to speak. Finally he said, "What have you got to say for yourself?"

"Sir, I wasn't intending to disobey an order. I just thought that Paulson didn't understand that I was busy teaching Stanski to make his pack."

"And you thought 'fuck you' was going to explain it to him?"

"No, sir. I was just pissed at his attitude, like I wasn't doing my part or something. I never intended it as a refusal to help clean the head, sir."

"You can't go around telling your superior to go fuck himself just because you're pissed. This puts me in a hard place. Two days ago I put you on the list of recruits I was recommending for PFC. But I'm having a hard time thinking about promoting some maggot who can't even do what he's told.

"Still, if I go back to the Captain and tell him that I want to take your name off the list, he's going to think that I don't know what I'm doing, so your fuck up will become my fuck up.

"So I've decided to give you one more chance. For the rest of the week I'm going to be on you like stink on shit. If I see any sign of disobedience, laziness, arrogance, or anything else that I don't like, I'm taking your name off the list. If you can prove to me that you can do what you're told, immediately and with enthusiasm you might make PFC. And you might not. I'll probably take your name off the list anyway. It just depends on how I feel about it when we get back from the field."

He didn't want a response from me, so he didn't tell me to speak. He just started to walk more slowly, probably waiting for the rest of the platoon to pass, to make sure there were no stragglers.

For a moment I felt actual joy, the best I'd felt since the night I got to

Parris Island. I was swinging my arms and legs with energy, breathing deeply. The weight of the pack pulling my shoulders back only made it easier to gather air into my chest. They had written me up for a promotion when only ten percent of the recruits make PFC at Parris Island. One slot is always reserved for the Platoon Guide, who carries the platoon colors in parade and is the recruit leader of the platoon. One slot is always reserved for the house mouse, who is responsible for keeping the DI's quarters cleaned up, and who is usually a person of short stature – most platoons have plenty of short people to choose from. For our platoon of a hundred and ten, that left just nine PFC slots, and I was one of the nine. I felt honored, to be selected as one of the best at a hard thing.

Then I remembered that, due to my own actions, my name would probably be withdrawn. Suddenly I was plodding along behind the recruit in front of me, struggling not to fall behind. The pack weighed me down and distorted my breathing. I felt a deep sadness that was out of all proportion to the joy I had felt a moment before. It enveloped me physically, making my chest and stomach ache.

Fortunately, by the time we marched to the bivouac area, the physical exercise had taken the edge off my depression. It still encompassed me, but as more of a spiritual gloominess than a physical ache. I was able to attempt perfection for a few days.

I'm not sure how close I came to being a perfect recruit, but on the night before graduation I was one of the eleven who was handed a set of PFC stripes to sew onto his uniform for the graduation parade. I had no idea whether Hickox felt that I deserved the stripe, or if he was just trying to cover up his mistake of nominating me in the first place. That detracted from the pleasure, but at least the days of gloominess ended. I was happy with my success.

On graduation day we took to the parade ground and marched proudly to

"The Stars and Stripes Forever", our rows and columns perfectly aligned. We precisely executed the drill instructors commands, every arm and leg in perfect rhythm with the music and the DI's cadence. It was a happy day. I was relieved to be done with the worst of the training, and thought that it would be easy from then on. To this day, whenever I hear "The Stars and Stripes Forever," I smile and remember how beautiful we looked that day.

I remember nothing else about the graduation ceremony, except that some officer gave a speech where, for the first time, we were called Marines. After eight weeks of being called nothing but nasty names, it sounded good. After the ceremony we were given the rest of the day off, free to roam the base at will in our sparkling new uniforms. It felt like going to heaven after an extended stay in purgatory.

Stateside

The next day they put us on a bus for Camp Geiger in North Carolina, where we would get three weeks of basic infantry training. When the bus pulled in at our new barracks, my brother, John, who was stationed a few miles away at Marine Corps Air Facility, New River, was waiting. They let him talk to me for only a few minutes because, after the long bus ride, they had to take us to chow right away, but it was great to see him. It was so nice to talk to someone from home, and it meant a lot to me that he had taken the time on a Saturday morning to come see me. Although our talk was brief, he had probably been waiting there for hours, since it was impossible to predict the precise time that the bus would arrive.

Those few minutes with my brother made the next few weeks easier to handle. Not that the basic infantry training itself was particularly difficult. Because I was in such good shape after Parris Island, I found the physical part of the training less challenging than what I had gotten used to. It seemed to have been designed more to keep us in shape than to improve our physical fitness.

The skills we had to learn were generally easier to acquire as well. We were basically given the opportunity to use a variety of weapons, so that we would be familiar with all the weapons normally used by infantrymen. Each day we would go to a different firing range and use a different weapon, but we wouldn't be responsible for knowing the weapon inside out. So, for example, one day we fired an M-60 machine gun, but we didn't learn how to break it down completely or clean it. Those skills would be learned later by Marines with an MOS of machine gunner. We just needed to know how to fire it and clear a jam, so that if we ever had to use one in a fire fight, say if the fully trained machine gun team had been killed or wounded, we would be able to do it. It was all in keeping with the Marine Corps philosophy that every Marine is an infantryman at heart.

It was at Camp Geiger that I came to understand the fuller implications of the concept of fire power. When a group of Marines is charged with taking a fortified objective, for example a bunker, it is fire power that makes it possible to do so. The idea is that if you can shoot at the opening of the bunker often enough, the people in the bunker won't be able to shoot back, because they'll be forced to duck down. At Geiger, we learned the teamwork that would make it possible to keep sufficient fire power on an objective, so that a member of the team could approach it with a satchel charge of explosives or a hand grenade. During the training it occurred to me that the enemy within the bunker would be completely helpless, disabled by the withering fire pouring into the opening, until finally someone got close enough to deliver the coup de grace and exploded them into smithereens. The idea of killing men who, however temporarily, were helpless to do harm, was bothersome, but I could see no way around it, because, if you let up for even a few seconds, that would be long enough for them to stick their heads up and start shooting back.

It wasn't the hard lessons about how cruel combat needed to be in order to be successful that made Geiger difficult. The hardest lesson was that my two year enlistment wasn't going to be eight difficult weeks followed by twenty-two months of normalcy. I had thought that Parris Island was the big hurdle, and that life in the Marine Corps would be pretty regular after that. I found out that although Geiger had significant advantages over Parris Island - we could smoke more freely, we could talk pretty much anytime we wanted to, and we could count our free time in hours rather than minutes - we were still not respected. My twenty-four months in the Marine Corps were all going to be unpleasant.

There was less name calling; for example, nobody called you a maggot at Geiger. Instead the trainers called you "Marine", but in the same tone that the Parris Island DI's used when they called you fuckup, or pussy, or asshole. At Geiger I would begin to hate the word Marine, because it was so often used in a demeaning way, or to give an order to do menial tasks, "Marine, sweep the barracks." "Marine, police the lawn for cigarette butts." Marine was what they called you when they couldn't bother to use your proper name, even though it was clearly stenciled above the pocket on your uniform.

It was the way it was said that made it demeaning. The message wasn't supposed to be a request for cooperation in the important task of cleaning up after ourselves, a basic necessity for any group of humans living in close quarters. The message was the imposition of hierarchy, a demand for subordination. The fact that the area got cleaned up was almost secondary.

At Geiger I had my first incidence of food poisoning. We were about halfway through the three weeks of training, and had our evening meal in the mess hall near our barracks. The food tasted normal and, after our evening free time, we went to bed as usual at about 9:30 or 10:00 P.M. I woke up at about 1:30 A.M. with severe intestinal cramps. The toilets were in a building across the road from our barracks. I barely made it to the commode, one of six lined up without partitions between them along one side of the lavatory. When I got there, two of the six toilets were occupied, unusual for that hour of the night. As soon as I had my skivvies down far enough, I sat and gushed a foul, one hundred percent liquid bowel movement. As relieved as I was that I had made it to the toilet in time, the first gush didn't relieve the intestinal cramping. I sat and waited, knowing that there was more to come. Soon all six commodes were in use, and a line was forming at the door. As much as I wanted to accommodate the Marines who were waiting in line, I knew that once I got off the can, it would be a long time before a commode would be available again. Finally, after about fifteen minutes, and several more liquid movements of gradually decreasing volume, the cramps began to subside, and I felt confident that I was done for the night. I wiped and got out of the way as fast as I could. I walked past the line of Marines who were grimacing in pain while they waited, hoping their turns would come in time.

I saw several desperate Marines who couldn't wait, squatting over the drains in the shower area. Two bare bottomed Marines had actually climbed up onto the counter top that held the wash basins, and were squatting over two of the sinks where we shaved. I went to a sink as far from the two as I could get, washed my hands carefully, and left.

Back at the barracks, not a single Marine was left asleep in his rack. The next morning we had a normal training day. There was no time in the accelerated schedule to adjust for the drained state of the men in my platoon.

The other memorable event from the training at Geiger was the day we went to the tear gas chamber. It was a hot day and we ran most of the way there, so by the time we were in formation outside of the gas mask storage building, everyone was sweaty. I think this was intentional and part of the training protocol, so that the tear gas would irritate all our exposed skin, not just our lungs when we breathed it.

Somehow I had the misfortune to be one of the two people chosen to distribute gas masks. I say misfortune, because it was clear by the time that most of the platoon had their masks, that we had a few more Marines than gas masks. We were instructed to distribute all the masks, and that we, and a few unlucky Marines at the end of the line, would be going into the chamber without the benefit of a gas mask. This meant that, even though we would be the last ones in and the first ones out, we would get to breath more than our share of tear gas.

When all the masks were gone, we lined up in single file, ready to jog into the gas chamber, those of us without masks at the back of the line. Just as the front of the line started moving into the chamber, a jeep with several officers in it pulled up. As soon as the trainer saw the officers getting out of the jeep, he came over to the back of the line and told those of us without masks to fall out. We weren't going to be going into the gas chamber. Our misfortune had turned to good fortune.

A few minutes later I saw just how fortunate we were. The door to the gas chamber flew open and the line of Marines came streaming out, gas masks in hand. Their arms were raised over their heads and they were yelling as loud as they could, trying to expel the burning gas from their lungs. Tears were streaming from their eyes and running down their red faces to mix with the snot from their congested noses and the saliva from their screaming mouths.

The officers got back into their jeep and drove away, without having spoken to anyone. Why they had come was anybody's guess, but I couldn't come up with a single explanation that would have been complementary to them.

One testament to how intense was the pain caused by the gas came from a Marine I had met at Parris Island the night before graduation, when those of us who made PFC were gathered at the radio station to make brief statements for distribution to radio stations and newspapers at home. I had gotten to know him a little better at Geiger, where, on several occasions, he had expressed his love of the Marine Corps.

After the gas chamber, at least during the few weeks that I knew him before the Marine Corps sent us on our separate ways, he hated the Corps, and said so several times. Even though he had endured enormous pain during all the training prior to the gas chamber, and come through it all with a PFC stripe and a gung ho attitude, he couldn't get over the fact that the Marine Corps had deliberately caused him the intense pain of exposure to tear gas. In those few minutes in the gas chamber, his attitude had changed completely.

After Geiger I went home on leave for two weeks, and then on to three weeks of field radio operator training at Camp Pendleton, California. From there I flew back east to Camp Lejeune, North Carolina. There the accommodations were nearly the same as they had been in my three previous duty stations. I slept on the bottom half of a metal bunk bed. A wooden footlocker and half of an upright metal locker held all my belongings. I was allowed to keep personal belongings like civilian clothes in my locker, but the locker and footlocker had to be neat and were subject to inspection at anytime. So, in reality, I could have only a few personal items or I would never be able to pass the numerous inspections.

In the middle of the squad bay were three long tables with benches. These were shared by everyone, and used for writing letters home, playing cards, etc. On the first floor was a recreation room with a few chairs, a television, a ping pong table, and a pool table.

The physical training was not demanding, just sufficient to keep us in shape. The work was boring, mostly keeping the barracks clean, doing preventive maintenance on the equipment, and preparing for the numerous inspections. The treatment was better than at my previous duty stations, but with the same emphasis on rank and obedience. Even though many of those with higher rank talked to us in a normal manner, there were others who seemed to feel that respect flowed in only one direction, up the chain of command. Those of lower rank were to be treated with indifference at best, and often with scorn. There was never a question of appealing to the nice guys to control the jerks. They just would have closed ranks and all become jerks. Each week seemed to bring a few situations where the best thing to do was to shut up and do what I was told.

Always in the background were the dual threats of non-judicial punishment and court martial. Non-judicial punishment would result in evening and weekend work of a most unpleasant nature. You could never forget about it because most evenings someone would be spending his "free" time polishing a waste receptacle to a metallic gleam, or giving the head an extra, unnecessary scouring. The alternative, for those who committed major infractions or seemed unrepentant of minor infractions was judicial punishment, court martial. You couldn't forget that either, because every couple of weeks there would be a formation where we would stand and have the infractions and punishments of those who had been recently court martialled read to us. The usual punishment was brig time, loss of rank, and loss of pay. The brig time didn't count against your enlistment time, so, if you didn't get dishonorably discharged too, you still had the remainder of your enlistment to do when you got out of jail. I never heard of anyone who got court martialled and was found innocent of the charges. The judicial process was just a rubber stamp.

Since I was trying to send half my pay home every month, and since my pay as a PFC barely exceeded $100 a month, I could afford to leave the base only every other weekend. But since the "Marine, sweep the floor," stuff didn't end on weekends, there was no question of staying on base during any weekend when I could afford to leave and wasn't on duty. I don't think I could have made it through without those two normal days out of every fourteen.

The trip to Washington, D.C., the swoop, actually lasted about sixty-three hours, from roughly 1600 hours on Friday, when weekend liberty passes were handed out, to 0700 hours on Monday, which was the next roll call. Base security ran a ride sharing service every Friday afternoon. Each Rider would show his liberty pass to the Shore Patrol, and get a number. Drivers would arrive and announce their destination. The riders with the lowest numbers who were interested in going to that destination would fill the car.

Fortunately, the Shore Patrol never bothered to check the length of your

Stephen G. MacDonald

pass, since it was illegal to go as far as D.C. on a two day pass. In order to be available during national emergencies, we were required to stay within a specific radius of the base, the length of the radius depending on the duration of the liberty pass. Still, being an enlisted man in the Marine Corps was a high risk, low pay job that did not enhance your chances with women. D.C. was a preferred liberty port because, in the days before computers, the various government offices there employed such vast numbers of young women that the ratio of women to men offset the bias against the military, and you could actually find a woman who wanted to go out with you. That's why many Marines were willing to go technically AWOL on the weekends. Actually, in the Marine Corps, it wasn't just a technicality. If you were caught in D.C. on a two day pass from Camp LeJeune, you would be prosecuted as Absent Without Leave, so we were always careful to avoid situations where we might have a run in with the Shore Patrol. For me the draw wasn't just any woman. John's fiancé, Kathleen, had introduced me to her friend Joan, and I was happy to make the three hundred fifty mile trip to see her as often as I could.

The seven or eight hour ride was spent cramped shoulder to shoulder in the back seat of a car with two other Marines. Usually all five or six of the Marines in the car would be total strangers. For most of the ride it was too dark to read, and all of us were too fixated on our destination to make any kind of conversation. The highlight of the trip was the fifteen-minute stretch at the first general store after we passed over the North Carolina/Virginia state line. We'd make a pit stop, wolf down some junk food to replace the supper we'd missed, and pile back into the car for the second half of the trip.

Usually sometime between midnight and 1:00 A.M. we would get to D.C. I would ring Joan's doorbell, and she would buzz me in. We would hug as if we'd been separated for years instead of only twelve days. We were so happy to be together that we would talk all night that first night, finally going to bed when the dawn light would begin to show on the edges of the curtains.

But we wouldn't sleep long. Usually by nine or so we were up and about, getting ready to meet John and Kathleen for breakfast. John and I always coordinated our visits to D.C.

All the things we would do on a weekend needed to be inexpensive, because John had the same financial constraints that I did, so breakfast, and all the other meals, were usually either at Joan's place or at Kathleen's. We spent a lot of time hanging around one apartment or the other, just talking and laughing. When we needed to get aired out, the order of the day was free activities like a walk at Rock Creek Park. Sometimes John and I would leave the girls to do their own thing, and we'd take the bus to visit our mother, who lived in D.C. In the evenings we would usually just hang around talking or playing parlor games. Ordinary things, but those weekends were such a treat.

But 8:00 P.M. on Sunday would always come, and John and I would kiss Kathleen and Joan goodbye, and leave to meet our ride at a nearby restaurant. The trip back was relatively pleasant compared to the ride to D.C., because John always rode with some friends from New River, so at least there was a little conversation to pass the time. We also slept on the way back, that being the main sleep any of us would get on Sunday night. They would drop me at the main gate to Camp Lejeune at about 5:00 A.M. on Monday, and continue on to New River. I would get a maximum of one hour of sleep in my rack, and then it was reveille and the beginning of 12 more days in the stateside Marine Corps, another very blue Monday in the green machine.

After only six weeks at Camp Lejeune I received orders, effective in two weeks time, to take three weeks leave and then to proceed to the Staging Battalion at Camp Pendleton, where I would receive my final training before being shipped to WESTPAC for a thirteen month tour of duty. Technically, WESTPAC stood for Western Pacific, but everybody knew that it really meant Vietnam.

That weekend John and I were riding the bus to see our mother. He said, "I wish it was me going instead of you."

I said, "I know you're worried about me, but don't be. I'm happy to be going. I hate the stateside Marine Corps. Everybody says it's better in Vietnam. I feel sorry for you, having to stay here and put up with all their crap. As long as I make it back OK, I'll have had it a lot better than you."

"Yeah, as long as you make it back OK."

"Hey, you work with a lot of guys who've been to Nam and made it back. Why not me? I'm going as a Marine. We know what we're doing."

"You sound like that Parris Island brainwashing really worked on you. Don't forget that the Marines always seem to end up in some pretty bad places."

"Sure, they send us there because we're disciplined, so we can deal with a tough situation. Since I'm going to Vietnam, I'd still rather be a Marine than anything else."

"You got that right. Shit, listen to me. I guess there's not much doubt that we were both brainwashed."

"Brainwashed or not, here's the way I feel about it. I've spent all my life getting ready to do things, year after year of school, just getting ready. Even all the Marine Corps training was just getting ready. Back at Lejeune, all we really do all day is to make sure that we're ready and that the radio equipment is ready. Finally, in going to Vietnam and helping to keep the South Vietnamese people free, I'll be actually doing something. I'm glad I'm going. I can't wait to get there and see what it's like."

"I hear you. Good luck, man."

A couple of weeks later when I would go home on leave, I would be wished good luck many times, usually as I would see each person for the last time before leaving. After the first few times, it began to sober me about the seriousness of going to Vietnam. I began to dislike saying goodbye to people not just for the obvious reason, but because each time somebody said good luck to me, my anxiety ratcheted up a notch. I kept telling people that I was well trained and that I would be okay. As in the conversation with John, I was trying both to sooth them and to convince myself.

Just before I left Lejeune to start my leave, I was told that I had been put in for a promotion to Lance Corporal, but that the paper work hadn't come back yet. They said they would forward it to California when it arrived.

I was pleased. Only six months in the Marine Corps, and I was already a Lance Corporal.

I wanted to spend my last few days of leave with Joan, so I hitchhiked to D.C. because I didn't have the money for bus fare. It was easy to get rides. I just dressed in my uniform, put my sea bag on my shoulder, and took public transit to the Mass. Ave. on-ramp to the Massachusetts Turnpike in Boston. It was illegal to hitchhike on the highway, but the cops didn't bother you if you waited at entrances and tolls, where the traffic was moving slowly. I walked to the bottom of the ramp, stuck out my thumb, and displayed my "D.C." sign. Within a few minutes I got my first ride. The whole way down, I never waited more than a few minutes between lifts. Half the people who picked me up were former Marines, doing their "Semper Fidelis" thing.

Those last few days with Joan were bitter sweet. As much as I enjoyed being with her, knowing that I was going away for so long was making us both sad. I couldn't find anything to say to make her feel better. Somehow the tack that I'd taken with all the others, trying to convince them that I was off to a great adventure, just didn't seem to apply.

It was the same when I went to visit my mother. On the bus ride back to Joan's, I thought about it and realized it had been the same with Vee, a woman at home who had become a mother to me when my own mother left. Clearly the women in my life were not taking the Steve goes to Vietnam thing very well.

On the night before I was due to leave, Joan and I stayed up most of the night, trying to get the most out of the short time left. After breakfast the next morning, I put on my uniform and packed my sea bag, making sure that I had my orders to proceed to Camp Pendleton on top so that I could fly military standby. Then it was time to go. I called a cab, and we went downstairs to wait. Neither of us spoke, the separation already beginning. When the taxi pulled into the curb Joan and I kissed one last time and then I threw my sea bag into the back seat and climbed in after it. I began my adventure, and the people who loved me began their wait.

Staging

When I got to California, I was placed in the Staging Battalion for my final training before going overseas. About halfway through staging they gave us escape and evasion training. In the morning they taught us the rules that apply to prisoners of war during and after an escape from a POW camp and they showed us how to avoid detection in the woods. After a lunch of C-rations, they gathered us together for our final instructions before releasing us into the forest.

The trainer said, "For this exercise, you are presumed to be an escapee from a POW camp. You are unarmed, and have only the clothes on your back. You are located five miles east of your supper, which will be prepared for you at a camp on the beach on the other side of this forest. If you maintain your sense of direction, you will find the camp.

"There are armed hostiles in the woods who will attempt to capture you and return you to the camp as a POW. POWs will be put in a cage at the camp and will be subject to verbal harassment. POWs will not be fed supper.

"Each Marine will be released into the woods alone at five-minute intervals. If you do not get to the camp within four hours of your departure time, you will not get supper. That is more than enough time to move undetected through five miles of woods."

When my turn came I headed off into the woods. It was a sunny day, so it was pretty easy to keep track of which way was west just by keeping the midday sun generally on my left. I couldn't always see the sun through the tree tops so I checked for moss on the north side of trees too, but I didn't feel like I could always rely on this, probably because I was only trying to use it where there wasn't much sun anyway, where it would be least reliable.

Whenever I came to a thinning of the forest or a clearing I rechecked my orientation with the sun. One of the tricks they had taught us was that if you point the hour hand on an analog watch toward the sun, then south will always be about halfway between the sun and twelve o'clock on the watch.

Eventually I came across a trail that seemed to be heading generally west, so I got on it. The trail was wide enough that it was easy to walk without making noise. After a few minutes I began to relax. If this trail kept heading west, it was going to be a piece of cake to get to camp before my four hours were up. Even counting the time I'd already spent bushwhacking, I'd be there in less than two hours.

I began to enjoy the walk. It was a sunny November afternoon in Southern California and the temperature was nearly perfect. To my right I saw an area that had been blackened fairly recently by a small wild fire that must have burned itself out. Maybe a thunder storm had lit it with a lightning strike and immediately doused it with rain. I expected to smell some hint of smokiness from the charred wood, but all I sensed was the fragrance of a nearby stand of pines. As I continued west into woods that hadn't been burned, the only sounds were from my own boots, and the occasional rustle of a small animal disturbed by my passing. What a gorgeous day.

Suddenly, two hostiles stood in the path in front of me. I sensed a motion, and then they were there. I think they must have leapt from behind a boulder that stood beside the trail, but I was paying so little attention to the exercise that I wasn't sure. I was caught totally by surprise.

They started running toward me and one of them yelled, "Halt."

My normal reaction would have been to just give in to authority, but the thought of going without supper, and especially the thought of standing in a cage being harassed by the trainers and by any of my peers who felt like it, energized me. I bolted into the woods on my right, running as fast as I could.

Fortunately there wasn't much underbrush there.

After a few seconds I looked back and saw that they weren't closing any distance on me. I'm not a fast runner, but I had the advantage of not carrying any gear, while each of them was loaded down with a rifle, and canteens of water. But I wasn't getting away from them either. My only hope was that they would tire before I did. I had a little adrenalin kick that they probably weren't feeling, and maybe it would be enough to keep me from exhausting myself before they gave up.

After running for about a minute, I could see that, although there were trees in front of me, I could see through them to a place where there were no trees, and then, further away, I could see trees again. That's when I realized that I was approaching a cliff. Unfortunately, I couldn't tell how high the cliff was. I was running towards it, full tilt, and the hostiles were so close that if I slowed down to assess the situation, they would catch me. I hoped that there would be some way to stop myself at the last minute once I knew how far the drop was. Soon I was three steps from the edge, my last chance to stop, but I still couldn't see the ground beyond the cliff edge. That meant it was a pretty good drop, at least ten or twelve feet, but maybe a lot more.

I was not going to be captured. I ran headlong off the cliff and fell about fifteen or eighteen feet, fortunately into a good sized bush that broke my fall. One fairly large branch broke off and gave me a scrape near my left kidney, bruising my back muscles, but fortunately it did not pierce them. I disentangled myself from the bushes, and looked up at the top of the cliff. The two hostiles stood there, neither of them willing to jump.

I ran into the woods, making a wide circle so that I wouldn't come across the same two men again. I was much more careful during the rest of the exercise, keeping to the forest and away from trails. I made it to the camp in time for supper without seeing anyone else.

I think that running off that cliff may have been the stupidest thing I've done in my life. The potential gain, getting fed and escaping a night of harassment, was so miniscule compared to the injuries I could have suffered, that it made no sense to jump, and yet, in desperation, I did jump.

As I wrote the previous paragraph, the thought occurred to me that if I substituted joining the Marine Corps in a time of war for running off the cliff, and getting the GI Bill for getting fed, the paragraph still sounded true. I was certainly desperate on the day I quit college. But the analogy works only partially because it leaves out so much. I believed, and still believe, that fighting my country's battles is a patriotic duty that should be shared by everyone. I wanted to know what it was like to be in combat, to see if I could do it. I wanted to be a Marine.

Another incident I remember from my time in staging battalion was when I ran into Paulson, my platoon guide from boot camp. I was standing in line outside the sickbay, waiting with the rest of my platoon for what I hoped was my last set of vaccinations.

A Marine walked up to me and said, "Hey, MacDonald, how're you doing?"

I turned around and there was Paulson. We exchanged information about our various duty stations since Parris Island and then I asked, "Are you getting ready to ship out to Vietnam, too?"

"No, I refuse to go over there. They can't make me."

I didn't know what to make of the statement. It just didn't make sense to me. "What do you mean you refuse?"

"They gave me orders to go, and last week I was in staging just like you, getting shots right here, and I just got fed up with the whole idea of going to Vietnam. Some mouthy corpsman started getting in my face. He was a real asshole anyway. I'd had a run in with him the week before too. I just got pissed, and I hauled off and decked the guy. Suckered him. Him and his fucking vaccination gun went down like a ton of bricks with one punch.

"Now I'm on administrative hold. My unit's shipping out next week, but

I'm staying here for my court martial. When it's all over, they'll give me six months in the brig, six months at half pay, and boot me out of the Marine Corps. The old six, six, and a kick."

"Yeah, but they always review those sentences. What if they drop the kick?"

"Then I'll punch somebody else in the face, and do another six months in the brig. Either way I'm not going to Vietnam and get killed. I'll still be out in a year, probably sooner."

"Yeah, but with a dishonorable discharge."

"Yeah, but I'll be alive and in one piece, not some honorable dead motherfucker."

I reached out and shook his hand. "Good luck, man. I hope you make it through. You've got a lot of balls."

I meant it. I had seen a brig rat while I was stationed at Camp Lejeune. He was out on the base, getting something from one of the administrative offices. A beefy looking brig chaser, carrying a loaded .45 caliber pistol in his holster and holding a drawn nightstick in one hand, walked one pace behind the prisoner, who was handcuffed, his head shaved, no rank on his utilities - shades of Parris Island. The brig rat's face had a slackness to it that said that he hadn't used his smile muscles for a long time. His body seemed to droop down from his shoulders, dragging them down in defeat. He was the unhappiest looking man I'd ever seen in my life. As I waited for my vaccinations, I remembered that man's dead eyes, and it occurred to me that Paulson had chosen a very hard road for himself.

One of the last training exercises we had in staging battalion was practice taking a hill. The night before, we set up a perimeter on a nearby knoll. I had watch in the middle of the night, but I fell asleep. Fortunately, I woke up before anyone caught me, but I felt guilty. What if I fell asleep in Vietnam and someone got killed because of it. How could I live with that?

Before dawn, we moved to the bottom of the objective hill and formed a skirmish line. Taking a hill is like taking a bunker, in that you are relying on being able to use enough fire power that the enemy has to keep ducking to avoid being killed. The only way to do this is to have a fairly straight line as you go up the hill. If people fall too far behind as the line advances up the hill, they eventually have Marines in front of them instead of at their sides, so they can't shoot. Available fire power gets reduced. If that happens to enough people, the enemy can stop ducking and begin taking careful aim and shooting.

When we went up that hill, we were told to walk at a fast pace, but not to run. It was a long steep hill. By about halfway up, I was getting tired, but my guilt about falling asleep the night before kept me going. I really wanted to get this exercise right. I did a good job of staying at the same level with the Marines on either side of me, but when I got to the top and turned around, it was clear that our skirmish line was so crooked that we probably would have lost half our fire power. Seeing that crooked, ineffective line of Marines made me worry. If we couldn't even get it right in training, with no real enemy opposing us, what were the odds of surviving if we ever had to take a hill in Vietnam?

In late November my promotion to lance corporal caught up with me. The effective date of the promotion was almost two months earlier, but with my three weeks pre-combat leave and the time it took for staging battalion to get duplicates of the lost paperwork for the promotion, I was almost eight months in the Corps before I put on the rank. Still, the effective date of the promotion was only six months after I joined. That meant I would have a shot at making corporal within a year of joining the Corps, which was excellent time. Before the buildup for the war, getting promoted that quickly wouldn't even have been possible, and, even with the war on, only the most squared away Marines got promoted that fast.

Okinawa

Two days later we took a bus to San Diego and boarded a troop ship to Vietnam. My thirteen months tour of duty in WESTPAC began on the day we sailed out of the harbor.

Although I felt sea sick for most of the two week voyage across the Pacific, and although the accommodations were not luxurious - the racks were three high, and didn't have mattresses on top of the canvas and steel beds - I loved the time on the troop ship.

For one thing, I had lucked out in my work assignment. I was the chaplain's assistant, and the total extent of my duties consisted of assisting at Mass each morning and making one or two announcements over the PA system each day. The rest of the day I was on my own.

So much free time was a luxury. I loved going to the fantail of the ship and watching our wake widen and dissipate and eventually disappear, so that if I looked back far enough I couldn't tell where our ship had parted the ocean. I could do this even at night, because the churning propellers caused algae that lived in the warm waters to give off a phosphorescent glow.

It could be that I had too much free time. On the third day at sea, I wrote Joan a dear Jane letter. This was some kind of a response to my being on the way to Vietnam. Somehow the impending danger caused me to begin some kind of a shutdown of my emotions. Perhaps the constant fear of what lay ahead just left no place for the more normal emotion of love. Whatever the reason, I just no longer felt that I loved her, and I told her so in the letter. As sad as that was, I felt better once I had sent the letter off. It liberated me, giving me the freedom to accept the danger. I felt alone, but, under the circumstances, it was good to be alone.

After two weeks at sea, including several uncomfortable days in a storm, the ship docked at Okinawa. This was where much of the gear that we wouldn't be using, things like winter uniforms, would be offloaded. They had issued each of us an extra sea bag, and given us detailed instructions about which gear was to be stored on Okinawa.

When I went topside after turning in my gear for storage, I thought I heard music, but it didn't seem to be coming from the ship's loud speakers. I looked down over the railing and saw a marching band playing on the dock. Leaning over the rail to listen, I watched the light sparkle on their polished instruments, and I felt honored that they had gone to so much trouble to greet and entertain us, especially since we were just passing through.

A few minutes later I found out that I wasn't just passing through. An announcement came over the PA ordering a few dozen Marines, including me, to report to the dock with all our gear. Within an hour I was boarding a bus for Camp Hansen, a large Marine base in the middle of the island. I wasn't going to Vietnam at all. I was going to be stationed on Okinawa.

It took me a couple of days to get used to the idea, but eventually I realized that I had dodged a bullet. Okinawa was not the stateside Marine Corps. People treated me well as long as I did my work, and I always did my work. This was the best of both worlds. I was being treated like a human being, but nobody was shooting at me. It didn't get any better then this in the Marine Corps.

And then it got even better. Once it was clear that I wasn't going to Vietnam, my emotions returned to normal. I was in love with Joan again. I wrote her a letter explaining everything and she understood. We even started planning for her to take her vacation on Okinawa so that we could see each other in the summer of 1967, rather than waiting for my full thirteen month

WESTPAC tour to finish at the end of the year.

And then it got even better. Several of us got assigned to a month of temporary duty at Kadena Air Base. We were to set up communications for a Marine helicopter unit stationed on the base, but Kadena was an Air Force base. That meant we didn't even have to make our own beds or clean our barracks; the Air Force allowed Okinawan women to come in and do all the cleaning. It only cost us a few dollars a week. All we had to do was our radio work, and when we weren't on watch we were free to do whatever we wanted. We even had a permanent liberty pass so we could leave the base and come back on at any hour. The mess hall was almost always open, and we could eat at any time of the day or night, except for a couple of brief periods each day when it was being cleaned.

And then it got even better. The temporary duty ended, but, because things had gone so smoothly, I was made a corporal, even though I had only five months in grade as a lance corporal. Eleven months after joining the Marine Corps, I was a non-commissioned officer. Even during the buildup for the war, you couldn't make rank any faster than that.

Then the other shoe fell. I was transferred to the radio section of H&S Company of a battalion that had come from Vietnam, were regrouping on Okinawa, and were soon headed back to Vietnam. I hadn't skated combat duty after all.

It took only a few days before I wrote Joan another dear Jane letter. Once again the thoughts of impending combat had caused me to shut down emotionally. Even now, I still feel badly that I jerked her around so much. The only thing I can say in my defense is that I would never have hurt her if I could have avoided it, but that it would have been wrong to string her along if I no longer loved her. The Marine Corps was jerking me around too, and it was the situation that caused my emotions to run hot and cold.

Corporal John Tackett - another arrival to Okinawa from the same troop ship as me, who had also just made corporal - was transferred with me. His nickname, based on word play on his last name, was Sharpie, and it described him well. As we went together through the several days long process of signing out of our old unit and into the new, he was the one who came up with a credible theory as to why I had made corporal so quickly, and why he was being shipped to Vietnam with only four months left to do in the Marine Corps.

Shortly after what was to become our new battalion arrived on Okinawa, nearly all the members of the radio section had been involved in a bar brawl. It took a few weeks for justice to be done, but the end result was that all but one corporal from the radio section was demoted, and the battalion put out a requisition for two field radio operators with the rank of corporal.

Meanwhile our first sergeant on Okinawa heard about the brawl, figured out what was likely to happen, and promoted Sharpie and me, two new guys - just off the boat, as the saying goes - to corporal. When the requisition for two corporals came through, the first sergeant just transferred his two least senior corporals, thus protecting from combat duty all the men who had been with him for a while. A cynical analysis, but it did seem to fit the facts we knew.

Regardless of how it happened, Sharpie and I were going into a tough situation. Most of the men we would be in charge of were already combat veterans, but Sharpie and I were not. Several of the men we would be in charge of were former corporals, the men who used to be in charge and knew how to run things, while Sharpie and I were now in charge, but didn't really have any idea how the radio section of an infantry battalion ran. This was not an ideal situation in an organization as hierarchical as the Marine Corps.

When we arrived at our new unit, the reception we received from the other radio operators was frigid. Essentially, nobody would talk to either Sharpie or me, except when the job required it. Integrating replacement troops into a unit that's been together for a while is always a problem, and maybe that's the main thing that was going on, but I believe that the rank differential exacerbated the situation. The only good thing about it was that Sharpie and I became closer than we had been, because nobody else would talk to either one of us.

Word came out that we had only a couple of weeks left on Okinawa. No one would tell us the exact date that we would be leaving, since that would be a security violation, but the work changed from assembling equipment to packing it up, and the experienced hands knew that meant our days on Okinawa were few. We wouldn't pack equipment if it would need to be unpacked for the next preventive maintenance cycle. The time was getting close.

I got a sudden desire to go into town and find a woman. It may sound funny to people only a few years younger than me, who grew up in the age of birth control, but in February of 1967 I was barely twenty years old and still a virgin. My intention had been to wait until I was married to have sex, but now I couldn't wait. I wasn't sure if I would be alive in a year, and I didn't want to go to my grave having never known a woman.

On payday Sharpie didn't want to go to town, so I left the base alone and went to a night club across the street from the main gate. The club was down a long flight of whitewashed cement stairs, in a large basement that ran the whole length and width of the building. As I descended, the music got louder until, at the entrance at the bottom of the stairs, it was deafening. Inside, every corner of the place was brightly lit, the seats as well as the stage. Because it was payday, there were few empty seats, so they squeezed me onto one end of a large circular booth that was already filled by three Marines and three Okinawan women.

When the band took a break I reached out my hand and introduced myself to the guy next to me. "This is my first time here, and I'm horny as hell. How do you get a girl?"

He shook my hand. "Glad to meet you. All you have to do is, when a hostess comes over to get you a drink, buy her a drink, too. She'll come and sit with you to drink it. They make their money off of tips and the drinks you buy them, because usually they just have the bartender give them tea, even though they've charged you for both drinks. If you're lucky, at the end of the night, the girl will take you home, but that's extra. Some do and some don't, and you have to buy drinks all night to find out."

"What do they charge if they do take you home?"

"It depends. Usually about eight or ten bucks. Be sure to find out ahead of time, or it could cost you twenty."

Just then an Okinawan woman came over. "Hi, I'm Sachiko. Can I get you a drink?"

"I'm Steve. Can I have a scotch and water, please? And can I buy you a drink too?"

"Sure. I'll be right back."

By the time Sachiko came back with the drinks, the band had started up again, and it was too noisy to talk, so we just sipped our drinks and watched the band.

At the next intermission, she went for more drinks. While she was gone, I noticed that two of the women seemed to be vying for the affection of one of the other Marines at the table. The two women spoke with Japanese accents, but I finally figured out that they were interested in the Marine because he was cherry, a fellow virgin. I decided that maybe my sexual status was an advantage in this situation, although I wasn't about to announce it at this table of strangers.

When Sachiko returned we made small talk until the band started up again. They played the last set of the night – the bars all closed at 11:30 because the Marines all had to be back on base by midnight – but, when they began their last song, a beautiful young Okinawan woman came on stage and stripped while dancing to the music. That was in keeping with my mood for the night.

People started to leave as soon as the strip show was over, but I nursed my drink until Sachiko and I were alone at the table. I was as nervous as a boy asking for a prom date when I said, "Sachiko, I'd like to take you home tonight. I'm cherry." I figured I might as well tell her, since if she said yes there'd be no fooling her anyway, and, if she would have said no, maybe she'd say yes instead.

She looked at me carefully for a moment before answering, I think trying to figure out if I was telling her the truth or not. Then she said, "OK, eight dollars for a cherry boy. Let's go." We hustled up the whitewashed stairs to the street.

As soon as we got off the main street, there were no streetlights. Even though the moon was up, it still seemed very dark after the brightness of the club, until my eyes began to adjust. We walked only a couple of blocks into the residential area before she opened a gate on a tall fence. She closed the gate behind us, and we walked a few steps beside the house, when she stopped and whispered, "Wait here."

She was gone for a few minutes while I stood and thought about how dark it was, and how nobody knew where I was, and how, with the high fence, I wasn't visible from the street. Finally she returned, fortunately alone. "Where did you go?"

She giggled a little as she answered, "To the toilet." Then I remembered that many of the houses on Okinawa had outhouses, without running water. Much of the human waste was gathered by trucks and carefully composted and used as fertilizer.

She slid back an opening on the side of the house, and we entered a room. I stood near the entrance while she slid the door back, and then she groped her way to a small lamp. When she lit the lamp I could see that the room was nearly empty, except for the lamp on a small table and two quilts on a mat in the center of the room. The bed.

I took off my Marine Corps issue raincoat and laid it on the floor beside the bed. I went into my wallet to get the money and realized that all I had was a twenty dollar bill. I was afraid that, if I gave her the twenty, I'd never see my twelve dollars back, and I couldn't afford to pay her that much. Even after my promotion to corporal, twenty dollars was still half of a week's pay. While I was in my wallet, I took out a condom.

She looked at it, grabbed it out of my hand, and threw it across the room. She said, "You won't need that," then she turned out the lamp. There was no way I was going to find the safe in the dark, so I told myself it would be alright.

We undressed and got between the quilts. I knew I'd better settle the twenty dollar bill situation beforehand, and I thought I had a good solution. "Sachiko, I just looked in my wallet and all I have is a twenty dollar bill. So what I'll do is to leave you my Marine Corps raincoat. That's worth more than eight dollars, and then tomorrow night, I'll give you the eight, and you can give me back my raincoat." By now I was on top of her, but I didn't really know what to do next.

"No, give me the twenty dollars, and tomorrow I'll give you back the twelve." Perhaps as a way of convincing me to go along, she reached down and guided me into place.

I began to move in her. It felt incredibly warm and slippery, but I needed to make it clear to her that I hadn't agreed to her terms. "No, I'll leave you the coat. I'll be in big trouble on the base if I don't come back and get it. You don't have to worry, you'll get the money."

"No, I want the money tonight, not the coat."

Just as she finished saying that, I climaxed. I guess she hadn't planned on my finishing so soon, and thought she'd have a little more time to bargain. As soon as I stopped moving and she realized what had happened, she said, "I'll take the coat."

So that was my initiation into sex. Not very romantic, but then I guess paid sex usually isn't. Still, it felt like I had set some kind of a record for unromantic that night. The next night I met Sachiko at the bar and redeemed the coat as I'd promised.

A few days later I was taking a shower and decided to check my penis for any sores, just in case. I was surprised and horrified to find that there was a dark red spot on the head. Both in basic training and again at staging battalion they had shown us scary movies about venereal disease, and combined them with scarier lectures about new, incurable strains of VD that were showing up. I didn't know if it was a syphilis sore or a chancre or something incurable, but I was scared. I didn't want either the pain or the embarrassment of some of the treatments they had described to us, but it was clear that I had no choice but to see the doctor about it.

Once everything was packed up and loaded onto trucks, we boarded a troop ship. This was one that was specially designed for amphibious landings. It was built almost like a catamaran with an area in the center that held tracked amphibious armored landing craft. We did a practice amphibious landing on a beach in Okinawa before we left. It was a little close in the AMTRAK once it was packed with Marines, but it made the landing a piece of cake. We got on the AMTRAK in the middle of the ship, rode it through the water up onto the beach, then the armored doors parted at a presumably safe part of the beach and we ran off. We didn't even have to get our feet wet.

Once the ship was a day out of Okinawa, I reported to sick bay. I told the corpsman I had a sore on my penis, and he let me in to see the doctor.

"What's the problem, corporal?"

"Sir, last week I was taking a shower, and I noticed that there's a red spot on my dick."

"OK, drop trou. Let me take a look." He examined my penis, and then asked, "Have you had sex without a condom?"

"Yes, sir, that's why I was checking myself out when I found the spot. I tried to use a safe, but she said I wouldn't need it."

"Oh, and you just believed her. You knew she was pure and truthful because she had white socks on?"

I knew that was supposed to be a joke, because most of the Okinawan women wore white socks, but I wasn't laughing. I just answered, "No, sir."

"Did you experience any kind of pain or a burning sensation during intercourse?"

"No, sir."

"Is this the first time that you've examined your penis so carefully, looking for problems?

"Yes, sir."

"Well, what you have isn't any kind of VD. It looks like a hemangioma, just a bunch of small blood vessels that have always been there, probably since you were born. It's very similar in structure to the port wine birthmark on your face. You just noticed it last week because you happened to check. Since it doesn't cause you any discomfort during intercourse, I'd say just leave it alone."

"Thank you, sir. I'm very glad to hear that."

"I just have one question. You're obviously very relieved that this isn't anything that needs treatment, or that you should worry about. Yet you noticed it last week. Why did you wait so long to come to sick bay?"

"Sir, I was afraid that if it was VD, they'd leave me on Okinawa while they treated it, and I'd miss the chance to go to Vietnam."

"I figured you'd say something like that. Next time use a condom, no matter what she says. And if you think you might have VD, come to sick bay right away. You can end up with a case that's much more difficult to treat if you wait too long."

"Aye, aye, sir. Thank you, sir."

Stephen G. MacDonald

Camp Carroll

After several more days at sea, it was our last night on the ship. Sharpie and I went up on deck to try to see the sunset, but the sky was just a continuous sheet of gray, with no color to it. You couldn't even be sure where the sky ended and the South China Sea began, so we just headed for the fantail instead.

It was hard to concentrate on what Sharpie was saying because I was distracted by my stomach, my usual seasickness compounded by tension due to the ships location, a few hours east of the coast of Vietnam, and headed west. As Sharpie talked on, I pressed my belly against the railing, and got a moment of relief as the vibrations from the ship's engines passed into my gut, but then the nausea returned.

Sharpie said, "I was talking to one of the squids who steers the ship. I guess we won't be going on the AMTRAKS tomorrow because the sea's going to be too rough. They're going to send us in on regular Navy LST landing craft instead."

"Oh, yeah? Do they leave from the middle of the ship too, like the AMTRAKS?"

"No, it's going to be over the side and down the nets."

"Wow, just like on 'Victory at Sea'. When I was a kid I used to watch that show every Sunday with my family. I can't tell you how many times I've seen Marines go down the nets to the strains of orchestral music. I feel sort of like I'm carrying on some kind of tradition or something."

"Yeah, right."

84

"No, really," I said. I was a little put off by Sharpie's attitude, but I wanted him to understand. "I mean I'm sort of from a Marine Corps family. One of my brothers is a Marine. My cousin was in the Marine Corps in the Korean War. One of my great uncles was in the Spanish American War in the Marine Corps. I think he was Admiral Dewey's aide or something. I feel like I'm doing my part being here like this. I wouldn't mind if we got shot at tomorrow, maybe one or two rounds of sniper fire. Enough so we could get a medal for an opposed landing. What do you think?"

Sharpie looked at me closely for a moment before he answered. "What do I think? I think you're crazy."

"No," I said, thinking that Sharpie must have misunderstood. "I don't mean anybody gets hit or anything. I mean like that sniper they were telling us about that couldn't shoot worth a shit. The one that they eventually stopped shooting back at, because they figured out that if they ever killed him, he might be replaced by someone who could shoot."

"I don't want to get shot at, period," Sharpie said. "I don't even want to make the landing tomorrow, and I sure don't want to make an opposed landing."

"What the hell," I said. "It'd be a free medal."

"Steve, you can take your free medal and stick it where the sun don't shine. I'm going to try and get some sleep." He pushed off from the railing and headed for the hatchway without waiting to hear my reply.

"Hey, see you tomorrow," I yelled after him.

I was bothered that Sharpie didn't understand. I couldn't afford to have Sharpie mad at me too. I needed someone to talk to.

After a few more minutes on the fantail, I decided to try to get some rest myself. I hated going to the squad bay because there was no room. The racks were five high, floor to ceiling, each eighteen inches below the one above. In that eighteen inches we had to sleep and stow all our gear. Like everyone else,

I slept with my legs on top of my sea bag, if you can call that sleeping.

When I got to the squad bay, it was in an uproar. Marines were climbing all over the racks, leaping from rack stand to rack stand, chasing each other from side to side and top to bottom of the room, like monkeys in a zoo. It seemed to be some kind of a three dimensional game of tag, but with the tag delivered with a fist, to make it more interesting. It differed from a normal game of tag in another way as well. Once the prey was selected by whoever was it, the object of the game became to chase that one person. All the other would-be prey became spectators for that round, cheering each jump or swerve by the current target and jeering each near miss by the chaser.

The game made me nervous, because I didn't want to go leaping about in front of a lot of strangers. It was a relief to be left out of this game, although it took me a little while to realize that neither Sharpie nor I was going to be included.

As I watched I began to get even more worried about the next day. I could see that the amount of energy going into this game was way out of proportion to the game itself, and it became clear to me that these guys were even more nervous than I was. That was frightening because most of them were returning to Vietnam. They knew what they were going back to. It took a long time after the game wore itself down before I finally got to sleep.

The next day I saw Sharpie for only a minute, because we were going to be in separate parts of the landing. Sharpie was going with some lieutenant in logistics and would remain in Dong Ha for a few days, providing communications, while all the battalion's "you don't carry it on your back" supplies were unloaded. I was going in with the troops and would have a radio, but would provide communications for no one. They weren't about to trust the battalion communications during the landing to a newbie, even a newbie corporal.

My group was ready to go by 10:00, but then we just sat on the deck.

"Hurry up and wait" was the story of our lives as Marines. Nobody talked much. When it got late enough, word began to be passed that we would be eating lunch on the ship. This was always followed by word that we would not be eating on the ship. Finally, word came down that we could eat C-rations for lunch, but we could have no fires to cook. Everybody broke out the stuff that wouldn't be too bad cold, mostly crackers and cheese or cookies. A few really hungry people opened an entree, if they had something good like ham steak or meatballs. Nobody ate ham and lima beans. Very few people liked them, and those that did kept it a secret, because a decent entree could generally be traded for ham and limas plus a premium, say ham and limas plus cookies for meatballs. If anyone had ever admitted to liking ham and limas, and eating them cold would certainly be seen as such an admission, he would have come under considerable pressure to trade all the time, and without receiving a premium. Nobody was that foolish.

Finally about 1:00 word came down to saddle up, and this time it wasn't followed by word to stand down. At 1:25 I was standing at the rail, next to go over. Two landing craft heaved about twenty to twenty-five feet below, depending on whether they were riding on the crest or in the trough of a wave. As I climbed over the rail above my landing craft, I saw that nobody was going down the net into the other boat. A Marine lay unconscious in the bottom, his arms and legs sticking out at unusual angles. At the moment, nobody seemed to be helping him. Maybe they were waiting for the corpsman to get his gear together and go down next.

I decided that I'd better concentrate on what I was doing, if I didn't want to end up the same way. I was surprised at how hard it was to get down the net, how loose the rope ladder felt as I placed each foot or hand on the next lower crosspiece. I was careful to have only one limb at a time not on the rope. The gear on my back made me top heavy, pulling my upper body away from the ship, so when I had to let go with one hand, I gripped especially hard with the other. It was clear from the way my body pulled back that, if I lost my grip, I'd end up hitting the boat head first and backward, probably what had happened to the guy lying in the other boat.

Finally I was just above the highest point that the side of the boat was reaching, as it thrashed against the side of the ship. I'd been trained that it wasn't safe to step on the side of the landing craft, because of the danger of getting your foot caught between the boat and the ship. The correct technique was to jump down into the bottom of the boat. The idea was to time it so that the boat was at the top of its rise, and just starting to fall. Jump too soon and the boat was still rising and you crashed into it. Jump too late and the boat was falling fast and you had to fall a lot further, chasing the boat down, accelerating all the way. I watched the boat rise and fall a couple of times to get a sense of the rhythm. At what looked to be close to the peak I jumped. I got it just right, but, when I hit the bottom of the boat, the bottom of my feet still stung as if someone had taken a stick to them. I was unhurt except for the pain, but that was bad enough to make me wonder what it must be like if the boat did something unexpected, and you hit wrong.

I immediately moved off to the side, so the next Marine could start down the net. Watching the next guy come down, I was reminded of the "Victory at Sea" TV show again. Still, watching it was different from doing it. On TV they'd never shown a shot of an unconscious man in the bottom of the landing craft. I missed the music too.

As soon as everyone was on board and counted, the boat left the side of the ship and headed for the mouth of the Cua Viet River, the only visible break in the perfect sandy beach that stretched in front of us once the landing craft rounded the end of the ship. As we got further from the ship, the bucking caused by the proximity of the two vessels settled to a gentle but nauseating roll as the swells of the South China Sea lifted first one end then the other of the landing craft. I was relieved when we started up the river, which was brown from the spring rains, but nearly flat.

We moved so slowly that the strongest children from the villages we passed could briefly swim beside the boat begging, "Hey, G.I., give food," or "Over here, soldier." Whenever someone would throw a can of C-rations in the water, any nearby swimmers would race for it. If two of them got to the can at the same time, they would fight over it. A few guys threw coins as well, and the children dived and fought for them just as hard as for the food. Apparently American money had value here.

Occasionally I found myself getting engrossed in the swimmers' competition and I would have to consciously draw myself away, to remember that we weren't just floating along on this river. We were making a military landing. Then I would realize that, at the pace we were moving, we were a perfect target for anyone on the shore with a gun, but not a target without its defenses. I was comforted by the quad 50's, four fifty-caliber machine guns that worked together to lay down a deadly base of fire, mounted on the boat. Only a fool would attack the boat with small arms fire. I alternated between wondering if there was anyone that foolish out there, and wondering at the sights on the river. Real sampans, housing real people, floated down the river, or were tied together sharing the limited dock space. These were not in a geography book, but right out there on the water, bobbing up and down, their chimneys smoking. People waved from one of them. I thought, 'This is like being in a foreign land.' I smiled at my inane thought.

Several villages along the river had Buddhist temples with stone stairs that went from the temples right down into the river. One temple was on a high bank, and had about twenty stairs visible above the water. They looked like marble, but maybe that was just the way the sun was shining on the stone. Looking up at it from the boat, I felt the way I had the first time I had looked up the stairs at the Capitol Building in Washington, D.C., seeing a familiar thing in person for the first time. I felt like a tourist, wishing I'd brought my camera so I could take a picture of the graceful curves of the temple roof warding off evil spirits. As cameras all around me clicked away, I wondered what it was that compelled tourists to take snapshots of the things they had seen so many times in pictures shot by professionals.

I saw a boy running behind a water buffalo, and was brought back to reality. I wondered why the boy was running. Was he trying to get away from something that was about to happen? I became conscious again of how slowly the boat moved up the river. I moved a step closer to the quad-50's, being too inexperienced to know that the enemy would try to take them out first. I was reassured when the camera shutters started clicking again, as the Marines around me took pictures of the boy and his water buffalo.

A short time later the boat turned in to the shore, grounded itself at a newly constructed beachhead, and dropped its front to let us off. I stepped onto the soil of Vietnam for the first time. I was counted for the ninth, tenth, and eleventh time that day, as I was placed in several different groups. While I stood around, I heard a couple of the Marines from Dong Ha talking about a company of Marines that had just had the shit kicked out of them. It was springtime, and apparently the NVA, the North Vietnamese Army, was on the move. This made me even more nervous. Finally everyone was happy with the way we were divided up, and we began boarding trucks for Camp Carroll.

We headed west from Dong Ha along Highway 9, which seemed to be mostly dirt road. The rural terrain was largely uninhabited, because a large area south of the DMZ had been evacuated, the residents concentrated in just a few towns to make it easier to defend them. Since this part of Vietnam was a tropical rain forest, the jungle was reclaiming the land.

Ours was the last truck in the group, which made me uncomfortable. I felt isolated whenever we would get to a curve in the road and I couldn't see the other trucks. We didn't follow very closely, partly to let the road dust settle between trucks, and partly to ensure that one land mine would get only one truck.

When we were on an open stretch of road I got the feeling that we were being watched. The trucks beds were uncovered, so that we could get out of them quickly in any direction if we came under fire, but that also meant that we were completely visible to anyone in the woods. I felt like a target again.

I got especially jumpy when we had to cross a stream on a low pontoon bridge. It was next to where the high bridge had been, before it was blown up. If they could blow up a high bridge, they could blow up a low bridge with a truck on it. It felt good to get off the bridge and back up on the road, but then I remembered the possibility of land mines again. Finally I decided that there wasn't much I could do about it anyway, so I might as well try to enjoy the trip until something happened.

A few minutes later the truck pulled through the barbed wire gates of Camp Carroll. As the truck rolled past the artillery and mortar batteries, the huge tents, the Marines going carelessly about their business, I began to feel safe. The landing was over. I would feel safe there for five more days.

On our sixth day in Vietnam, Sharpie and I were digging a zigzag trench. Sharpie had just gotten to Camp Carroll that afternoon, his work in Dong Ha finished a day ahead of schedule. He'd taken a mini-tour of our tent, the two rows of cots sitting up on wooden pallets, each cot holding an air mattress with a poncho liner on top for a blanket, each Marine's helmet, flak jacket, and sea bag stored under his cot. He'd stowed his gear under his own cot, then walked around the outside of the tent, noting that no sandbags surrounded the tent and that the z-trench outside the tent was so shallow that you would need to lie down in it to be protected. Without even sitting down and resting, he asked me to help him work on the trench. He wanted it three and a half to four feet deep, so that we could get our heads below ground level without lying down. That way there would be room in the trench for everyone.

It wasn't bad work. We had a real pick, not just an entrenching tool pick, and we were young. I was twenty; Sharpie was twenty-two. It was early March, and not too hot yet. The soil was mostly clay, but it was still moist enough to be soft. The work went fast, and we could stop and talk if we felt like it.

At the end of the initial burst of work, when I started feeling tired, I stopped and leaned on my shovel. "So what did they have you doing down in Dong Ha?"

Sharpie answered in short snatches, after each time his pick sunk into the ground, while he was rotating it to loosen the soil. "Mostly just moving things from here to there and there to here." A pause as he inhaled and lifted the pick over his head, then thunk as it wedged into the ground. "They did all the communication by phone, so they didn't use us as radio operators at all." Pause, thunk. "We just did bull work. But at least all the radio stuff is here now ..." Pause, thunk. "not buried under a ton of other stuff down at Dong Ha."

I was starting to feel guilty about doing nothing while Sharpie worked, so I began digging again. I could talk as I worked because I didn't hold my breath with each exertion like Sharpie did. "This is the most physical work I've done since I got here. Mostly we've just been standing watches, 6 hours on, 12 hours off. The rest of the time we pretty much do what we want. Read, do laundry, shoot the shit, write letters, sleep, whatever. A couple of times someone's been grabbed for a detail, but I've been lucky so far. I got off watch just before you got here, and I don't have to go on again until midnight."

"Yeah," Sharpie said, "they already told me I was on from 6 to midnight. What do you do anyway?" He stopped and leaned on the pick while I answered.

"Oh it's mostly just monitoring the radios and writing down or relaying messages. We just take care of the operational stuff for the battalion. The forward air control and artillery units are separate. The radio operators from FAC are in the tent next to ours. The artillery radio operators are part of the artillery units and sleep back with them."

Just then, as if responding to its name, one of the eight inch guns that was positioned about a hundred feet behind our tent fired. I flinched at the boom, and then broke up laughing as I saw Sharpie dive to the bottom of the trench.

When Sharpie looked up and saw me still standing, and laughing too, he stood up himself. "What the fuck was that?"

"That was an eight inch gun, you know like they have on battleships. One of the artillery units is a battery of eight inch guns, but it's right here on land, right back there." I pointed toward the puff of blue-gray smoke that was rising above the gun position.

"Jesus," Sharpie started laughing too. "That thing shook the ground. I thought we were getting hit."

"Get ready for more of the same," I said. "They never just fire once." On cue, four more rounds went out, these in rapid succession.

"That was a spotter round, followed by a fire for effect, so someone must have just called in a fire mission," I explained. "The other pattern they seem to use is just four rounds, one after the other. I think those are when they're firing an H and I mission."

"What's an H and I mission?" Sharpie asked.

"Harassment and Interdiction. They don't have a particular target, just an area where the VC might be, and where we're not. So every now and then they fire a few rounds in there, in the hope of hitting something. They do it a few times a night. It really pisses me off when they wake me up shooting at nothing."

"Man, how'd you like to own an ammunition company?" Sharpie said.

"I'd rather own one than work in one," I answered.

"Yeah, really," Sharpie laughed as he started digging again. "So what else do I need to know?"

I took over the pick as I gave him a thumbnail sketch. "Camp Carroll is a fire base, and our battalion is responsible for perimeter defense. Usually one of the line companies takes care of it, but right now they're all out in the field, so Headquarters Company has it. We have three outposts, OP Red, OP

Green, and OP Blue, on the three hills surrounding this one." I pointed to a small hill northeast of the Z trench. "You can see OP Red right over there.

"Besides the OP's they usually have one or two patrols out, and one or two ambushes. You just take in the calls from everyone every half hour, and let the operations officer know if anyone changes position, or if anyone hasn't called in for a while."

"Sounds easy enough," Sharpie said.

"It is, especially after the next piece of information I'm about to give you," I paused for effect, and then laid it on him, "Sitrepalphasierra."

"What's that?" Sharpie couldn't even say it.

"Sitrepalphasierra. On my first night on watch I was on with Harrington. I guess Jackson figured he knew what he was doing, because he'd been in the Nam before. But he'd been in artillery so he only knew part of the story. Anyway, we took over the radios and in a little while people started calling in sitrepalphasierra. It took us a couple of hours to figure out that they were calling in situation reports. We finally figured it out because one guy called in 'sit rep all secure.' Sitrepalphasierra was sit-rep-alpha-sierra, situation report all secure. Fortunately we figured it out and changed the radio logs before anyone saw what we'd been writing down for log entries. Also fortunately, nothing happened that night, because for the first couple of hours we didn't even know we were taking in status reports. If the operations officer had come over and asked us something like 'What's happening on OP Red?' we would have made real fools of ourselves."

"Well," Sharpie said, "At least I'll be on with someone who knows what he's doing, even if it is Jackson."

I understood. I didn't like Jackson very much either. He was the head corporal, and since we didn't have a sergeant in the group, he was the guy who really ran things day to day. He didn't treat any of the new guys very well. He didn't talk to us except to give orders, and all of his orders to new guys seemed to have an implicit I'm-the-boss-and-you-aren't-worth-anything in them.

A few minutes later, I hoisted myself out of the trench. This time I didn't go back to the other end to start another pass. I had been through four times, twice shoveling out the soil Sharpie had loosened and twice loosening soil for Sharpie to shovel out. The trench was just over four feet deep. I leaned on the pick as Sharpie threw out the last few shovels of dirt and then threw the shovel itself out.

Sharpie seemed to have a little trouble getting himself out of the hole. Like many Marines, he was a few inches shorter than average. "There," he grunted, as he finally wriggled his weight up over his hands and lifted himself out, "That's a trench."

"Yeah. I can't wait to use it."

"No, really," Sharpie said. "I'm surprised there isn't more digging going on. If you look around, most of the areas don't have anything better than this hole was when we started. Some have even less. It's sort of surprising because this base camp's been here for a long time."

I hadn't even noticed the holes, having been too busy reading and writing letters, but there had to be a good reason why they weren't in better shape. "Well, maybe the holes were better, but the dirt got washed back into them by the monsoons."

"Maybe," Sharpie answered, "but I doubt it. Besides, the monsoons are over, and Charlie's on the move. That's why all the line companies are out in the field now. If some of these cooks and typists don't get their asses in gear, there's going to be a lot of people hurt."

I still felt safe at Camp Carroll, and believed that Sharpie was being overly dramatic, but I didn't really care, so I changed the subject. "Come on, I'll show you where the showers and mess hall are. After that, it'll be time for you to go on watch."

It was cold at 11:45 when I heard Jackson waking Harrington. Even

Stephen G. MacDonald

though there were three guys asleep in the tent who wouldn't be getting up for watch then, Jackson had turned on the bare bulb in the center of the tent.

I sat up and hung my feet over the side of the cot to one of the pallets it rested on, touching the cold wood with my big toes only, to minimize the heat loss. Normally I liked to lay in bed for a few seconds, but I didn't want to give Jackson an excuse for shaking me. As I reached down for my boots, Jackson yelled over to me, "Come on, MacDonald, get up. It's time for your watch," as if I weren't already sitting up. Of course the guys who were still trying to sleep didn't know I was already up, so they probably thought I was the one being a pain in the ass.

I slipped my feet into the cold leather - I still hadn't been issued a pair of canvas jungle boots - and immediately began to chill as the boots sucked the heat from my feet. Before stooping to lace them, I reached under my cot for my field jacket. The cold had already penetrated through the thin cotton of my jungle utility shirt. Like everyone else there, I wore just the single thin layer of jungle utilities, no skivvies to hold in moisture and cause crotch or arm pit rot. Just then I heard the concussion of what I thought was one of the eight inch guns.

Jackson said, "Is that incoming?" in a normal tone of voice, as if he was asking about the air temperature.

Before I could make a fool of myself by offering my opinion that it was just the eight inch guns, the next round landed and Jackson started yelling, "Incoming, incoming, everybody in the hole."

I reached under the cot for my helmet and put it on my head. I tugged at my flak jacket too, but it was under my sea bag and wouldn't come loose. I thought how stupid it was to not have it ready. It must have been stuck on part of a pallet, a corner or nail or something. Rounds were still coming in. I wanted my flak jacket on me, but I wasn't sure I could free it quickly. I left it and ran down the center aisle of the tent.

When I was at the tent flap I heard Jackson say, "Douse the light. They'll use it to sight on." I turned left at the flap and was about to take another left at the corner of the tent, but before I could gauge the angle or distance to the zigzag trench Sharpie and I had worked on that afternoon, I heard the bulb break as someone slapped it on the way by.

There was no more light. I had lost my night vision to the now defunct bulb, and I could see nothing. I took a few normal steps, then began baby stepping when I thought I was close to the hole. I wanted to be down in the hole, but I wasn't even sure I was heading for it. I felt that the next round was going to land right next to me and tear me apart, me without a flak jacket, but I couldn't find the hole. I couldn't even find the courage to take normal sized steps, for fear of falling into the hole and breaking my leg. I thought I should have been there by now. I must have missed it. I wondered if I should change direction, but I had no way of knowing which way to turn, so I continued in what I thought was a straight line.

Finally I heard Harrington whisper, "It's right in front of you." From below, he must have been able to see me silhouetted against the starlit sky.

I remembered the depth of the hole from the afternoon's digging, and jumped as if I could see the bottom, not wanting to take the time to find the edge with my hands. I landed safely and scuttled past Harrington to the other end of the trench. It was such a relief to be down in the hole. Within the next minute everyone from the tent had made it in.

We huddled there for a few minutes. When there was a lull in the incoming, I stuck my head up and looked around. I heard a lot of firing from the base perimeter and was afraid that we were being overrun. I thought perhaps that the lull in the incoming had been planned to give Charlie time to make a ground attack, and the firing on the lines indicated that this was it. I kept looking all around, but concentrating mostly to the north, where most of the firing seemed to be coming from. I didn't want to get caught ducking when I should be looking.

Jackson yelled at me, "MacDonald, get you're head down."

I yelled back, "What about a ground attack? We won't even see them coming."

"There's no ground attack," Jackson answered.

"Well what's all the shooting on the perimeter about then?" I asked, as I ducked back into the trench.

"That's just the Dual-40's and Quad-50's laying down a base of fire. It's just a precaution, and doesn't even mean they've seen anything. If they were getting hit, there'd be a lot of small arms fire too."

"Okay." I concentrated on the sounds so I'd be able to recognize them next time.

A few minutes later the incoming started again. After a few rounds I heard someone at the other end of the trench say, "Ah shit, it sounds like they're walking them in on us."

I listened and sure enough the rounds were coming regularly, about every eight or ten seconds, and each one was closer than the last, whistle BOOM - 60 yards ... whistle BOOM - 40 yards ... whistle BOOM - 20 yards. This time we were showered with dirt from the blast. This was it. The next one would be right on us. I counted the seconds off to myself. Ten ... nine ... eight ... seven ... I wanted to get out of the hole but there was no place to go. It wasn't safe in there but it would be worse up top in a few seconds. I'd never have time to get away. Six ... five ... four ... three ... anytime now ... two ... let it land in the other end, not this end ... one ... ah shit ... zero ... no whistle. A few more seconds and still no whistle. I was starting to think it wasn't coming. Maybe that mortar crew had used up all their rounds. Maybe they were shooting at something else. Maybe it was still coming, but I didn't think so. Of course, I didn't know very much about it either.

I noticed that my hand was shaking. I rested it against my leg to steady it, so no one would see. I furtively looked over at Smitty, the guy who had come in the trench after me, to see if he'd noticed my trembling. He was the only other guy I could see. Everyone else was around the first corner of the trench, so if Smitty hadn't seen my hand, I'd gotten away with it.

Smitty was looking the other way. Even if he had noticed, maybe he wouldn't say anything. He was one of the few guys I liked. He always treated Sharpie and me well. I respected him too. He was a combat veteran and knew what he was doing. Then I looked down at Smitty's hand. It was shaking as badly as mine had been. I took my hand off my leg and let it shake.

A few minutes later it was clear that we were in another lull. Smitty turned to me and said, "So how's it feel to lose your combat cherry?"

The only thing I could think of to say was, "Good." It was true too. I felt like I had just passed the initiation into an exclusive club, although I didn't think it was over yet. Now when all those World War II veterans and Korean War veterans wanted to tell war stories, I wouldn't have to feel guilty or wonder how you got through something like that. I was making it through OK. Maybe in a few more minutes I was going to be blown to bits, but I was feeling happy now.

That feeling didn't last very long. Someone said, "Shut up everyone. I think I hear someone."

Everyone listened, and sure enough there was a moaning sound. It was coming from the Forward Air Control radio operators' tent, on the other side of our own. It was pretty weak most of the time, probably more of a response to the pain than a cry for help. Twice the wounded Marine screamed out, "Corpsman, my leg."

Someone said, "I think it's Moorehouse."

Knowing the wounded man's name made having to sit in relative safety and listen to his cries for help that much harder for me. Even though I didn't really know Moorehouse, I had met him once or twice and could visualize his features with every yell, but by now rounds were coming in again, and we could do nothing but wait.

Finally another lull came. After about two minutes without an incoming round, and another scream from Moorehouse, I stuck my head up out of the hole. I was trying to decide what were the chances that I could go out and get him before the next barrage. I was at one end of the hole, and probably the closest to him in travel distance, since I'd have to go around our tent to get to the FAC tent. Clearly it was my responsibility to go out and get him.

"MacDonald get your fucking head down, now," Jackson said.

"What about Moorehouse?" I asked.

"You just get your head down. We'll get Moorehouse out when it stops. Nobody leaves this hole until I say so. That's an order."

I pulled my head back into the hole. I remembered being taught at Parris Island that the Marines won't leave you out there alone, but here we were leaving Moorehouse out there, maybe to be hit by another round. I kept thinking about my cousin who had saved a wounded Marine under fire during the Korean War. How could it be right to just crouch here in the relative safety of the trench while Moorehouse bled without first aid a few yards away.

I blamed Jackson for my inaction. The direct order took it out of my hands. Every time Moorehouse cried out I converted my relief at not having to leave the hole and my shame at not going to help into hatred for Jackson. Of course nothing would come of that hatred. In the Marine Corps you often hated and despised your superiors, but you always obeyed them.

Finally there was a long lull. After five full minutes had passed without any incoming, Jackson started giving orders. Two men were sent to get Moorehouse. I was sent to the Battalion Aid Station, the BAS, to get a corpsman. I ran part of the way, but slowed down after I tripped in a shallow hole in the dirt road. I had my night vision now, and there was enough moonlight that I could see pretty well, but not so well that I could run safely. I could walk nearly as fast as I could jog anyway.

The scene at the BAS, one of the few wooden buildings in the camp, was chaotic. Wounded marines were laying on every flat surface, including the bare plywood floor. Except for a narrow pathway to the treatment room in back, all available floor space was occupied. Yet, as soon as I got in the door, a corpsman came over and asked, "What can I do for you?" as if I were the only person there.

"We've got a wounded Marine up by the radio operators' tents," I said.

"Is he hurt bad? What's the matter with him?" The corpsman asked the two questions together, I guess to save time, and let me know the kind of information he needed.

I answered as well as I could, considering that I hadn't waited around while they went for Moorehouse. "I don't know for sure, but I think it's his leg. He yelled that out a couple of times. It must be pretty bad because he couldn't make it over to the hole on his own. I think he's in a lot of pain too. He was screaming and moaning a lot."

"Okay," the corpsman said. He yelled into the back room, "Butler, go with this Marine and see what's wrong with his friend. Bring a stretcher."

I told Butler what I knew as we hurried back to Moorehouse. We had to stop and get down once when an incoming rocket roared by, but otherwise made good time getting back to the tent. When we got there, we found that Moorehouse was laying in the bottom of the Z trench, where they'd put him to protect him from getting hit again.

The corpsman jumped down into the trench and tried to treat Moorehouse, but he didn't have enough room. There was no room to get the stretcher under him either, so the corpsman asked Jackson and Smitty to lift Moorehouse out. They knelt straddling the trench, and reached down and grabbed Moorehouse's arms and legs, but as soon as they tried to lift him, Moorehouse started screaming, "My leg. My leg. Let go my leg. Oh, Jesus, LET GO MY LEG!"

There was a thud as his legs hit the bottom of the trench. Smitty had dropped them both, not knowing which one was hurt. They made two more tries to get him out in the same way, by his arms and legs, but each ended as horribly as the first.

Then the corpsman told Smitty and Jackson to each grab an arm. They began pulling him up by his arms, and, when they had him partway up, the corpsman somehow managed to get his arms under his middle and the three of them lifted him out. Moorehouse screamed the whole time, but the corpsman didn't drop him. I don't know how he was able to hold on through those screams, but he did. Once they had him on level ground they rolled him onto the stretcher.

The corpsman gave Moorehouse a shot, maybe a painkiller or an antibiotic, and began cutting away his torn utility trousers. He put sulfur powder on the dirty wounds, and covered them with field dressings. While he was in the middle of all this, the characteristic whistle warned us that a mortar round was going to land nearby. Everyone got down on the ground or in the hole, except the corpsman, who covered Moorehouse's body with his own.

Once the corpsman had completed his first aid, Smitty and Jackson carried Moorehouse down to the BAS. I went into the tent and dug my flak jacket out from under my sea bag – what a stupid place for it - and then Harrington and I walked to the Battalion Command and Operations Center tent, the COC, to start our watch.

At the COC they wouldn't even allow Harrington or me to man a radio, because we were still taking in an occasional round of incoming, usually a rocket. I thought the main issue was our inexperience, i.e. that they wouldn't risk any lost communications during an attack, but in the future I would learn that it was typical for the radio operators not to switch off in the middle of a battle. Too much context could get lost in the switch, making misunderstandings more likely. Harrington and I ran an occasional errand, but mostly sat around the COC doing nothing. Around 1:00 A.M. I went out to the communication supply tent, about a hundred yards away, to pick up some spare batteries.

Just as I got there, we got a few rounds in, and I had to sit tight for a few minutes before I could bring the batteries back. By then Harrington was gone. One of the rounds had severed the telephone line to OP Red, so they'd sent Harrington up there to provide radio communications. I hung around for the rest of the night, doing nothing, until, at the end of my watch, the dawn light began to leak through the shrapnel holes torn in the tent.

For the next three nights and days I was on six hours on and six hours off watches at the COC, because we were short handed, with three of our radio operators out at the three outposts. When I wasn't on watch, they still wanted the spare radio operators near the COC, at least until things calmed down a little, so on my first morning off I dug myself a little hole about halfway between the COC and the communications supply tent. Since I had used up half of my six hours off time digging and eating breakfast, I was still pretty tired when they came to wake me up for my next watch at noon.

When I got back to my hole at 1800 hours I found out that Phillips had worked on it all afternoon, making it much deeper and adding a few logs and a layer of sandbags on the top. The roof made it substantially safer, and it also made it quite cozy, because it blocked the night air, which, in early March, was usually chilly.

I ate my supper and went back to the hole and wrapped myself up in my snoopy blanket, which is what we called our poncho liners. I was asleep within a minute.

The second night I had to share the hole with Phillips, even though it was really only a one-man hole. It was so narrow that one of us always had to be on his side. The ventilation was so poor that, after an hour of multiple occupancy, the air was dank. It smelled of us and of moist soil. The dirt smell would have been pleasant if a hint of it had wafted up at spring planting time, but when it saturated the air as it did in that hole, it was overpowering.

On the third night I got the hole to myself again, because Phillips schedule and mine were out of sync, and fortunately would overlap only every other night, but by then the air in the hole was almost as dank as when I'd had to share it. I think the entrance opening was just too small to let in enough ventilation.

Fortunately they let us return to the tent for sleeping the next day. By then the whole camp was more secure than it had been on the night of the attack. Everyone was working long hours beyond their regular watches digging holes and filling sandbags. Every tent was going to be surrounded by rows of sandbags. Right now the rows were low, but in a couple of weeks they would be three feet high.

The old COC tent had been replaced by the new COC bunker, built completely below ground level in a hole dug by bulldozers. A construction company – I don't know if they were Marine Combat Engineers or Navy CBs – had arrived the second day after the attack and constructed it with huge wooden beams and plywood. Covered with multiple layers of sandbags, the COC bunker would be able to take a direct hit by anything they had, except maybe a rocket, and still protect the people inside.

As soon as I was told that I could leave the COC area, I headed for the sleeping tent to fill sandbags. When I got there, I found Sharpie taking a break, so I made myself a cup of C-ration coffee and had some cookies with him. Sharpie needed the break because he'd been doing mostly physical work since the attack. Because he'd had only one watch on the radios before the attack, they didn't trust him to man the radios yet. Tonight would be his first radio watch since the attack, an indication that things were getting back to normal.

After our break, Sharpie filled the sandbags, which I held, tied, carried and placed on the low row. The bags were placed like bricks with the middle of one bag on top of the joint between the two bags beneath it, so that the wall would be even.

I brought up the subject of the Z trench. "You know, I can't help but think how lucky we all are that you got back from Dong Ha a day early and decided to work on that trench. There just wouldn't have been enough room for all of us otherwise."

"Not really," Sharpie replied, "That was just a matter of preparation. We were more ready because we worked at it, not because of luck."

"No, really," I said. "If you'd come back a day later, the hole wouldn't have been ready."

"Yeah, well if you want to feel lucky, think about this. The attack started when you were getting up to go on watch. What if it had started ten minutes earlier?"

"What do you mean?" I asked.

"Haven't you looked at your rack yet?"

"No." I began to feel a sense of dread as I walked over to my cot. When I'd come in, I had thrown my helmet and flak jacket on it without really looking. Now I could see that my air mattress was lying flat on the cot, all the air that I'd dizzied myself to put inside it had escaped. I pulled the blanket and useless air mattress back and saw that there were holes in the cot where shrapnel had passed through. I looked under the cot and saw that my sea bag also had many holes in it.

Sharpie had followed me to my cot. He walked over to the side of the tent at the head of the cot, and lowered the shrapnel pocked canvas. Each of the dozens of points of light that appeared was a cut made by a piece of hot metal. He lifted the canvas and retied it, then pointed down to a small crater where the mortar that had aerated the tent side had exploded. It was directly in line with my rack, and about seven feet away. "It was the same round that got Moorehouse. His rack was right over there." Sharpie pointed past the crater to the damaged side of the Forward Air Control tent.

"Jesus." I sat down on my cot as I looked at the crater. I kept coming back to the same thought. Why had I been so lucky? The answer was always the same. There was no reason. It was just luck. Luck that could change, run out, be gone in an instant, for the same reason it had come in the first place. No reason.

This was a difficult answer for me. At the time I believed in logic and reason more than any other way of understanding the world. In school my favorite subject had been geometry, my favorite part of geometry syllogisms. If A then B; if B then C; A is true; therefore, C is true. Where was the chain of reasoning here? I was saved because the attack happened at 11:50 and not 11:40. There were effects, dire consequences, but no chain of causes back to some cause I could control. All there was was luck, and you can't woo luck. You can only suffer or enjoy her whimsy.

The next step was obvious. It was clear to me that I was probably going to die in Vietnam. It was obvious because it was just too far fetched to think that I would continue to have the kind of luck I had had a few nights before. I could see that my survival for the ten months that remained in my WESTPAC tour was a long shot.

Although it made me sad to think that I would probably never see my family again, it also took a great deal of pressure off of me. Not that I could become careless. I still believed that I could get myself killed sooner by doing something stupid. I was afraid of that, as well as of getting some others killed by my stupidity. The difference was that now I could see that when I did things right, I was only delaying the inevitable. If I did somehow get myself killed, it would be only minutes, or days, or at most months sooner than I would be killed anyway. That was basically different from getting yourself killed fifty or sixty years too soon. I accepted my death.

Sharpie had gone back to work alone while I sat on my cot. Now he came over and broke into my thoughts. "Are you okay, Steve?"

"Yeah, I'm okay," I answered, putting on a cheery voice. "Whoa, baby. That was a close call the other night." I got up and started carrying the first of several sandbags Sharpie had filled and tied while I sat. As I worked, I wondered why I needed to hide my thoughts from Sharpie. Was it really so crazy to accept the inevitable? It was a relief.

A while later a truck convoy rolled past our tent. It was Mike Company returning from the field to man the perimeter and outposts. They hadn't seen any action in the field. Everyone stopped working for a minute until the dust cloud raised by the trucks rolled past. I looked at them sitting on the trucks, filthy from their nine days in the field. Normally I would have felt guilty, because I had been relatively comfortable here at the base camp, while they had been somewhere out in the jungle looking for Charlie. Instead I felt superior because Mike Company hadn't seen any action, while we had had serious casualties. What an odd place, this war zone.

About ten minutes after the trucks drove past, Harrington came walking down the road from OP Red with a radio on his back. He joined Sharpie and me, so that we were a three-man team. Since filling sandbags was really only a two-man job, we switched off after every sandbag. Each of us would shovel dirt into one bag, then hold, tie and place a second bag, and then take a short break until the third sandbag was filled and the shovel became available.

Sharpie asked Harrington, "So what have you been doing for the last few days. I haven't seen you since the night of the attack?"

"I was up on OP Red. It wasn't bad out there. At least they were already dug in, so there weren't all these sandbags to fill."

"Yeah, I know what you mean," I said, as I started to tie the bag I'd been holding open for Sharpie.

"What are you talking about?" Sharpie broke in. "You may have stood a lot of radio watches, but you just started filling sandbags an hour ago."

"Yeah, but I was thinking about you busting your hump here the whole time. It was awful. I felt so guilty," I laughed.

Sharpie had been about to pass the shovel to Harrington before picking up an empty sandbag. Instead he stomped the blade down into the ground one more time and picked up another shovel full of dirt. He brought the shovel over my bent head, and then called me so I would look up from the sandbag I was tying. I saw the dirt falling in time to be startled, but too late to move out of the way. The dirt rained down on my head, rolled onto my neck and shoulders, and, when I stood up to try and get away, made its way down my back, some of it on the inside of my shirt.

I grabbed the sandbag I had been tying and went after Sharpie who dropped the shovel and ran. I chased him around the tent three times, losing dirt from the untied sandbag all the way. When I finally caught up and emptied the remainder of the bag on Sharpie, there were only a few unsatisfying handfuls mounded on one shoulder. I missed his head and neck completely because he was one of those little quick guys, and he dodged at the last minute.

Harrington laughed, "Hey when you two get to the showers tonight, they won't be able to tell you from the guys who've been out in the field."

We all got back to work. After a while Harrington started talking, more or less in a monologue. "This is a lot harder than OP Red. Up there you can just sit around and read all day, because they're already dug in. The toughest part was getting out to the hill on the night of the artillery attack. They didn't have a radio and the telephone line had been cut during the attack. I was just hanging around anyway; they wouldn't let us on the radios that night. When Steve was off picking up some spare radios and batteries, Jackson sent me to the outpost.

"I've never been so scared in my life. It was dark as hell. I'd wrecked my night vision with the lights in the COC, but I couldn't wait for it to come back. I had to crawl up the road on my belly, and there was no way to tell them ahead of time that I was coming. I could just barely see in front of me. All the way up I kept yelling to let them know I was a friendly. At the same time I wanted to be as quiet as I could, because we didn't know if the landline had been cut by a round or by Charlie.

"One time right after I yelled, I heard something moving in the bush beside the road. I thought I was a goner, but it must have just been an animal, because it didn't shoot me. I was afraid to shoot at the noise, because I figured, if I fired a round, the lines would let loose on me.

"I was so happy to get inside the perimeter without getting shot. I was so sure I was going to get it from our own guys."

"Yeah," I said. "I'd hate that."

"Bullshit," Sharpie broke in. "It doesn't matter who shoots you if you're dead."

"Bullshit, 'bullshit'," I contradicted him, encouraged because Harrington felt the same way. "You know it matters."

"Bullshit, 'bullshit bullshit'," Sharpie replied. "If you're dead you're dead. It don't matter how you got that way."

I didn't want to go to four bullshits, then six, then ten, and it was pretty clear to me that Sharpie was willing to say odd numbers of bullshits to my even numbers of bullshits indefinitely, so I just let it go. But I knew for sure that, if I got killed, it really did matter who did it.

That night, even though the sandbag wall wasn't completed, we slept in the tent. It felt like air conditioning compared to the musty hole of the previous nights.

A few nights later I went through my sea bag to see if any of my personal gear had made it through the attack. I had one set of civilian clothes that I had intended to use when I went on my R&R. They were ruined. I decided not to worry about it since there was no certainty that I'd make it through the minimum of six months in country that I'd need to earn my R&R.

I had a transistor radio that I'd bought on Okinawa. It had one piece of shrapnel embedded in its leather case, but was otherwise unharmed. It was somewhat useless in the sense that reception of the armed forces station was marginal in the northernmost part of South Vietnam, but it worked as well as it had before the attack.

The only other thing in the sea bag that mattered to me was a small train set. My mother had given it to me shortly before I left for Vietnam. I think that somehow, in her mind, the presence of a child's toy made Vietnam a safer place. I imagine that the idea went somewhat like this. 'Oh sure, they have there guns and grenades over there, but they're really just boys at heart, and therefore they shouldn't be hurt.'

I got some weird looks when I got down on one of the pallets that formed the flooring in our tent and assembled the track. There were a couple of flip comments as I wound up the locomotive, as I knew there probably would be, but I really wanted to know if it was still working. What surprised me was that when I hooked up the locomotive and set the train running, almost everyone gathered around to see it go. It had survived the attack unscathed. I was glad for that. And somehow I got the feeling that the rest of the guys were glad too. Even though the train didn't mean squat to them, they wanted it to run for their own reasons, probably related to a normal manifestation of the transportation gene on their Y-chromosomes.

A few days later someone came back from the showers and told us that a Marine from one of the line companies had just been killed. Two guys were joking around, and one of them pointed his M-14 rifle at the other from just a few feet away, pretending to shoot him. When he pulled the trigger, there was a round in the chamber, which fired and tore into the other guy's chest, and that was that. It went in making a hole the size of a dime, but by the time it came out the other side it was carrying enough pieces of shattered bone that it made a hole the size of a small grapefruit.

It was like something you'd hear about two little kids who find their father's loaded gun, but it had happened to two Marines. Now one was dead and the other was probably torn up in his mind. He was going to jail because that's what happens to a Marine who accidentally discharges his weapon, even if the round doesn't hit anybody, but especially if it does. This happened totally out of the blue, and it made no sense. I began to think of Vietnam as a place where anything could happen, and the world, meaning my home in Somerville, Massachusetts, U.S.A., as a place where things like this didn't happen.

A few days later M Company went back into the field. I was sent up to OP Red to provide radio communications back to the COC. It was my first duty on one of the outposts, and I loved it. The outpost was already fully dug in, so there was no work to do. I read a book for half the day, and spent the rest of the day writing letters. Then, at 1600 I went down the hill to meet Sharpie for supper. We had gotten into the habit of eating supper together whenever we could. We talked about the article from the "Stars and Stripes" military newspaper that described the artillery attack of the week before as the largest to hit Camp Carroll since the beginning of the war.

Next we talked about the bread. It was homemade bread, baked fresh, but it had some kind of small black insects in it. I wasn't too sure about it; I hated bugs. Finally, when one of the cooks came around and assured us that the bugs had been in the flour and were well cooked and quite dead, I gave it a try. The bread was excellent, as long as you didn't look at it. It was delicious with a thick layer of butter, and that made it easy to imagine that the crunching sensation was coming from small pieces of well-baked crust. The bugs didn't seem to alter the flavor of the bread in any way.

After supper I went up the hill to OP Red. I tried to get some rock music on the armed forces radio station, because we could sometimes get it around dusk, but that night the reception was bad. I re-tuned the station often. As the sun set, the static got worse, until finally there were times when I couldn't find the music at all. Needing to get some sleep before my midnight watch, I gave up and went to bed.

It didn't seem that long before somebody was shaking me awake. I thought the guy wasn't saying anything because he didn't know my name, but, once I was sitting up, he whispered in my ear, "I think there's somebody out there."

I took a mental count of how many of us were on the outpost. Five marines, plus a few army guys who manned the dual-40s. I was fully awake at the thought that it wouldn't take much to take a hill with only five Marines on it. I checked my watch to see how long we'd have to hold out. It was only 11:30.

The artillery attack had been at 11:50.

"What's your name?" I whispered.

"Bill Simmonds."

"Okay, Bill, you did the right thing to wake me up early, but don't wake anyone else up yet. Did you call in on the radio yet?"

"No, not yet. I wasn't sure if there was anything out there or not."

"Okay, let's see." In order to stay low, I duck walked over to the window, a hole in the sandbagged wall. I slowly rose up and looked out, but the ground outside dropped off so rapidly I could see nothing but the tops of the closest trees. Whoever had sited the bunker must have been thinking of it as an artillery observation post, because it was near the crest and therefore well suited for seeing long distances in all directions. For observing what was happening on the hill itself though, a bunker placed more on the side of the hill would have been better.

It was cloudy, and what moonlight and starlight there was barely lightened the clouds without filtering through to the ground. The treetops appeared black against the dimly lit gray sky. I looked until my eyes ached from trying to focus on nothing, but I couldn't tell whether there was anything between the foliage and the bunker. My eyes were useless.

I pulled my head back down partway, sat quietly and listened. There was a gentle breeze rustling the leaves on the trees, but it wasn't enough to mask out other noises. After a while I began to hear a rhythmic scraping sound, what could have been someone digging a hole with a shovel. I listen to it for a minute, hoping I could get a better idea of what it was.

I ducked all the way down behind the sandbag wall and whispered, "Is that it, the scraping sound?"

"Yeah," Simmonds whispered back.

"How long have you been hearing it?"

"About fifteen minutes now. That's why I got you up early, because of the noise."

"We better call it in." I picked up the radio hand set, depressed the transmit switch, and whispered the call name of the battalion COC into the handset, "Oldfield, this is OP Red. We have movement on the hill below us."

"This is Oldfield. What kind of movement?"

"It sounds like some kind of a scraping noise, maybe an entrenching tool. It sounds like it's about half way down the hill."

"What direction?"

"North and maybe a little west."

"Roger." A minute later the response came back. "OP Red this is Oldfield. We have no units in the area. Keep us informed."

"Roger." There went the hope that it was just one of our ambushes getting themselves dug in. I went over to the window and listened again. The scraping continued. I listened every few minutes for the next half hour, and heard the sound each time. Then it stopped. I heard some rustling in the bushes, and then silence, no noise except the wind in the leaves and the faint murmur of the brook at the bottom of the hill. When the noise didn't return, I convinced myself that it had only been an animal digging a hole, and I began to calm down.

Near the end of my watch, I began to notice moving lights to the east of the outpost. Right away I began to wonder if we were being surrounded, earlier someone digging in on the north, now lights to the east. Quite a few lights, and only five of us out here on the outpost. I called them in. Oldfield, this is OP Red. We have moving lights to the east."

"This is Oldfield. How many lights? How far?"

"I can't tell for sure how far. With no moon, it's too dark to see anything in between. Maybe two kilometers. Usually two or three lights at a time."

"Roger."

I waited while the operations officer looked at his map to see if there were any friendly units in the area.

"OP Red, this is Oldfield. We think you're looking at lights of our trucks at Dong Ha."

"Roger," I answered. I was immediately relieved to hear that we weren't being slowly surrounded by the enemy, but then I was embarrassed. What would Charlie be doing shining lights our way anyway?

They must be having a good laugh at the COC, taking the calls from the new guys on the outpost, who get spooked by an animal, and then think that lights that are miles away are only a couple of kilometers away. The distance I'd given them was so far off that they'd actually felt free to tell me what the lights were, apparently believing that there was no danger in giving out the location of Oldfield as being two kilometers west of Dong Ha, because we were actually so much further west.

A few minutes later I woke up my relief, told him about the animal, pointed out the lights, told him what they were, and hit the rack. The last thought that drifted through my mind before I fell asleep, was the hope that nobody at the COC had recognized my voice.

About a week later I was working in the COC, and the following radio transmissions came through from L Company's commanding officer.

"Oldfield, this is Lima 6. I have a report of heavy contact."

I answered, "Roger, this is Oldfield, wait one." I yelled across the room to the operations officer, who was plotting the positions of all the units, based on their latest situation reports. "Major, Lima's C.O. is on the hook. He's got heavy contact."

"Let me talk to him." Major Sterling walked over and took the handset I offered him. "Lima, this is Oldfield 3. What have you got?"

"This is Lima 6. I just got a report that one of my ambushes has heavy contact. Details are still a little sketchy, but I thought you'd want to know right away."

"Roger, Lima. Fill us in as soon as you know more. I'll alert the skipper. Out." The major sent someone to get the Colonel.

Before he could get back to plotting positions, the second call came in.

"Oldfield, this is Lima 6. We just got a report from a patrol. They're under heavy fire and have taken several casualties. They're in the same sector as the ambush, but about a kilometer away. It looks like Charlie's on the move in a big way. Over."

"Roger, Lima. This is Oldfield. The Skipper is on the way. He'll want to know what's going on when he gets here."

"Roger, Oldfield. I'm going back to the company radio now. I'll call back when I have more details. Be ready with some artillery and maybe a medevac. Over."

"Roger. Out." Major Sterling handed the handset back. As he went to the phone line that connected to the regimental headquarters, he yelled across the COC to the artillery section, "Get ready for a mission. Have a white phosphor marker round ready to fire in the 105s and in the 81s. We may be passing the coordinates through here rather than through Lima's forward artillery observer, so be ready. That goes for you too radio."

He quickly checked the map and continued, "Approximate coordinates will be 110 217. Aim the guns, but do not fire anything yet."

"Aye aye, sir."

The major picked up the phone and turned the crank a few times to make it ring on the other end. "I need a medevac chopper standing by, to go to the vicinity of Cam Lo...Yeah, tonight...I'll get back to you when I know for sure how many will be coming out tonight."

Just then Colonel James arrived. He and Major Sterling talked quietly for a few minutes, occasionally fingering some feature on the map, trying to figure out what might be going on. The Colonel came over and asked me for the battalion handset.

"Lima, this is Oldfield 6, put the 6 on, over."

"Roger." When Lima's C.O. came on the radio his voice was shaking noticeably. "Oldfield 6, this is Lima 6. I'm afraid I have some bad news sir. It turns out that one of my ambush squads has ambushed one of my patrol squads. As far as I can tell, we have no enemy contact at this time. Most of the patrol has been hit and is down. At least two are dead at this time. I'm trying to get word now as to how badly the wounded are hurt. Over."

"What the hell happened?"

"That's not clear at this time, sir. I'll call back as soon as I find out more. We should have the casualty figures in the next few minutes, over."

"Roger, see if you can find a decent landing zone near the ambush site too, over."

"Roger, Out."

The skipper went back to the map and Major Sterling. A minute later Sterling yelled over to the artillery section, "Cancel my order for white phosphorous."

"Aye aye, sir."

A few minutes later the final call came from L Company. "Oldfield 6, this is Lima 6, over."

I yelled, "Skipper, Lima's on the hook." and answered, to save time, "Lima, this is Oldfield. The 6 is on the way and listening. Go Ahead, over."

"Roger. We need a medevac for three seriously wounded. We have two others wounded who can wait till morning. We have five dead."

The transmission stopped. I wondered if maybe Lima's C.O. was losing it. Major Sterling didn't wait. He picked up the phone to regiment and called for the chopper.

The colonel took the handset. "This is Oldfield 6. Go ahead Lima 6."

"Roger. The ambush is bringing the wounded to what looks on the map like a passable LZ at 110 215. They should be there in about twenty minutes. They'll put out a white phosphor grenade when they hear the chopper. Over"

"Roger, Lima, we're calling for the chopper now. It should be there in about ten minutes. You need anything else?"

"No, sir."

"What the hell happened? Over"

"There was a last minute change in the assignments. The ambush happened where I had originally told the patrol to go. After I looked at the map some more, I decided to move the patrol further south, and put an ambush in the original location. The radio operator passed the word to the ambush, but not to the patrol, so they both ended up in the same place."

As he heard this, the Colonel gave me an angry look, as if I had been the radio operator who didn't pass the word. I was angry about the dirty look for a moment, but that quickly gave way to relief that I wasn't the one who got the five guys killed. How could you live with something like that?

That night I dreamt about the L Company ambush. The dream felt very real, and although I usually can't remember my dreams, I remember this one. Sometimes I think that maybe it wasn't even a dream, maybe it was just my thoughts as I began to drift into sleep, but then I remember details like the fact that I was carrying a rifle in the dream, and I know it was a dream because in real life, and therefore in my conscious thoughts, I always carried a pistol. Here's the dream.

It was dusk and we wanted to be set in before dark. Twilight didn't last long in the woods. We were following a wet trail through the soaking forest, hurrying more than we should have been, making too much noise. Fortunately most of the noise was masked by the sound of the light rain. It would be a miserable night for sleeping.

We found the spot we were looking for, a bend of nearly ninety degrees in the trail, with only twenty minutes of dim light left. There was no apparent reason for the bend to be there. Perhaps it pointed to the former location of a village, or maybe it had originally been worn through the jungle by the whim of a few water buffalo. It would suit our purposes.

There were eleven of us in the squad, and we set up an L shaped ambush with the bend of the trail at the bend of the L. Eight of us were along the trail at about ten foot intervals, the long part of the L, with the remaining three, including the M60 machine gun crew, close to each other at the bottom of the L, where they could see directly down the path.

Everyone dug in just far enough back from the trail so that we wouldn't be seen. The jungle was thick enough that fifteen feet provided good cover for a man who was holding still, while still letting us see glimpses of the trail, and anything that moved on it. We didn't dig deep holes, just sort of pushed enough dirt to the side and front to form a depression deep enough to provide some protection. By the time it was dark, we were all lying in place, wrapped in our ponchos and poncho liners. Fortunately the poncho liners provided some insulation even when they were wet, because, we were all soaked to the skin by the cool rain and our own sweat. We kept our rifles inside our ponchos even though it wasn't much dryer there than on the outside.

Each man was connected to the next by a piece of string. This would allow us to communicate with each other without speaking. We would serve two man, two hour watches, with those not on watch sleeping, or trying to. We were so tired all the time that normally we would sleep soundly on an ambush, but on a night like this it would be difficult.

It was 10:50 when the strings were pulled, not just for the next watch, but all the way up and down the line. Someone was coming down the trail.

I was the fifth Marine of the eight in the long part of the L. When I was awakened by the string on my finger, I immediately heard the enemy coming down the trail. I pulled back on the string to let number four know I was awake, and began repeatedly pulling back and forth on the string of number six, until I felt the responding tug on the line.

I was very scared. I hoped there weren't many of the enemy. Even in an ambush I didn't want to be outnumbered. Now I was glad it was raining because the wet leaves and twigs didn't make any noise as I rolled over to free my rifle. I already had a round in the chamber, so all I had to do was take off the safety. I did it slowly enough so that it didn't cause a metallic click. I was ready to fire.

When the enemy was passing by me, I sighted on each shadow as it walked by. I felt awful. There was incredible tension, fear that we would be seen before all the enemy was in the kill zone. There was also incredible guilt as I sighted on each passing shadow, waiting for the sound of the machine gun to signal that it was time. They seemed so helpless as they walked by, unsuspecting, defenseless as targets in a shooting gallery.

I had to keep reminding myself that if I didn't get my man, my man might start shooting back. Still I felt a momentary relief each time I moved my sites off one of the shadows, until I was lined up on the next.

As I lined up on the sixth man to go by, the machine gun started firing. I was ready, gave a quick squeeze, then another. I was sure I'd gotten my man with the first round, but I didn't know about the second, because just as it squeezed off, my man was hit by several M60 rounds that jerked him out of my sights.

I couldn't see anyone else standing so I sprayed single rounds up and down the part of the trail I could see, being careful not to fire so far down the trail that I would get the bottom of the L.

My magazine was empty, and I released it, flipped it over, and jammed it back in. I always kept my magazines of ammo in pairs, taped back to back. As I chambered the first round, I wondered if it would go home. Sometimes it was hard to keep the rounds in the exposed magazine clean. This was no time for a jam.

As I sighted down the trail, I heard the first cry. "Corpsman."

I wasn't sure I'd heard it until I heard it again. "Corpsman."

Was it a trick. My mind raced, trying to figure out if Charlie could be laying there yelling for medical help in English, without any trace of an accent.

Everyone continued to fire.

I waited, listened. When I heard the call for the third time, I was sure. Those were Marines being shot to pieces in the kill zone. I yelled, "Hold your fire."

When two men at the end continued to shoot, I stood up and yelled it again. "Hold your fire."

The firing stopped.

I got down on the ground again, just in case I was wrong. "Who are you?"

No one answered, maybe they thought it was Charlie who had ambushed them. I tried again, using a longer sentence so they'd be sure to realize I had no accent. "Are you Marines? Where you from?"

The answer came back, weak, obviously talking in spite of pain, but understandable. "We're from Lima Company, on a patrol out of Cam Lo."

I heard someone from the ambush say, "Ah, shit."

Someone else said, "A perfect fucken ambush, but it's us."

I couldn't speak. I felt a weight of guilt, pressing down on me and in on me. My stomach knotted, my throat tightened, my arms and legs weakened. I forced myself to get up again, and started walking the few feet to the kill zone. I didn't want to see what was there, but I had to see if I could help the survivors. How could anyone have survived that?

That was when I woke up. I was immediately relieved, the guilt lifted. For me it had only been a bad dream.

A few days later Mike Company was sent out to the field again, so H&S

Company was going to be responsible for manning the perimeter of Camp Carroll. On my way to watch at the COC, I stopped in at Sergeant Miser's tent and reminded him that it was probably a good idea to send radio operators out to each of the outposts. He seemed to be drunk a good part of the time, and I didn't want him to forget. I liked the OP duty now that I was used to it, and I was hoping that I would get assigned to an outpost.

When I got back to the radio operators tent after watch, Jackson was in a rage. He'd just been told to redo the watch list to include radio watches on the outposts. When he saw me, he said, "You can all thank MacDonald for having to go to six on and six off watches. He's the one who reminded Miser about the outposts."

I wanted to say something but I kept my mouth shut. Jackson and I were both corporals, but he was senior, and technically I worked for him, so I had to play it cool.

But that wasn't going to work. Jackson came over to where I was standing and started yelling, "Don't you ever go behind my back again. If you have something to say to Miser, you say it to me first."

"I didn't go behind your back. I was on my way to watch and I saw Mike Company getting onto trucks, and I figured that they were leaving the lines to us, so I stopped in at Miser's tent to remind him about the outposts. It had nothing to do with you."

"Well now we all have extra watches so we'll have enough people to cover the outposts."

The realization that he was giving me a hard time just because he was too lazy to stand extra watches got to me, and I lost my cool. "Don't lay it on me because Mike Company had to go out to the field. You just don't give a fuck about the outposts, because if the land lines get cut in an attack again, you're not the one who's going to have to go crawling up there on your belly, hoping not to get shot by your own men."

I guess Jackson could see that he'd look pretty foolish if he tried to bring charges against me, because he backed off. "Get a radio and batteries, and get your ass up to OP Red. Now."

I did what I was told.

At chow about a week later, I was telling Sharpie what had happened to India Company. "I came on watch at 1800, but Smitty wouldn't give up the radio. The shit had just hit the fan for India Company. Smitty ended up staying in the COC all night, until he heard that the radio operator from India, a guy named Markham, had been evacuated. I guess Markham was a friend of his.

"Anyway, nobody really figured out what was happening until the next morning when Mike Company was able to get in and relieve India. Charlie had cut out by then. It turns out that the NVA had a perimeter set up on a hill, and India Company started setting up a perimeter on the same hill, and the shit hit the fan. I don't quite get how it could happen, but somehow the two perimeters intersected, so India had some NVA inside its perimeter, and the NVA had part of India Company inside its perimeter.

"The first calls came in from the commanding officer, saying they had heavy contact. Next thing we know Markham, the radio operator, is on the hook saying the CO is unconscious, who do we want to be the acting CO? They told him to find some lieutenant - I forget the guy's name - which he did.

"Next thing he's on the hook again. The lieutenant is dead, and he is wounded himself. Who should he find next? They told him to find the first sergeant, who, fortunately, lasted through the night. Not that it did them much good to have the radio there. It was too crazy, with firefights in every direction, so they couldn't figure out what was going on.

"We relayed some artillery fire for them, because the artillery forward observer was dead, but they couldn't shoot too close, because they were in the same place as Charlie. They tried a couple of Huey's before it got too dark, but there was no clear way to mark where they were and where the enemy was, because they were all mixed in together. They couldn't even land a chopper to take out wounded, because there was no secure LZ. So what was left of India just stayed out there all night, until Mike Company arrived the next morning."

Sharpie didn't say anything for a couple of minutes. I started working up to the other thing I wanted to tell him. The pause was long enough that I finally got it out. "Sharpie, I've decided to go out in the field."

"What do you mean you're going out in the field? You're a corporal; they can't make you go out in the field."

"They're not making me. I volunteered. I already talked to Sergeant Miser. I'm going out with Mike Company when the radio operators rotate in a couple of weeks."

"Why'd you do that?" Sharpie asked.

"I'm tired of Jackson giving me a hard time, and I'm tired of almost everyone else ignoring me. I just can't take it anymore. I'm supposed to be a corporal here, but all the people who are supposed to be taking orders from me don't think much of me because I have no field experience. I don't think much of myself for the same reason. I mean I pretty much know what I'm doing now, but it's just not right for me to be sitting back here warm and dry and safe in the COC, until I've done my time in the field like everyone else."

"Bullshit," Sharpie answered. "You have no obligation to go out there and get shot up, if they don't make you."

"I'm not going out there to get shot up. It's just to do my part, so that if I make it back, and I'm in the COC, and the shit hits the fan, I won't have to feel guilty, like maybe some radio operator's out there doing my job. I'll have done my time, taken my chances."

"Bullshit."

I thought that Sharpie's second "bullshit" had been sort of half-hearted. I wondered if he had also felt guilty about having it too easy. I continued on,

123

encouraged. "I've been thinking about it for a while now, since Lima ambushed its own patrol. I keep wondering if maybe I could have done the job better."

"What are you talking about? That radio operator is just a fucking scapegoat. The real problem is that Lima's captain doesn't know his ass from his elbow. If he's going to go shifting the night patrols all over the place, he's got to make sure that the word is passed. It's just like when we pass coordinates to the operations group in the COC, and they put them on the map. They know where everybody is. We don't have a map, and we would have no idea if two units are getting too close to each other. That radio operator didn't have a map either."

"Yeah, your right. I've really been wondering more if I might end up in that kind of deep shit too. I guess I'm willing to take that chance, because I want to see what it's like out there. The clincher came the other night, when I was listening to what was happening with India Company. I just can't take the guilt anymore. I went to see Miser today, and that's that."

"What about me? What am I supposed to do here alone?" Sharpie asked.

I knew I was deserting Sharpie, and I felt guilty about that too, which is probably why I responded angrily. "What about me? You're going to be gone in two months, but I'll still have a lot of time left to do here alone. I want to do it as someone with field experience." I got up from the table and left to start my watch at the COC.

The next day I heard that McGreggor had killed himself. Although he'd always worked as the radio supply guy, making sure we had radios, parts, and batteries, he was actually a radio operator. He had been assigned to a line company, but, the night before he was scheduled to go out, he shot himself in the head. One version of the story was that he was cleaning his weapon and it went off accidentally. Another was that he was despondent over receiving a Dear John letter from his wife and had killed himself deliberately. A third version said that he was afraid to go out in the field and so had killed himself.

At the time, the third version of the story didn't make sense to me. How could a man who was afraid to go out in the field, summon the courage to kill himself? Now I realize that the motivating fear wouldn't necessarily be fear of death. It could also be fear of not being able to keep it together during combat, of letting your fellow Marines down, and maybe getting a bunch of them killed. Fear of not being able to control your fear.

Whatever the reason, or lack of reason, if it was just an accident, McGreggor was dead, and some poor lieutenant, who was unfortunate enough to be walking past McGreggor's tent at the wrong moment, had a shattered elbow, broken to smithereens by the round that had just passed through McGreggor's head. A .45 caliber pistol is a powerful weapon at close range.

One night just before I was due to join Mike company, I was making a tape to send home to my family. As usual ,I asked that everybody stop saying "fuck and suck" for a while, since I was taping, and, as usual, my request was met by what I had come to think of as "the fuck and suck serenade." This lasted through several rewinds of the tape, until finally the chorus tired of obscenity and returned to their card game. As he was dealing the next hand, Harrington said, "Oh, by the way, Steve, I heard this afternoon that Sharpie is going out with Kilo Company tomorrow."

"Oh yeah?"

"Yeah, he volunteered, just like you. You two must be crazy."

"Maybe so," I answered, nonchalantly, not letting on that the news really bothered me. I felt like I was responsible for Sharpie going out. What if he got killed? Would it be my fault?

After a few minutes I put it out of my mind and went back to taping. I didn't know if I'd be able to write as often once I was out in the field, so I wanted to at least start out caught up with my correspondence.

I got so caught up in the taping that I didn't realize at first that something was going on, but even I couldn't ignore the foot falling only two inches from my tape recorder, or the Marine that was attached to it, frantically evading three other Marines, two of whom were soaking wet. When the three trapped the one, they picked him up and carried him to a large crater full of muddy water and threw him in. Then all four of them came for me.

I bolted for the front exit from the tent, just barely managing to get moving before they reached me. The four of them got smart and began chasing me in pairs, two resting and two running, always managing to turn me back toward the resting pair.

When I was too tired to run any more, I panted, "Okay, I'll go in. Just let me take my boots off so they don't get wet." They agreed, and I took off my boots and placed them and my wallet in a small pile near the crater. When the first guy grabbed my arm a little too roughly, I instinctively tried to break loose, but it was too late. They were all on me. I fought hard, but, once they got to where each Marine had one of my limbs, it was hopeless. All I could do was be an accordion, pulling the two guys on my legs closer to the two guys on my arms, and then pushing them away again, but they didn't lose their grip or fall down. The four of them staggered to the edge of the crater. I knew if I kept fighting them then, they might accidentally miss the crater and toss me onto the ground. I finally had to relax and let it happen. They swung me back and forth, one - two - three, and then I sailed up and out, splashing down in the center of the crater. A second later my boots and wallet landed beside me in the filthy water, punishment for not going in easily, when I said I would. The wallet was wrapped in a plastic bag, so it wouldn't mildew from my sweat, so it floated, as did the boots because they landed with temporary air pockets. I quickly recovered them before they sank. If they had ever dropped completely below the opaque surface of the water, I might never have found them again. I swam a few strokes to the edge of the crater, and slipped and crawled my way up the loose dirt on the side. As I poured the water out of my boots, I wondered if they would have tried to dunk me if I hadn't volunteered for field duty.

I wasn't sure I was totally pleased with the results of this new camaraderie, especially since the showers wouldn't be open until morning, but I felt more accepted. I was absolutely certain I'd made the right move in volunteering to go to the field the following week. I wondered if Sharpie felt the same way.

I can't remember how the conversation got started, but, on the night before I was due to go out with Mike Company, Hayes and Miller, neither of whom I liked very much, started telling me war stories from their first stretch in-country. The battalion had been stationed further south then, and the main enemy had been the Viet Cong, not the North Vietnamese Army, as it was near the DMZ. I still remember three of the stories they told me. Supposedly one or the other of them participated in the events in the stories, but I later heard two of the stories from other sources, and believe that they are mythical.

In the first story, Miller was riding on the back of a tank that was rumbling through a town that was believed to be supporting the Viet Cong. Suddenly a woman carrying something wrapped up in a shawl ran out from between two huts, headed straight for the tank. Because of the reputation of the town, Miller took off the safety on his rifle, and sighted in on her.

She kept running toward the tank, and Miller started yelling for her to halt, but he didn't know any Vietnamese, and the tank was making an awful lot of noise, and she just kept on coming. As she got closer to the tank, he knew he was going to have to shoot her, but he was afraid that what she was carrying in her arms was a baby, and that all she really wanted was to show them her baby was hungry and needed food.

Just above his sights he saw her face, but he couldn't read her intentions.

Why didn't she stop? She was looking right at him now, could see that he had her, but she wouldn't stop.

As he began to squeeze the trigger, he cursed her for being so stupid, but still raised his sights a few inches to try and get her above where the baby's head must be. Her neck would be a tougher shot, and he'd been trained to shoot for the center of the body, but he was pretty sure that it was a baby now, and that baby hadn't done anything, stupid or otherwise. Besides she was only about twenty-five feet away now; he couldn't miss.

An instant before his rifle fired, he saw her arms began to swing open, and the shawl fall from her shoulders, exposing an AK-47. Then he felt the recoil of his M-14 rifle and saw her fall to the ground. There was no baby.

In the second story, Hayes was on a helicopter with an officer from intelligence and two Viet Cong prisoners. The prisoners were bound hand and foot, with their hands tied behind their backs.

The officer asked the first prisoner several questions in Vietnamese and when he didn't get any response, he hit the prisoner several times in the face, openhanded, but still hard enough to raise a welt and cause the Viet Cong's mouth to bleed.

The officer then went to the second prisoner and questioned and beat him, but in this case he hit him only in the body, where the bruises would be hidden by the man's clothing. He also beat him for a substantially longer time, delivering perhaps two dozen blows with his fists. At the time, Hayes didn't understand the significance of the difference in the two styles of beatings.

After the second beating, the officer went up and spoke to the pilot of the helicopter, and then the helicopter took off. It flew several miles from the base and up to a height of about five thousand feet. Then it just stopped where it was, hovering a mile above the jungle.

The officer grabbed the first prisoner by his black pajama top, and dragged him across the floor to the open door of the helicopter. He questioned him again, and when the prisoner wouldn't answer, he pushed him partway out the door, so that his head and shoulders were hanging out in the air.

The officer yelled his questions out the door, and, when the prisoner didn't answer, he pulled him in and beat him again, but this time severely, even going so far as to wrap his fingers in the man's hair and pound his head on the floor of the helicopter several times.

He pushed him out a second time, but this time all the way past his hips, so that more of the man was hanging outside the helicopter than inside. He yelled some more questions and, when the man didn't respond, he lifted his legs up in the air, and tipped him out the door.

The officer stood in the door looking down for what seemed to Hayes to be at least a minute, apparently waiting until the Viet Cong hit the ground. Then he casually walked over to the second prisoner, who was so terrified by what he'd just seen that his eyes were bugging out. The officer asked a question and the prisoner began speaking in a torrent of Vietnamese. Hayes couldn't understand Vietnamese, but it was clear to him from the cadence of questions and answers that followed that the man was answering all of the officer's questions at great length.

The third story is the most disturbing because I never heard it again, which makes me think that it might not be myth, that it actually happened. It took place when Hayes and Miller were out in the field. It was evening, and they were cooking their C-ration suppers. Because they were out of heat tabs, they were heating the water for their coffee by burning C-4, which was actually an explosive in the presence of a detonating cap. Somewhere along the line someone had discovered that C-4 would burn very hot if lighted with a match, and now whenever the Marines were out of heat tabs, or when the day was so windy that they couldn't effectively heat their food or water with a heat tab, they would use small balls of C-4 explosive instead, probably at ten times the cost to the tax payers.

Near Hayes and Miller, tied to a tree, was an old man suspected of being either a Viet Cong or a Viet Cong sympathizer. When he saw them eating, he began begging for food.

After a few minutes, Hayes grew tired of listening to the man, so he reached into the plastic bag of C-4 they'd been using for cooking, grabbed as much explosive as he could fit in his hand, and shaped it into a ball. He carried it over to the old man, and fed it to him. The man was grateful to get something to eat, and ate the whole ball.

Hayes sat down with Miller again and they both finished their supper and coffee in peace. Shortly after they were done, the old man began moaning, and eventually screaming. He screamed through most of the night, and was dead by first light.

After the third story, I left the tent and went for a walk. I'd understood the first story, and it seemed appropriate for training someone about to go out in the field, if that's what they'd had in mind, but I was disgusted by the other two stories. Why had they told them? Were they true? I'd certainly felt like they were as they'd been telling them, but now I wondered. If they were true, shouldn't I turn Hayes in? I walked around for half an hour, finally convincing myself that I had no way to know if the stories were true, and therefore I had no way of knowing whether I should turn Hayes in or not. That was the answer that I needed to get to, because I was pretty sure that a whistle blower would not have been greeted with open arms. I just wanted to get out in the field and earn my way into the group, not do something that would alienate me from the group forever.

In the Field

It was my second day with Mike Company. I knew I hadn't made the error, and yet here was the skipper, Captain Carrington, questioning me in an accusatory tone.

"Are you sure you passed the word to the lines that the patrol was coming in?"

I doubted myself momentarily, wondered for an instant if I really had passed the word, and then I was sure again. "Yes, sir. I rogered the transmission from the patrol, called in to battalion to let them know, and then called out to first, second, and third platoon to let them know. All three platoons rogered my transmission."

"Are you sure that second platoon rogered?"

It made me uneasy that Captain Carrington was asking me a question that I had just answered. Had he detected the momentary hesitation before my reply? Was there a contradictory statement made by someone else? This had shades of the Lima company ambush about it. A Marine in a patrol about to come back inside the perimeter had just been wounded by shrapnel from a grenade thrown by a Marine on the perimeter. A few shots were fired as well, but fortunately nobody was hit by any of them.

Was I going to get blamed, even though I was sure I'd done my job? Suddenly I realized that I still hadn't answered the question. "Yes, sir. Second platoon responded that they had received the transmission."

I was getting worried now. I could see that I was not coming across as believable here. I watched Captain Carrington turn and walk out of the tent, without bothering to acknowledge my reply.

I sat down on my cot. Why did this have to happen on my watch, especially now? Being so new to Mike Company, I had no credibility yet. I wondered if they'd court martial me. The guy had caught a lot of shrapnel in his leg, and had to be medevaced, so it wasn't just a local problem anymore. I went over the radio transmissions in my mind, to see if anyone would be able to corroborate my story; maybe the guy from first platoon, or third was paying close attention to all the transmissions. I wished that Mike Company kept a radio log like they did at the COC for transmissions at the battalion level. That would at least be some evidence.

After a while, Red came into the tent. Although we were from different worlds - he from rural Georgia, me from a city in the northeast - in the two days that I'd known him, I had gotten to like him. He was from the battalion telephone group, providing landline support to Mike Company. Usually there wasn't much to do in that department, so he helped out with the radios. Red's nickname could just as easily have been short for redneck as what it really was, a reference to the color of his hair. It could have been a reference to his skin color too. Except for the freckles, his skin always seemed to be flushed from the heat, or the wind, or the sun.

He'd had the watch before mine, but had heard about the trouble and started nosing around to see what was going on. As soon as he found out what had really happened, he'd come to tell me. "Well it looks like you're in the clear, Steve. The Captain found out that right after you radioed to second platoon, they changed watches. The guy waking up wasn't really awake when the guy you talked to told him about the patrol. When he heard the patrol coming in, he thought it was Charlie and threw a grenade and started shooting. Luckily, he heard the guys from the patrol yelling that they were friendlies. He was just about to set off a Claymore mine on them. He had the hellbox in his hand, and was just about to turn the crank to send the juice down the line. Could have been much worse if he had turned that crank."

As I spoke I breathed out heavily, releasing the excess air that had somehow accumulated in my lungs during the previous twenty minutes. "Oh, man," I sighed, "thanks for telling me. I was sweating it."

"Yeah I figured you were. That's why I came over to let you know as soon as I heard. That asshole Carrington might have left you in the dark."

"Really? How long's he been around anyway? He seems sort of new."

"He got here the day before you did," Red replied, "but it doesn't take that long to spot a really big asshole. You let me know if he gets word to you about what happened anytime soon. I've got five bucks that says he won't."

It was pretty clear to me that nobody could be that inconsiderate, especially after practically accusing me outright of being the cause of someone getting seriously wounded, but I didn't want to take Red's money, so I answered, "No bet. It wouldn't be fair to take your money on a sure thing."

Red replied, "You must be a good man, Steve, because you think everyone else is good. That just saved you five bucks."

And so it did. Carrington never got back to me about the cause of the accident.

The next morning we were told to saddle up. We were going to a place called Khe Sanh, which was a Marine base camp currently surrounded by the North Vietnamese Army. I had known we would be going out soon, but this sudden move was a change of plans. The base at Khe Sanh was under considerable pressure, and Kilo and Mike Companies were to be temporarily attached to another regiment at Khe Sanh to help force Charlie to back off.

I began feeling tense, wondering how bad it must be to force this change of plans. I emptied my bowels, knowing that, as the tension mounted, I would need to know that I had already gone to the bathroom.

I tied my gear on the pack frame the previous radio operator had given me three days before. In the days to come, when the weight of the pack seemed too much, and I wondered how guys who didn't have a pack frame to distribute the weight could make it, I would bless my predecessor for passing it on to me. Besides the radio and spare batteries that were the tools of my trade, I packed several C-ration meals, a poncho, poncho liner, entrenching shovel, and 3 canteens of water. All of this weighed more than fifty pounds. The one luxury I carried was a rotary can opener, which weighed only a couple of ounces. I carried it throughout my time in the field, as if to convince myself that as long as I could still carry this extra item, I wasn't overloaded.

When I was finished packing, I went to the bathroom again, getting back just as the trucks arrived to take us to the airfield at Dong Ha. A few minutes later as we drove beside the blown up bridge that had spooked me on the way to Camp Carroll, I felt like I had to go to the bathroom a third time, but I just had to hold it. I was glad I had already gone twice.

At Dong Ha we sweltered beside the runway, standing in formation, unprotected from the midday sun. In about fifteen minutes, a C-123 cargo plane taxied up. The back of the plane swung down to the ground to form a loading ramp. I was on that first plane because I was the captain's radio operator to battalion, and the skipper needed to get to Khe Sanh as quickly as possible to be briefed about the operation.

Since I was one of the first to board, I got one of the fold down canvas seats along the sides of the cargo area. The last Marines to get on had to sit on the floor. Two members of the plane's crew strung a few lines back and forth, so the passengers in the middle would have something to hold onto.

Before they restarted the engines, one of the crew came back and told us that when we landed, and the cargo ramp went down, we should hit the tarmac running. The airstrip was surrounded by mountains, which were currently under NVA control. It was often under fire by both artillery and small arms fire. My bowels knotted again.

As soon as the speaker left for the cockpit, the plane's engines started, and the cargo ramp was raised to form the back wall of the cargo area. The plane taxied down the runway, and was airborne within a minute. Immediately the whole cargo bay filled with fog, as the humid air inside cooled to below its dew point. I couldn't see anything more than two feet away. The men sitting on either side of me were barely shadows in the cloud, and the men beyond them were totally invisible. It was impossible to hear or be heard over the din of the planes engines. I felt totally isolated until the air conditioning dried the air and it became transparent again.

Suddenly, when we had been in the air about ten minutes, the plane started to bank and dive steeply, and I heard a loud thump. The cargo door opened part way. I looked out the door, but all I could see was blue sky. We were falling like a rock. I thought we'd been hit, and were going down.

Then I heard the hydraulics as the cargo door opened about two thirds of the way. That's where the thump had been; yet it seemed to be working normally. Suddenly the plane began to level off and I saw steep mountains rise to fill the view out the cargo door. Then I understood. This was how you landed an airplane at Khe Sanh, straight down through the mountains that surrounded the air strip on three sides.

When the tires hit the runway, the cargo ramp lowered the rest of the way. The brakes brought the plane to a jarring stop. As soon as the Marines nearest the door could get on their feet, they began running hard down the ramp. Suddenly I could see that the comfort of a seat on the plane had its price. We had to sit there in the plane and wait for the last Marines in to be the first out. I felt like I was sitting in the center of a bulls-eye.

When nobody shot at the first few Marines to hit the runway, the rest slowed down to a jog. The last few, including Captain Carrington and I, just walked off.

I followed the Captain to the Command and Operations Center. While the Captain was briefed, I hung around shooting the breeze with the radio operators. I knew one of them from Okinawa. It seemed like a small world.

A few hours later, when we were digging in for the night on a hill just outside the perimeter of the camp, it seemed like an even smaller world. I was about halfway through digging my hole, when I heard someone say, "Maxie."

This was one of my nicknames in high school, and no one had called me that since graduation. I looked up to see Chris O'Brien. "Chris, what are you doing here?" I asked. "I didn't know you were in the Marine Corps."

"Me neither," Chris answered, meaning he didn't know I'd joined either. We exchanged reminiscences about high school, and stories about what everyone was doing now. Then Chris asked, "Are you going out there tomorrow?"

I thought that there was some kind of fear or foreboding in the question, as if out there wasn't a very nice place to be. "Yeah, why, is it bad?"

"Yeah, 3/3 just got the shit kicked out of them."

"Is that who you're with?"

"No, I'm with 2/9. I'm a chaplain's assistant. I'll be staying right here to identify the bodies when they come back. I guess they figure a chaplain's assistant will have seen a lot of the guys in church."

"Well, I'm glad you know me from the world, because I haven't been to church much lately."

"Yeah. Hey, man, I got to run. Good luck tomorrow." The good luck wish made me more nervous than all the horror stories in the world could have.

"Thanks, man," I said. "I hope I'm standing up next time I see you."

"As long as you can see me, you're okay. Most of the guys I see can't look back."

The next morning we were up at first light. Wisps of mist still hung in every depression, although they would disappear as soon as the sun climbed over the hills to the east. It would be a windless, hot, humid day. I took a few salt tablets with breakfast, hoping they'd help keep me from getting dehydrated. I wished I'd thought to take the tablets over the previous two weeks, so that I could have gradually built up my salt level.

After breakfast I packed my gear, filled my canteens at a water tank that had been flown in by helicopter, and sat around with everyone else to wait for the trucks. After about an hour of waiting we got the word to move out on foot.

The terrain was hilly. Several times when we went down into hollows I couldn't even keep radio communications with battalion. Once I even put on the ten foot antenna, but it didn't help. That was just as well, because I hated using the longer antenna because it made me stand out. If all the radio operators providing communications within Mike Company had two foot antennas, and I had a ten footer, Charlie could easily figure out that I was the radio operator who was providing communications back to battalion headquarters.

Usually the bad communications only lasted for a few minutes, but on two occasions, when we came up to higher ground, I found that battalion had been trying to reach us for the previous ten minutes. I explained the situation to the radio operator at the other end, being careful not to compromise our position in my explanation of the terrain. Anyone tuned to the right frequency could listen in on a radio conversation, including Charlie.

By lunch time I was getting pretty tired, and I was glad to take my pack off and sit for a while. I'd been sweating a lot, so I took a few more salt tablets with my water. After lunch the heat was worse, and I got tired again almost immediately. We sweltered whether we were in the woods, where we were protected from the sun, but there wasn't much air movement, or in the open, where there was a slight breeze but the sun poured down on us.

I relayed a couple of messages requesting medevac choppers. Guys were starting to pass out from the heat. When the helicopter picked up a guy with heat exhaustion, it would fly straight up to cooler air to revive him, and then fly him away to the hospital.

I felt sick to my stomach, and I wondered if I was going to be able to make it. I kept telling myself that I felt sick only because I had taken too many salt tablets, but I knew that nausea was one of the symptoms of heat stroke. I came close to calling it quits, afraid that I was frying my brain by going on, but I didn't have the courage to just sit down and let them get me out of there. I decided that I wouldn't burn that many more brain cells if I waited until I fell down. I thought back to boot camp when Hickox had told us that, if you fell down, you better end up with a bloody nose from where your face hit the ground. So I kept on going, one step at a time, hoping the next break would come soon. If they were going to pack me in ice, they'd have to save a piece for my face.

The last hill of the day was the steepest. We were heading for high ground, to be in a defensible position for the night. I was using my arms now, as well as my legs, but they weren't nearly as strong, so it didn't help very much after the first few minutes. About two thirds of the way up, we came across a stream of clean water and rested for a few minutes. The skipper didn't want to lose anyone else to the heat when we were so close to settling in for the night.

I finished all my water, filled all three canteens in the stream, and added a water purifier tablet to each one. Then I just sat on a rock, forearms resting on my thighs, trying to conserve every remaining quantum of energy for the last push. I wanted that last break to be a long one, but in a few minutes we began climbing again. Still, it was enough; I made it to the top. I took a short break, but then I had to start digging my hole for the night. That's the way it was in the field. When you set up for the night, job one was to dig yourself a fighting hole, just in case you got hit during the night. Sometimes the ground was soft, and it wasn't too tough a job, but the ground on that hill was a mixture of rock and clay, very tough digging, just when I had almost nothing left.

After I had been at it for about twenty minutes, I noticed that the radio handset was making a static noise every few seconds. I picked it up, and found that battalion had been trying to reach us for almost ten minutes. I apologized and explained that I had been digging my hole and hadn't heard the call. Apparently that wasn't good enough, especially in light of the communication losses earlier in the day, because the battalion commander came on.

"Marine, I want you to know that if there is one more loss of communications with Mike Company, I'll see that you are relieved, and I'll personally meet the chopper that I send to take you to your court martial, and I'll shove a radio handset up your ass. Have you got that?"

"Yes, sir."

"Okay then, put the skipper on."

"Roger." I called Captain Carrington to the radio. When he gave the handset back to me, he gave me a dirty look.

I was embarrassed and angry. I had thought I was doing a pretty good job. I didn't know how they expected me to closely monitor the radio while I was digging my hole, but I knew that I didn't want to get sent back from the field in disgrace, and that I certainly didn't want to go to the brig. Luckily Red came by just then.

"How's it going, Steve?" he drawled.

"It sucks, man, that's how it's going."

"What's the problem, boy?"

"These assholes at battalion, sitting on their fat fucking asses with their feet up in front of their radios with speakers attached to them, are getting on my ass because I don't answer the radio the first time they call. How the fuck am I supposed to hear them if I'm down in a gully, or if I'm a few feet away from the radio digging my hole?"

"I hear you, but that's what you got to do. I think I've got just what you need. Be right back."

A few minutes later he returned with a piece of heavy wire, about the thickness of coat hanger wire. He wrapped it around the narrow part of the handset, just below the ear piece, twisted it together with his linemen's pliers, and made a hook out of the twisted part. As he handed it to me, he said, "Stick that hook in the top button hole of your utility shirt, and it'll keep the handset up near your ear. You'll never miss another call."

"Thanks, Red. I'll give it a try." Sure enough, when I bent down to dig, the earphone part of the handset fell down close to my ear. The coiled wire attaching the handset to the radio made digging more difficult, but when the next call came in, I heard it right away.

I was teamed up with the captain's other radio operator, Benson, who carried the radio for communications between the captain and his platoon leaders. When we were done digging our holes, we made our hooch for the night. I put my poncho down as a ground cover, and Benson rigged his above it with a long stick he cut from a nearby tree. This made a makeshift tent, but, instead of staking the poncho sides to the ground, we tied strings to the corners and staked them out. This put the bottom of Benson's poncho about two feet above mine, so we could feel any breeze that might come by.

Benson, Red, and I had supper, and, once I ate, my stomach started to feel better. We divided the radio watches, and I lucked out and got the last watch, so I was able to get all my sleep in one uninterrupted block. I was in the hooch and asleep on my poncho liner before it was completely dark.

The next morning it was Mike Company's turn to be the point company, leading the way through the forest and over the hills. I was sore from the workout of the day before, but I didn't seem to be as tired. I was taking fewer salt tablets, and my stomach wasn't bothering me any more.

We were going through a part of the mountains that was moist and tropical, with trees growing in all different directions where the eroding soil had been unable to hold the tree trunks straight up. At several steep places I used the trunks of sideways trees or hanging vines to pull myself up, because the damp, crumbly soil gave way if I tried to climb with just my legs.

The lushness of the forest dried up when we went through an area that had been defoliated. What leaves remained on the trees were sparse and brown, making them look like the winter oaks at home, where some of the dead leaves stay on the trees until the new foliage arrives in the spring.

Late in the morning we moved through what somebody said was a deserted rubber plantation. It was defoliated, so the sun lighted it almost as if it were an open field. We walked between two rows of tall, evenly spaced tree trunks that threw parallel shadows across the trail. I thought that these must be the rubber trees, but in retrospect I realize that they were so perfectly spaced, and majestic that they were probably planted as some kind of a welcoming archway at the entrance to the plantation, only now without their foliage, the arches had disappeared, leaving only the tree trunk columns. I felt as if I were walking in a church, but one that had burned down, leaving only the supporting structure, still reaching to the heavens, but no longer bearing any weight.

Shortly after leaving the plantation, I heard gunshots. Everyone got down on the ground. Captain Carrington got the situation from one of his platoon leaders over the company radio, and passed it on up to battalion using my radio, so I heard everything that was going on. The lead platoon had two men shot and a couple more pinned down by at least two NVA who were shooting at them from the cover of a cave. The captain asked for priority on an artillery mission and got it.

The artillery forward observer was with the skipper and me, and he could see the two NVA through some brush if he stood up. He called in his mission and got no response. He called it in twice more, still nothing. Finally he yelled over to Carrington, "Hey, Skipper, we can't get our arty mission. There's some South Vietnamese general flying around in a helicopter near the 105's and they won't fire for fear of hitting him."

Carrington asked, "How about the company's 60 millimeter mortars. Will they be able to get in there?"

"Maybe, but it'd be a tough shot for a high arc weapon like that. I guess it's better than just waiting for the general to land."

Carrington got on the company radio and ordered the mortars forward. I watched the FO bobbing up and down ten feet away, trying to keep under cover, but needing to observe the situation in case his mission started, so he'd know if any adjustments were needed. Suddenly he stood straight up, dropped his radio handset and began feeling up and down his chest and stomach with both hands, almost like a smoker who feels for his pack of cigarettes, but more urgently. Before he found the place where the bullet had entered him, he fell limply to the ground, and someone started yelling for the corpsman. The corpsman was there, working on him within a few seconds, and they had him on a medevac chopper within ten minutes. We would learn later that they even got him back to the hospital, which usually meant that you would be saved, but he died there. He had been shot in the side, and the bullet passed through both lungs, and cleanly out the other side, perhaps hitting something painful in the middle, because he had searched for the wound on his front, but he had no exterior wound there.

I had never seen anyone shot before, and throughout the whole time the thought kept coming into my head that this was real, and not a movie. It had been very sudden. One minute he was trying to call in an arty mission, and the next minute the bullet arrived and he was down. Once he was shot, the arty FO never spoke a single word, and then he was gone, soon to be gone forever, without uttering any last brave thoughts or encouragement for his surviving comrades. What brought home the reality of it for me was that the guy was hurt but he couldn't find the entrance wound. In all the thousands of TV and movie deaths I'd witnessed, I had never seen anyone looking in the wrong place for the bullet hole. Shouldn't you at least be able to know that much of what's going on, to know where you've been shot?

A few minutes later our artillery mission came in. The platoon leader switched his radio to the arty frequency for a few minutes to make adjustments, and then he ordered a fire for effect, and it was over. It took about an hour to evacuate all the wounded - several more had been hit during the firefight - and then we were on our way again.

As we began to move out we went by one Marine who was sitting alone on the side of the hill, in a fetal position, arms wrapped around his knees, head down on his arms, rocking back and forth. He was sobbing quietly. I assumed they would have to medevac him too, because I didn't think he was about to come out of it and fall in with his platoon.

As soon as we got to some high ground, we stopped and had lunch. We were in no rush now because Kilo Company had taken the point while we were tied up with the firefight, and now we were in reserve. This turned out to be exceedingly good luck for us, at least those of us who hadn't been killed or wounded in the firefight that had caused the change in order.

The next morning Mike Company was still held in reserve while Kilo Company and a company from another regiment tried to take Hill 881. They went up in the late morning, but they took heavy casualties and had to come back down. We were sent to help them get down off the hill.

We got there in mid-afternoon, and found them in a bad way. Most of the wounded were on a small hill at the foot of 881, and they were being carried to a nearby hill that was a little higher than the small hill, and set further back, so that the back side of the hill couldn't be seen from 881. They had managed to set up a landing zone there. Not enough able-bodied Marines were left in the two companies to carry all the wounded out, so we pitched in.

I told Captain Carrington I wanted to help evacuate the wounded, gave him the radio, and went across to the small hill. There were only a few stretchers and many wounded so most of us had to carry the wounded on ponchos. I teamed up with a guy standing at one end of a poncho with a Marine already lying on it. As soon as we picked up the two ends of the rain gear, it sagged in the middle. In order to keep from dragging the wounded man on the ground as we moved, we not only had to lift up, but also to pull against each other, all while trying to make progress toward the landing zone over uneven terrain.

My arms were aching and burning before we had the first man even halfway to the LZ, but I didn't want to ask for a break, because it was important to get the wounded to the choppers as quickly as possible. Finally, when we were about two thirds of the way to the LZ, the other guy couldn't take it anymore and said he had to have a break. I didn't try to talk him into going on, because I was exhausted myself. Even though I knew that there was no way that I would have the strength to make it all the way to the chopper in one carry, I was relieved that I wasn't the first one to give in to the searing pain in my muscles. We took a brief, guilty break, while the man on the poncho groaned and bled. We got him to the chopper, and then went back for someone else. The second time we stopped at about the halfway point, totally spent, unable to do otherwise, but guilty nonetheless.

When we went back for a third Marine to carry, I was relieved to find that there were no more. Just as I was about to head back to find Captain Carrington on the more protected hill, mortars started whistling and crashing in on us. Everyone ran for a nearby twenty-foot bomb crater. As the rounds came in, I started to become angry. We had only finished getting the wounded out of the area a minute before, and now we were under mortar fire. It wasn't right to try and kill men who were already wounded.

The thought flashed through my mind that perhaps the NVA had granted us a military courtesy and deliberately waited until the wounded were out of the way before firing on us, but I immediately put it out of my mind, replacing it with hatred for them, for their inhumanity, convincing myself that they had really intended to finish off the wounded Marines. It would be too confusing for me to think of the enemy as honorable men, caught in war as I was, but following civilized codes of conduct. Better to just think of them as the enemy.

The man next to me caught a piece of shrapnel in the neck. He quickly put his hand up to the wound, and came away with some blood on his palm. He yelled for a corpsman, but they were all at the landing zone, attending to the wounded who hadn't made it onto choppers yet. He applied direct pressure to the wound with his bare hand for a few minutes, and the bleeding stopped. Once he was sure he was going to be okay, he started laughing and talking to me, even though he didn't know me. "Hey, man, I just got my first purple heart. One down, two to go." He was referring to the fact that you would be sent home if you were wounded in action three times and lived through it, even if none of the wounds was severe.

I couldn't help thinking about the arty FO the previous day. It occurred to me that next to me was not a very safe place to be lately. After about fifteen minutes, the mortars stopped and we all ran as fast as we could to the more protected hill, chased by two last mortar rounds that didn't get anybody. When I found Captain Carrington, the first words out of his mouth were, "Where the hell have you been all this time. This radio is getting heavy."

"Okay, give it here skipper," I replied. I was angry at the skipper's reaction, at the implication that I'd been screwing off somewhere, when in fact I'd been rescuing wounded Marines from enemy fire, but I knew better than to let my anger show. In the Marine Corps, the officer is always right. "Sorry, sir," I apologized in my most consoling manner, "but as soon as we got everyone off the hill, they started shooting mortars at us. You probably heard them. We were stuck in a bomb crater for the last fifteen minutes."

I spent the next forty-five minutes following Captain Carrington as he talked to various people from the two companies that had gone up the hill, trying to account for all the missing men. It seemed to me that the gist of each conversation was that Carrington wanted to hear that there were no

Marines left alive on Hill 881. He asked questions like, "So you think he was pretty seriously wounded when you saw him. Not much chance of getting him out alive then, huh?" and "I guess he must have been hit pretty bad or he'd have made it back down by now, huh?" The desired answer was always implicit in the question.

We'd been taught at boot camp that we'd never be left out there to die, that someone would always come and get us. If we did get killed someone would come and get our bodies. We were Marines, and Marines didn't leave their own in the hands of the enemy, but that wasn't what I was hearing here. I'm not certain that the respondents were necessarily influenced by Carrington's line of questioning, but given the authoritarian nature of the Corps, I can't imagine that they weren't.

After several of these heavy-handed conversations, Carrington went to confer with Kilo Company's commanding officer. I wasn't in on the conversation, but that wasn't exceptional. Whenever the officers got together, they usually had the radio operators within shouting distance, but not within hearing. That was fine with me. If I ever got captured, the less I knew, the better. Half an hour later the meeting broke up, and the bombardment of Hill 881 began. Presumably there were no Marines left alive there, so it was OK to bomb the top right off the hill.

The initial bombardment came from artillery mission after artillery mission. When the first long lull in the artillery came, it was so that Phantom jets carrying napalm and 500 pound bombs could run air strikes. As soon as the Phantoms left, the artillery started again.

After watching the air strike, I began digging my hole for the night. I dug unusually deep, afraid that the NVA might come down off of 881 and take this relatively small hill. It occurred to me that the NVA probably knew the terrain, because I had seen a dead NVA when I was coming back from helping with the wounded. I wondered if this little hill might have been an outpost for them.

Later, while Red and I were shooting the breeze, there was a lull in the artillery. We speculated as to whether that would be it for the night. Then the first B-52 dropped its bombs. The B-52 run wasn't on Hill 881 itself - we were too close for that - but somewhere just beyond it. The rumble of explosion after explosion lasted for more than a minute. I wondered if one plane could carry all those bombs. Red was of the opinion that a B-52 could. As if to settle the issue, another plane came and dropped its bombs for a minute or so. Then a lull and another.

The planes flew so high that we couldn't hear their engines, only the whistle of the falling bombs, and the explosions when the bombs landed. As the targets got further away, we couldn't even hear the bombs fall. There was only the rumble of the explosions.

After the B-52s were done, the artillery started up again. It continued for two nights and a day, stopping only when there were Phantom jets nearby. During that time we had nothing to do but watch the bombardment. I enjoyed watching the air strikes, even from my less than ideal vantage point below Hill 881. The jets flew differently depending on what they were dropping.

On the napalm runs they would come in low and flat, almost slowly, if a Phantom jet could ever be said to be flying slowly. The shiny canister of napalm would fall lazily from the silver wing, and tumble along the ground for a second or two. Suddenly the whole area where the canister had hit would be obliterated by yellow flames and thick black smoke.

On the bombing runs the planes would start from several thousand feet up, and fly nearly straight down at the target. At a few hundred feet the pilot would release a bomb and then pull the jet out of the dive, barely missing the treetops as the nose came up. The bomb would continue on the original path until it exploded on the target.

After one of the air strikes Red said, "Man, this is better than the Fourth of July."

I said, "I wonder how much more expensive it would be to make the shells and bombs burn in color, like on the Fourth. If Uncle Sam really wanted to make us happy, that's what he'd do."

Red said, "I know Uncle Sam wants you to be happy. That's why he gave you this great job in the Marine Corps. I heard they used to have the shells in color, but they had to stop. Too many dumb Yankees were getting killed when one that looked like the American flag would go off and they'd all stand at attention."

"Yeah," I said, "Uncle wouldn't pay for any that looked like the Confederate flag, so you southerners were safe."

Later Red watched the radio for me so I could go over to the section of the hill where Kilo had set up and talk to Sharpie. I was glad to see that he looked okay, no minor wounds or anything. I still felt responsible for him being there, even though it had been his own choice. "Hey, Sharpie, how you doing man?" I said.

"I'm okay," Sharpie answered coolly, not bothering to ask how I was doing.

"Hey, what's the matter man? You okay after yesterday?"

"Yeah, I'm okay. I'm just pissed off about yesterday. We lost half our company, and some of it was because of these fucking M-16s." He held up his rifle.

"Hey, where'd you get that?" I asked. The standard weapon for radio operators was a .45 caliber pistol, and here was Sharpie with one of the brand new M-16s the line companies had recently been issued to replace their M-14s.

"There was a pile of them," Sharpie answered. "During the fire fight guys who got hit and were trying to make it back down the hill just threw their M-16's into a pile. They just wanted out of there. Other guys who had their M-

16s jam, would take a working one out of the pile. When I decided I needed more than a .45, I had to try three rifles from the pile before I got one that worked.

"Today they came around and told everyone that the M-16 has to be kept very clean or it will jam. What kind of field weapon is that? And why the fuck didn't they tell us that before the fire fight?"

Sharpie went on and on, about how you could shoot an M-14 with a plug of dirt in the barrel (which I thought was probably bullshit, but I didn't say anything) about how the officers were doing a shitty job, not having them ready ahead of time for anything that happened, about how the whole Marine Corps sucked. Finally he wound down.

I got up. "Well, I have to get back now. It was real nice talking to you," I grinned.

Sharpie laughed. "Well, at least I feel better. I'll never have to worry about getting an ulcer from holding it all in."

"Really. See you tomorrow."

During the bombardment, I often found myself looking up at the hill. It seemed to be the focus of everyone's attention. Whenever people weren't doing something else they were looking at the hill. We knew that pretty soon we were going to have to take that hill. Except for all the U.S. firepower being used, it was quiet. During one lull we saw an NVA going down the side of the mountain, but he disappeared when someone started shooting at him. Other than that, there was no sign of activity from the NVA, no small arms fire, no more mortars.

The night before the assault, as I lay on the ground at the foot of Hill 881, trying to get to sleep, my thoughts kept returning to Paulson, the guy who'd smacked a corpsman in order to stay out of Vietnam. I wondered what it must be like to not laugh for six months straight. I laughed every day. I couldn't remember a single day when I hadn't, even in Vietnam - especially in

Vietnam. Was I just taking the easy way out? Some people would say Paulson was taking the easy way out, but I didn't think so. Some people would say the young men who left their homes and families and went to Canada were taking the easy way out, but I didn't think so. So what was left? Knowing we were going to try to take that hill the next day sure didn't feel like the easy way out. Maybe none of us were taking the easy way out. Maybe we were all just handling this war and the compulsory draft in whatever way we could. Vietnam, Canada, the brig, none of it was easy. We all paid our dues.

As I lay there, thinking about climbing a steep hill while the enemy would shoot down on us, I knew that I could refuse to go up the next day, do a little brig time, and get a well deserved dishonorable discharge, but that would ruin my plan. I wouldn't get any G.I. Bill benefits; it would be that much harder to get through college. My shot at a decent sized piece of the American pie would be seriously compromised. Was that it then, was I just putting myself in danger for a shot at more money?

That was part of it, but just as important was the idea of doing my part, fighting my country's battles like all those World War II veterans and Korean War veterans had done. I wanted to be able to face them when I got home and tell them that I'd fought too. I wanted to be able to face my family and friends, not as a guy who chickened out, but as a guy who hung in there with honor. And I couldn't imagine facing the guys from Mike Company the next day and telling them that I wasn't going up the hill with them. "Semper Fidelis" and all that. I guess you couldn't know that your "faithful" was really "always" unless you went through a little something to prove it.

It was eleven o'clock on the morning of our third day beside Hill 881, and there hadn't been any bombardment for several hours. It was hot, but less humid than it had been. I could smell the hay like dryness in the grass, as I stood at the bottom of the hill. I heard the summer hum of thousands of insects, frogs, birds, all the animals that were probably there the day before, but whose life sounds had been inhibited or drowned out by the explosions.

Mike Company and the remains of Kilo Company were assigned to take the hill. Mike would go up first, with Kilo in reserve to be used where needed. We were lined up along the northeastern side of the hill. Above us was two hundred meters of steep slope, with nothing growing on it but foot high grass. Beyond that was a tree line, and a gentler slope to the crest of the hill. I wondered why there were no trees on the lower slope. Had it been cultivated at one time, or used for grazing? Whatever the reason for the hill's grassy sides, the lack of trees was going to be a problem for us during the assault. We would have no cover until we were most of the way to the top.

As I stood there waiting for the signal to move up the hill, I thought that, in this high tech world, physically going up the hill was a pretty stupid way to find out if there was anyone still up there. Why not just use sensors and keep blowing the top off the hill until the sensors indicated there was no life left there? Obviously, we were expendable, just as the sensors and bombs were, and it was only a question of how many bombs, and the aviation fuel to deliver them, were equivalent to the life of a Marine.

I tried to concentrate on my anger at the Marine Corps for putting me in this position, because it helped me forget how scared I was. I was afraid because I knew that if the shit hit the fan, we'd be sitting ducks, just like Kilo Company had been two days before. I thought back to the time we had taken a hill in training at Camp Pendleton, how exhausted we were near the top, too tired to move quickly, just barely making it at all. This hill was much higher than the one at Pendleton had been, and we were carrying a lot more gear.

This was craziness. How could we hope to survive an assault on terrain this steep and open? As if to avoid answering my never asked question, Captain Carrington raised his arm, looked up and down the line, waited for his platoon leaders to raise their own arms to indicate their readiness, and then dropped his arm. His lieutenants dropped their arms to acknowledge, and Mike Company, 150 strong, started moving up the hill.

No one spoke. We walked slowly, conserving our energy for when the shooting started, and, even more important, being careful to maintain an even line going up the hill. If anybody got too far in front, it would make it impossible for the Marines behind to shoot in certain directions. An even line could deliver more firepower at any target that presented itself. Firepower was the key. It was the only thing that could save us if Charlie was still on the hill. If we could shoot enough bullets that Charlie would have to keep ducking and couldn't aim or shoot back, then we could take the hill. If Charlie was free to shoot at us, we didn't stand a chance.

As I walked up the hill, I kept thinking that right now Charlie was free to shoot at us. Until he fired, we wouldn't know where to direct our weapons. We could see nothing of his positions. He could see us, chose the best targets - the radio operators, the machine gunners, the officers. I knew that many of us would die or be maimed in the first few seconds if there was a fight. It was totally out of our control. I felt defenseless, a target. All I could do was walk up the hill, provide good radio communications, hope I survived, hope I wouldn't be blinded, hope I wouldn't have my balls shot off.

We were almost to the tree line now, and definitely in the sights of anyone who was up there. If there was to be a firefight, it would start soon. I looked up and down the line, from my perfect vantage point near the middle. There was one uneven spot, but the line was amazingly straight, straighter than it had ever been in training.

In spite of the fatigue, (they all must be tired, I was) in spite of the fear, (they all must know this was the moment when it would start) in spite of the heat, and the height, and the weight on our backs, we were moving inexorably up the hill, a force, a company, a unit. Mixed with my fear was a tremendous pride. We were taking a hill, just as thousands of Marines before us had taken their hills, when told to do so. I saw the line pass the lowest of the trees, and, a few seconds later, I ducked past the first of the trees on my part of the hill.

No firing. Charlie must have left the hill. A quick walk through the woods and we were on the summit. We had taken Hill 881. Although there were reports of sniper fire, I heard and saw nothing to indicate that we had been opposed.

The top of the hill was pock marked with craters from the bombardment. The explosions and shrapnel had removed much of the vegetation, yet some of the bunkers were still intact. Clearly, if Charlie had decided to stay, he would have killed many Marines before the survivors could have taken the hill. To knock out every single bunker, it probably would have taken a bombardment a hundred times the size of what was actually used. Using infantry really was the only way to take this kind of terrain.

Engineers came through now with explosive charges and blew the tops off some of the untouched bunkers. Some we would use ourselves. In one of the bunkers they found the body of a dead NVA soldier. Either he had been left accidentally in the confusion of their evacuation, or too many of the NVA soldiers were hurt in the bombardment, and they were unable to carry out all their dead. Because the body hadn't deteriorated much, I thought the soldier had probably been killed during the evacuation, and no one had seen it happen or missed him.

When I walked by, the engineers were going through the soldier's wallet. They found a picture of a pretty young Vietnamese woman, posed in a shimmering white *ao dai*, the ankle length tunic and pants that is the traditional formal dress of Vietnam. It was probably the dead soldier's sister, or maybe his wife. Perhaps it was even a wedding picture.

The engineers passed the picture around, making lewd comments about the woman, and what they would like to do to her. I was bothered by their callousness, but I didn't say anything. I didn't understand how they could go through the man's wallet without feeling worse about him being dead. It bothered me to think of him as someone with a family that would grieve for him when they found out he was dead, if they ever did find out for sure. I just wanted him to be the enemy, not a person.

I began wondering if the soldier was a draftee or a volunteer. Either way he was charged with the task of stopping the Yankee imperialists a few miles from his border, something he could believe in.

I was charged with stopping the spread of Communism 8000 miles from my border, something I believed in. As I looked along the devastated hill, and at the smaller hills beyond it in Laos, where the B-52's had dropped their bombs attempting to cut the Ho Chi Minh supply trail, but in fact only making huge brown craters in the otherwise lush hill, it almost made sense to be fighting so far from home. The devastation showed clearly that it was always better to have the war in the other guy's country.

A while later a crew came through to bag up the bodies of the Marines who'd been presumed dead and left on the hill two days before. I pointed out a body that was about 50 feet from my hole. Because of the extreme heat, the body was decomposing rapidly, and it had bloated to about three times its normal volume, completely filling and straining against the fabric of the Marine's normally loose fitting jungle utilities. At the waist, wrists, and ankles, where the clothes normally fit tightly, the corpse was further distorted because the swelling had been inhibited. The distortion was even more pronounced because the head, hands, and feet (someone had stolen his jungle boots) were free, and had bloated until the taut, grayish skin had started to crack in places. Dozens of huge flies buzzed about, feeding in those cracks, as well as near the eyes and anywhere else where moisture was escaping.

I was afraid to see something fall off the body when they picked it up, so I didn't watch while the crew checked the body for booby traps, and put it in the green vinyl body bag. The smell grew stronger while they worked to get the body into the bag – I wouldn't have thought it possible, but it did - and then gradually diminished once they zipped up the bag and carried it away to the landing zone. I would smell it for days. I don't know how much of that was due to occasional microscopic particles rising from the contaminated ground, and how much was due to particles trapped in my sinus cavities, but my brain was sensitized to the smell of corruption now, and it didn't take very many parts per million for me to notice it.

During my watch that night, the lieutenant from first platoon came by, sat down on the ground beside me, and started shooting the breeze. This made me uncomfortable, because fraternization between officers and enlisted men was discouraged in the Marine Corps. Perhaps this guy thought that he couldn't talk to any of his own men because of the fraternization rule, but he still needed to talk to someone. Out in the field, officers didn't get to talk together much, except to plan things.

Whatever his reasons, he just plunked himself down and said, "Puff sure is taking good care of us tonight." He pointed at one of the flares drifting down on its parachute. They were being dropped periodically by Puff, a dragon ship, so called because one of its armaments was a Gatling gun that could fire rounds so fast that the tracer rounds, only every fifth round, seemed to form a continuous stream. When the guns fired, it looked like it was flicking a long red tongue at its target.

"Yes, sir. You can read a book tonight without even waiting for the moon to come up."

The lieutenant put his helmet on the ground, leaned back and looked up at the stars, using the helmet to support his head. "Man, this is a great life, isn't it?" Before I could answer he went on. "You know, you spend a lot of your early life not being able to do anything. Your main job is to learn, and you never get to do. A year ago I was just a kid getting ready to graduate from college, and here I am now right in the middle of a life and death struggle, fighting Communism, making a difference in the world. And I owe it all to the Marine Corps. Where else could a 22 year old play an important part in history?"

I wanted to agree with him about learning vs doing, since it was the way I felt too, but, even more, I wanted to know what he meant by a part in history. "Do you mean the Vietnam War, sir?"

"Sure, the war, but this battle too. This will go down in Marine Corps history with Quadalcanal, Tarawa, Iwo Jima. The battle for hills 881."

"Is there more than one, sir?"

"Yeah. We're on hill 881 South. Two kilometers north of here is hill 881 North. The Second Battalion of the Third Marines is trying to take that one. They've gone up twice so far and got pushed back both times. They'll soften it up again tomorrow, and try again the next day. They'll keep trying until they take it. This is a big battle. Tomorrow's papers will probably have headlines like, 'MARINES TAKE HILL 881 SOUTH. BATTLE STILL RAGES FOR HILL 881 NORTH.' Imagine that, we've done something important enough to get in the papers." With that he got up and was on his way to wherever he'd been going when his excitement bubbled over. In my two years in the Marine Corps, that was the only friendly conversation I ever had with an officer.

I was a little spooked that night, because we were expecting a possible counter attack. That's why Puff was up there, floating flares all night, so we could see an attack coming. I thought about the other hill 881. The coincidence of the names got me thinking about how similar the situations were. Two different groups of Marines had tried to take two different hills, each 881 meters high.

My company was nearly intact, sitting on top of our hill 881. The other company was probably split up now, half sitting on some hill near the bottom of their hill 881, and half dispersed over all the aid stations, hospitals and morgues between there and Japan.

I wondered how long my luck could hold out. It had been a coin toss the other day, and Kilo had gotten the call, and gotten their asses kicked. It had been another coin toss today, and we had gotten the Hill 881 that the enemy had evacuated. How many times can the coin come down heads before it comes down tails?

One thing had become clear to me as I walked up the hill that day. There were situations that were completely out of my control. No matter what I knew, how strong I was, how careful, how courageous, how good at my job, there were circumstances that I wouldn't survive. Sure men died because they were foolish or stupid. I had to be careful. But being careful wasn't even close to a guarantee of survival, because men usually died mostly because they were unlucky. It was just a matter of being in the wrong place when the metal started to fly.

The next day a general arrived to check out the position. It made me angry. Where was this guy yesterday when we were taking the hill? He was back in the rear giving the orders that might have sent us to our deaths. Now he flies down in his helicopter to check out the morale of the troops.

When the general came by, I started giving him a dirty look, but when I saw him looking my way, I averted my gaze, hoping he'd keep on going, but it didn't work. The general came over, put himself right in my field of view, and asked, "How's it going, corporal?"

I wanted to stay angry, but I couldn't, partly because of the rank – Marine enlisted men didn't display their anger at generals - but mostly because of the way he had asked the question. I felt like he really cared how it was going for me, and that was very confusing. One day the man gives orders that treat me like so much cannon fodder, and the next day he asks, "How's it going?" and really seems to want to know the answer.

In my confusion, I fell back on military courtesy. I snapped to attention, just short of a salute - you don't salute officers in combat - and answered in my most military voice, "Very good, Sir."

The general looked at me for a second, replied, "Good," and continued on his original route.

The next afternoon a Catholic chaplain was helicoptered in to say Mass. He chose the 30 foot wide 1000 pound bomb crater near my hooch as the safest place to gather the faithful. The Marines came one or two at a time and went down into the hole. I was tempted to join them, probably would have joined them if my friend Chris O'Brien had been serving the Mass, but decided not to. I had lost my faith two years earlier, and wasn't about to go down into the hole now to hedge my bet, or maybe improve my luck.

For one thing I didn't think it would help much. I didn't know where I'd heard the saying, "There are no atheists in foxholes," but I knew that it didn't make sense to me. Everything about the war seemed to run counter to what I'd been taught about God. If the existence of the universe was the basis of one of Thomas Aquinas's proofs that God existed, not a real proof, but a proof for the edification of those who already believed, then the existence of war could certainly be the basis of a proof that God didn't exist, not a real proof, but a proof for the further disillusionment of atheists.

Clearly if there existed the God I had been told about, a God who was all knowing, who knew even when an individual leaf fell from a tree, and who was all powerful, who could do anything, if that God existed and yet let this go on, it was not a God that I could understand in any real way. It wasn't a he. It wasn't a she. It possessed no human qualities. If there was a God, It was not like us at all. It was something arbitrary, foreign, strange, so odd that there's no point in trying to understand or communicate with It.

My god was luck. I had to find a way to court luck, but I knew none. Besides, I already had luck, or I wouldn't be sitting on top of the hill. I needed to be careful to do nothing to destroy my luck.

The next day I went to the corpsman for an ulcer that had opened up on my hand. I told him that I had probably scratched it without realizing it, and that maybe a fly from one of the dead bodies had gotten into it. The corpsman didn't know what it was, but he treated it with Bacitracin ointment for the next four days so it wouldn't become infected. At the time neither he nor I knew anything about Agent Orange or the symptoms of dioxin poisoning. Neither of us related the open sore on my hand to the freshly defoliated areas we'd walked through six days before.

A few days later, the Second Battalion of the Third Marine Regiment took Hill 881 North. We stayed on hill 881 South for about a week. By then the airstrip at Khe Sanh was back in full operation, no longer under enemy fire. The First Battle of Khe Sanh was over. It became the first battle of Khe Sanh because, at the end of the week, we gathered our gear, blew the tops off the remaining bunkers, and walked off the hill. I wondered how long it would be before the NVA were on top of Hill 881 again. How did it make sense to pay so dearly for the high ground, and then just walk away from it? It took us about an hour to walk to route nine where we boarded trucks that carried us back to Camp Carroll.

I felt safe inside the barbed wire and mine field perimeter. Before I even went to the showers I stopped in to say hello to the other radio operators. Even though Mike and Kilo companies had been attached to another battalion for the operation, our battalion radio section had been monitoring the whole operation on the radios. I couldn't tell them much about it that they didn't already know, but they were still interested in hearing it from the horse's mouth.

I was sitting on my cot in the middle of the tent, and had been expounding for about fifteen minutes, when I began to notice a strange smell. Not wanting to break the spell - I couldn't believe the reception I was getting from these guys who had had no particular use for me only a few weeks before - I put up with it for a few minutes. When it seemed to be getting stronger, I asked, "What is that awful smell in here? Don't you guys clean anymore?"

Everybody broke up. Two guys answered, practically in unison, "It's you man. You stink. Go take a shower and then come back and tell us the rest."

I looked around and realized that although everyone was gathered around me and seemed happy to see me, the circle they had formed had about a five-foot radius. No one would get any closer because of the smell of my unwashed body. That's when it really hit that something was basically different about my relationship to this unit. I was a member now, part of the family. They would even put up with my stench to welcome me in from the field.

When I came back from the shower, I heard about Moorehouse. They'd received a letter from him a few days before. He'd spent several days on a hospital ship, then been flown out to Japan. There they'd tried for a week to save his leg, but there was too much infection, and too much damage to the tissue. It was impossible for him to beat the infection, even with all the antibiotics they'd given him, because of the damaged tissue. They had amputated his leg. Everything else was healing up nicely. In another week he'd be flying back to a stateside hospital. He'd heard that they try and put you as close to home as they could, and he was looking forward to seeing his family again.

I didn't say anything to anyone, so I must have realized somewhere in myself that my thoughts were crazy, or perhaps I was just inhibited in expressing them because everyone else seemed so bummed out by the news, but I was envious of Moorehouse. I would have traded places with him in a minute. He was out of Vietnam for good. He was alive and he would be home in a week. It was a sure thing and all he'd had to pay for it was one leg. It didn't seem like a lot to pay for an honorable way out of the war. It was clear to me that it would be incredibly presumptuous of me to think that I would have the luck to fare any better, and clearly I might do much worse. I thought of all the more serious wounds that I was still subject to - being blinded - loosing my balls - loosing my prick - loosing an arm - loosing both arms - loosing both legs - becoming a paraplegic - becoming a quadriplegic. The litany of awful things that could happen to a person in combat went on and on. And that's if I didn't get killed outright. But Moorehouse had skated it all and received the fabled million-dollar wound that sent him home.

From where I am now, safe, with all my limbs intact, I can see that Moorehouse paid a heavy price, and I envy him no more, but I was thinking differently then.

We stayed at Camp Carroll for about a week. By the end of it, I was almost glad to go out in the field again. I was tired of filling sandbags, and things had been so quiet at Camp Carroll recently that haircuts and boot polishing were becoming issues.

The kicker came the night before we were due to go out in the field. I woke up in the middle of the night, feeling a slight pressure on my chest. When I opened my eyes, I was staring directly into the eyes of a rat that was sitting on my chest, only a few inches from my throat. I didn't move a muscle, and neither did the rat.

After several minutes I was beginning to get sore from holding myself tightly in a single pose. I knew that I was going to have to move soon, but I was afraid that the rat would become frightened and bite my exposed throat. Finally I decided that if I rolled over very gently the rat would think I was still asleep. This was not very clear thinking on my part, since your average rat probably hasn't studied human activity and motivation extensively, and probably can't tell a benign motion from a threatening one. Fortunately, as soon as I started to move, the rat jumped off my chest, scurried across the pallet flooring of the tent, and wedged into a small pile of scrap building materials that probably hid the entrance to his nest.

I decided that going to the field the next day might not be so bad. Sleeping on the ground was better than sharing my bed with a rat.

Late the next morning we left Camp Carroll in a truck convoy. I was nervous about going out, but not as nervous as I had been. I barely got the jitters when we took the detour around the blown up bridge near the camp. The trucks stopped at the road to the village of Cam Lo and we got out. We were going to sweep the area near the road.

When we swept, we followed a trail through the woods that ran parallel to the road. We could never see more than a few feet on either side of the trail, so we found nothing.

Shortly before we were due to set in for the night, we were taking a break in a clearing near the fence for the Cam Lo refugee camp. Three old women came to the fence with loaves of homemade French bread and cans of soda to sell. I bought a loaf of bread to have later with my C-rations, but decided to try it right away. I broke off a chunk and had just taken a delicious bite of it, when Captain Carrington saw me.

"If you get sick from that bread, I will court martial you."

Even though Cam Lo was a friendly village, apparently Carrington didn't trust the civilians there. I had eaten one bite, and I was pretty sure the bread was fine, but to eat any more would have been defiant. That could end up causing trouble later, regardless of whether the bread was tainted.

Still, I didn't want to insult the Vietnamese women who had baked the bread, by throwing it away. I hoped that their English wasn't good enough that they understood what Carrington had just said. They had moved down the fence and were almost out of ear shot, so I responded in a low voice, to be sure that they wouldn't hear me, "OK, Skipper."

I put the bread in my pack, and when we set in for the night I buried the bread, making sure that I was in full view of Captain Carrington.

It was hot the next morning, and I was sweating heavily. Within two hours I had finished all the water in two of my canteens, and started on the third. I slowed down on this canteen because it was my last. We didn't come across any water all morning.

When we stopped for lunch, I finished all but a cup of my water. I hadn't been sweating as much since I'd slowed my water consumption, and now I was feeling hotter than usual. Fortunately, just before we had to move out, a helicopter came with a full water tank suspended below its belly.

I finished my last cup of warm, plastic tasting water while I waited in line at the water tank. When I got to the spigot, I filled all three of my canteens, and immediately went to the back of the line. While I waited to get to the tank for the second time, I began drinking the cool sweet water. I chug-a-lugged all of one canteen and started sipping on a second. Within a minute every inch of the thin fabric of my jungle utilities was completely saturated by my sweat, as if I'd been pouring the water on myself rather than into myself.

I drank all I could before I got to the spigot again, then refilled the two canteens I'd been drinking from, so that I had three full canteens when we moved out a few minutes later. My stomach ached from the weight of all the water I'd forced down, but I felt cooler than I had for several hours, even though it was now the hottest part of the day.

In the afternoon, the terrain was flat and open. It was mostly rice paddies, but the fields were not currently under cultivation, so they were dry and easy to walk on. In order to deny the Viet Cong access to food and a population that they could terrorize and recruit, all the civilians from the area had been moved to the refugee camp near Cam Lo. Apparently the strategy was working because, even though we often referred to the enemy as VC, the reality was that the enemy we contacted was always NVA, North Vietnamese Army.

Even with the easier walking, we didn't move any faster then we had in the morning. I lit up a cheap cigar and soon was on a nicotine high, enjoying the walk and the afternoon. At this pace, even the fifty pounds of gear I carried wasn't tiring. When we got to our camp site for the night, I felt like I could have done a few more kilometers if necessary.

There was a stream running through the perimeter we'd set up, and I went to refill my canteens. The water was a little muddy, but it was better than nothing. As I was adding a halogen water-purifying tablet to my first canteen, I saw something move on the lip. A leech. I flicked it off, nearly vomiting as I wondered if there were any more inside the canteen. I decided to wait a full hour for the halogen to purify the water, rather than the usual half hour. I also decided that if I drank directly from the canteen, I would strain the water through my teeth. I wasn't about to throw the water out though. In this heat, even the filthy muck in my canteens was better than running out of water altogether.

Just then a torrential rain shower began to pour down. I quickly took off my helmet, removed the liner, and turned the metal helmet upside down on the ground to gather water. Then I took off my utilities and boots, grabbed a small bar of soap from my pack, and took a shower. Most of the people around me did the same thing. I had just rinsed the soap off me when the rain stopped, just as suddenly as it had started. I poured the water from my helmet onto myself for a final rinse, reassembled the helmet and put it on my head. I put on my soaking utilities, and was clean for a few minutes.

I started digging my hole for the night. The idea of putting a lot of effort into digging a hole that I was just going to abandon the next morning always bothered me, so I usually dug the absolute minimum hole that I could convince myself would protect me from a nighttime artillery attack. Fortunately though, the tilled soil we had to dig in was unusually soft, and I felt good after the easy day and makeshift shower, so I ended up digging myself a pretty good hole in less time than I usually spent digging a marginal one. Just as I was finishing, we were hit by an artillery attack, and I jumped into the freshly dug foxhole. The problem with these flat open stretches was that we were visible over long distances. Charlie had probably spotted us hours earlier, but waited until dusk so that we wouldn't be able to call in air support to help find his artillery. Fortunately no one was hit by the first one or two rounds that landed while we were out of our holes, and apparently everyone else had done a good job on their holes as well, because no one was seriously hurt by any of the forty or so artillery shells that landed among us. I couldn't help thinking that it would have gone much worse an hour before, when none of us had holes dug, and most of us were standing around naked, without even our helmets on.

The next day we moved off of the rice paddies and began to make our way up into some low wooded hills. The trees gave us some shade, and again it was a pleasure to be out walking around.

As we moved along the trail, we went by a burned out tank. My apprehension grew as I looked at a million dollars or more of U.S. government equipment sitting in a tangled heap. Some combination of rust and the intense heat from the ammunition that had burned in the tank caused areas near the melted holes to be red, while most of the tank was soot black, even though it had been sitting out in the elements. If they could do a tank, they could do me.

We made contact shortly after lunch. The first platoon had the point. The lead squad was walking across an open meadow when they started taking fire from several different places in the wood line surrounding the field. Four men were killed, five others were wounded, and three men were cut off from the rest of the platoon.

The platoon couldn't get a clear firepower advantage because they had run into a system of mutually supporting bunkers. If they concentrated on one bunker and pinned down its occupant, the NVA in the two adjoining bunkers were free to fire. Captain Carrington didn't understand the situation well enough to find a way to break into the chain of bunkers. He was relying totally on his radio communications with the first platoon's lieutenant, and never moved up to see for himself what was going on.

The Company was at an impasse. We held our position for over an hour, more than a hundred men, waiting for something to happen. Nothing happened. Two attempts to flank the bunkers failed, but with no additional casualties. The men up front were being very careful now. When they tried to go around the bunkers, they found more. The three bunkers were actually part of a much larger system.

It was King who broke the impasse. He was a short timer, only twelve days left to go in the Nam. This was definitely his last operation. In a few days they would have sent him back, even if the operation was still going on. Until the firefight started that afternoon, he was probably thinking that he might actually make it home. Everybody said the last month was scary. There were a dozen stories of guys who almost made it, including the most bizarre of all, the story of the guy who got killed by a sniper bullet coming through the floor of the airplane as he was beginning his flight home. I've heard several versions of that one.

Nobody knows if King just lost patience with the pace of things, or if he thought some of the wounded guys couldn't wait any longer, or if he just wanted to be a hero and knew that this was his last chance, or if he just lost it, unable to take the tension any longer. Whatever his reasons, he got up off the ground, stood straight up, and began firing his M-60 machine gun from the hip, no easy task. This wasn't shooting blanks like in the movies, it was firing real 7.62mm NATO rounds, and it had a kickback. Most men aren't physically able to fire an M-60 like that, but King was strong. He walked toward the bunkers, firing short bursts at the mouth of each bunker - he had to keep them short or loose control of the gun. He was almost up to the first bunker when they got him, two AK-47 rounds in the chest. He went down right away. While he'd been firing and walking, other Marines had come in behind him, and from these new positions, they were able to keep up enough fire on the bunkers to get everyone out, even King himself.

The FAC, forward air controller, had choppers ready when they got the wounded back to us. The helicopters had been waiting for a while, and were so low on gas that they were just about to head back when King had broken it open. The FAC radio operator was tied up, perhaps trying to find out if there were any Phantom jets in the area that could give us air support, so I was told to bring in the medevac choppers.

I went to a clearing on the backside of the hill that they'd selected for a landing zone and switched my radio to the FAC frequency. I threw a white phosphorous grenade into the middle of the LZ and told the choppers to look for the white smoke. They responded but the message was so garbled that I couldn't understand anything they said. Regular FAC radio operators talked to the choppers all the time, and, with experience, learned to interpret what they heard, but I had no idea what the pilot had just said to me.

I was afraid to roger the message, because "Roger" means that you understand the previous transmission, but I needed to acknowledge that I could at least hear the transmission. I didn't want my inexperience to cause a chopper to crash, but I didn't want to slow things down either. Precious seconds that could make a difference to one of the wounded men were ticking by while I hesitated.

I decided that the only safe thing I could do was to admit that I hadn't understood the message, and retransmit my call about the white smoke, hoping they could hear me, and being careful not to say "Roger" in my transmission. Just as I was pressing the transmit button to do that, the first chopper appeared overhead, the prop wash from its rotors swirling the white smoke into spirals as it landed a few feet away. They had been able to understand my message, and fortunately, there had been no ambiguity to be resolved, such as someone else using a white phosphor grenade at the same time, so there was no need for back and forth communication. They just flew to the white smoke and landed.

They loaded the wounded into the two choppers. When the second chopper tried to take off, it moved into the air only about five feet, hovered there for a second, and then settled slowly back to the ground. It was so hot that the air was too thin to give them sufficient lift for a normal load. Two of the least seriously wounded - were they fortunate for that or unlucky under the circumstances? - were taken off the chopper to wait with King and the other dead bodies, and the bird flew away.

Before more helicopters arrived the regular FAC radio operator relieved me. I was glad. I didn't like trying to communicate without intelligible responses. There was just too much chance of an error not getting caught.

As soon as the second flight of choppers were out of the way, the artillery forward observer called in a massive artillery strike on the bunker system. Once he had placed his spotter rounds and given the order for a fire for effect, we headed out. It was almost dusk now, and we had to find a good place to set up a perimeter for the night.

Everyone was edgy as we swiftly retraced our path. We were just humping along, not having enough time before dark to exercise care as we moved. We were essentially gambling that Charlie hadn't come in behind us. Just after we went by the burned out tank we'd seen in the morning, Captain Carrington started yelling at me. "Why don't you have your pistol ready? Anything could happen here. I want you to carry your pistol. Got that Marine?"

I couldn't think of any reply that wouldn't get me into trouble. I knew that the military .45 caliber pistol I carried was inherently inaccurate except at point blank range, and I knew that my pistol wasn't particularly clean right then, and I knew that if something happened there would be lots of rifles laying around for me to pick up, and I knew that I had no intention of using the pistol except for close range self-defense, but I just answered, "Aye, aye, sir."

I took my pistol out of the holster, chambered a round and checked the safety. Carrington didn't say anything, but he seemed satisfied. He didn't speak again for the rest of the forty-five minute walk back to the small hill where we'd eaten lunch.

After a while I started to have trouble keeping radio contact. Finally the only way I could do it was to put on the 10-foot antenna. I hated to do that, because it made it clear that I was the battalion radio operator, the one who had to communicate over the longest distances. If Charlie was watching us and was about to strike, I would be a primary target of his first volley, even more than the other radio operators.

I moved to the side and let two more men get between myself and Captain Carrington. At least if they shot the men nearest to the battalion radio, they wouldn't get the skipper.

When we got to the small hill, we dug in well, expecting heavy contact, but we had a quiet night. I heard on the battalion radio that Kilo Company wasn't having a quiet night. They were overrun.

All during my watch my thoughts kept flitting back and forth between wondering if Sharpie was all right and remembering what a nice guy King had been. I was glad when my watch ended so I could stop thinking and go to sleep.

At first light Mike Company hustled to Kilo's position. I spotted Sharpie right away and went over to talk, keeping one eye on Captain Carrington the whole time, in case he needed the radio. "Are you okay?" I asked.

"Yeah, I made it through the night anyway," Sharpie said. "They breached the perimeter a little after midnight. It was scary. They were everywhere, but so were we, so you had to be careful of what you shot at. One of the machine guns pulled back to that hole after they broke through the line." Sharpie pointed to a hole with the idle muzzle of an M-60 machine gun sticking out of it. "Almost as soon as they got set up and started shooting again, the gunner got hit. His assistant took over the gun, and he got hit a minute later. Someone else jumped in the hole and started shooting, and he lasted a couple of minutes, but they got him too."

I thought that Sharpie was leading up to when he took over the gun, so I helped him along by asking, "So then you jumped in and took it over?"

Sharpie looked at me funny. "Are you crazy? Nobody went near that gun for the rest of the night. Three guys had held it, and all three got zapped. That was enough. You couldn't really use it anyway. With everyone all mixed in together like that, you couldn't lay down a field of fire without getting some of your own people.

"No, I just hung in there with the skipper, providing communications. That's my job. That and trying to stay alive. It wasn't easy. You had to be looking everywhere at once. After a while the skipper and I got back to back, crouching down in the hole.

"The worst of it was when someone threw a grenade in the hole with us. We couldn't find it right away, so we had to get out of the hole. Bullets flying everywhere, and all we could do is lay there in the open and wait for the grenade to go off. The fucking thing never did go off. It was a dud."

Sharpie reached down beside him and picked up a Chinese made grenade. He handed it to me by the wooden handle. "There it is."

I turned it over in my hands, awed. "No shit. How long did you wait outside the hole?"

"Over a minute," Sharpie answered. "And when we finally decided that it was safer in the hole, I just knew I was going to step on the fucking thing on the way back in, and blow myself up. The only way I got myself to do it was I told myself it must have just been a rock that fell down in the hole. Still, I wasn't surprised this morning to find it really was a grenade."

"What time did they leave?"

"About three in the morning. I guess they wanted to make a good getaway before it got light out. I'm tired, man. We didn't get any sleep."

"Why don't you get some shut eye?" I said. "We're going to be here for a while, because we didn't even eat breakfast yet. I'll keep an eye on the radios for as long as I can, probably a couple of hours."

"Thanks, Steve," Sharpie answered. "I appreciate it." He scrunched down into the bottom of the hole, almost in a fetal position, and pulled his poncho liner around himself and over his head.

Mike Company set up a perimeter that surrounded Kilo Company. We ate breakfast and then called in air and artillery attacks on the suspected NVA locations in the woods directly in front of us. The napalm runs were even more spectacular than at Hill 881, because this time we were slightly above the target, and the planes were coming from behind us and about three hundred feet to the side.

The Phantoms were flying only a few feet above the trees for the napalm runs, and when they got close, the scream of the jet engines was all I could hear. It was so loud I could feel the noise vibrating in my chest cavity. I think I even felt the heat of the flames as the gel ignited into a fireball taller than the trees.

Because the bombing runs were made from a dive, they didn't look any different than they had at Hill 881, except for one run. While the plane was still thousands of feet in the air, a small space seemed to open up between the plane and the bomb. I wasn't even sure at first that the space was there, but as the plane dove faster the space between it and the bomb grew wider, and it became clear that the pilot had accidentally released the bomb.

I was horrified to see that the bomb seemed to be coming straight at us, straight at me actually. As it fell I kept thinking how terrible it would be to go this way. I knew I was probably going to die here in Vietnam, but I didn't want to be killed by friendly fire. The closer the bomb got, the more terrifying it became. Everyone was getting down on the ground, balling up, yelling, "Hit it!" for the sake of the few guys who hadn't been watching the bomb run.

I didn't even have a hole to get into so I scrunched into a tight ball and waited for the impact, hoping I'd survive it. Finally it landed a hundred feet outside the perimeter. I was surprised that it was so far away. It had looked like it was going to land right on us. The blast was close enough that it woke Sharpie up. He threw back his poncho liner, looked around until he found me, and said, "What was that?"

"One of our Phantom jets just dropped a fucking bomb on us."

Sharpie said, "Are you alright Steve? You look as white as a ghost. How close was it."

"Not even that close," I answered, "but it sure did look like it was coming right at us. Jesus! I wouldn't want to be in the North Vietnamese Army. It must be a bitch getting bombed all the time."

Sharpie looked at me like he couldn't believe what he was hearing. "Fuck them, Steve. They'd just as soon kill you as look at you. I'm going back to sleep." He rolled up in his poncho liner again and went to sleep as if nothing had happened. Maybe nothing had. The reports came in on the radio a few minutes later. Nobody had been hurt.

After the planes and artillery had pulverized the forest for several hours, Mike Company got the word to move out. Kilo was going to stay in reserve at their present position.

Before my part of the column had even begun to move, word came in on the radio that the point platoon had contact. A sniper was keeping us from moving forward. It took over an hour for them to spot the sniper, move around him, and get him from behind. I was frustrated by the fact that one man was able to hold up a whole company of Marines for over an hour. The fact that the man had to pay a high price to do it didn't enter into it. Somehow it made me feel less powerful. Soon I started wondering why the NVA had sacrificed a man to hold us up for an hour. What was ahead that Charlie needed time to evacuate, or to fortify?

If Charlie was out there that afternoon, we didn't see him during the rest of our sweep, probably because, as usual, our sweep wasn't really a sweep at all. We never left the trail. If it wasn't visible from the trail, we didn't see it.

The next day we went back to Camp Carroll. Captain Carrington was relieved of duty as the company commander. He hadn't finished a normal field rotation, but he was assigned to do administrative work. Perhaps the powers that be were tired of Mike company getting into fire fights and always taking more casualties than they inflicted, or perhaps they were tired of Mike company going on sweeps and never finding anything until it found them, or perhaps they were tired of Mike company getting hung up for long periods of time by one or two NVA.

Whatever the reasons, Captain Carrington was assigned to do paperwork and Captain StCroix was assigned to Mike Company, even though he had only a month left to do in the Nam. StCroix had over a hundred confirmed NVA kills to his credit, with only a few of his own men killed in the process. The body count said he knew what he was doing. I started looking forward to my next trip to the field.

Operation Cimmeron started a few days later. Several battalions, including ours, swept out a large semicircle. It was rumored that the top of the semicircle was north of the DMZ, and that the circumference battalion tried to take a heavily fortified hill in North Vietnam, but was unsuccessful.

Captain StCroix turned out to be even better than I thought he would be. Many of his methods were different from Captain Carrington's. For example, when we swept an area, we didn't just stay on the trails. We spread out across the whole area. It was a lot harder. Sometimes we had to crawl on our hands and knees, or even our bellies, to get under thick underbrush. Still, no matter how flat against the ground I got, some piece of equipment was always snagging on a branch or tree trunk.

Part of the problem was my aversion to crawling on the ground. Even when there was incoming, I tended to squat down, rather than actually lie down on the ground like everyone else. I don't know why that was. It wasn't to keep clean, because I always seemed to be dirty anyway. Every time I put on a fresh set of utilities, some kind of dirty work came up, and I would get filthy right away. It happened even when we were at a base camp. I could cause a sandbag detail just by taking a shower and changing my clothes.

So I wasn't afraid of getting dirty, or dirtier, but I did have this aversion to putting my face right down on the ground. On the sweeps, I always seemed to be a little higher up than I should have been to avoid a snag. I would duck walk when I should have been on my hands and knees. I'd be on my hands and knees when I should have been on my belly.

Of course carrying a radio on my back didn't help. The corners of my radio seemed to have some kind of a tree limb magnet in them. I would gauge the distance between a limb and the ground and decide that I could get through on my hands and knees. I'd start under the branch, clearing nicely until the radio got near the branch. It would snag, and I'd be stuck. The harder I would push forward, the more stuck I would be. Finally I would end up going down on my belly and the branch would pop loose, unless I'd gotten myself really snagged, in which case I would have to get out of the back pack, free the radio, and drag it through after me.

This method of sweeping was exhausting. What was surprising was that it wasn't really any slower than Carrington's method of travel on the trails, where you could only travel as fast as the man on the point was willing to go. This usually couldn't be very fast since the NVA would watch the trails and have them booby-trapped. With StCroix's method, in the same amount of time we used to spend just observing an area as we passed through on the trails, we could truly sweep the area, covering it thoroughly, and in a way that was difficult for Charlie to defend against. Since we could arrive anywhere from any direction, and since many of the NVA booby traps and fortifications were designed on the assumption that the lazy Americans would stay on the trails, it was a lot safer for us.

StCroix was great in a firefight too, so different from Captain Carrington, who never seemed to understand exactly what was going on. We had only one fire fight on the operation, but it was a big one. We came across a major NVA base. The first contact came when Lima Company, traveling on the trails, got pinned down by one and then a second sniper in the trees. Mike Company was sent to get them out.

When the word came in to get Lima unstuck, the first thing StCroix did was to look at his map. Then he looked around for a few seconds to orient himself, looked in the direction where Lima's gunshots were coming from, then studied the map again, this time for nearly a minute. Then he strode off in the direction of the firing, giving orders over the company radio to his lieutenants, calling on my radio to have helicopter support in the area, in case we needed it.

On the way we passed through a clearing that was being used as a landing zone by Lima Company. A lieutenant from Lima was immobile on the ground, his body peppered with hundreds of small pieces of shrapnel from a booby trap. A corpsman was kneeling beside him applying bandage after bandage, but there were still dozens of places where the lieutenant's blood was oozing into his utilities.

StCroix spoke to the lieutenant to find out what he knew about the enemy placement, and, to my surprise, the lieutenant answered with some animation. As soon as we started to move on, the lieutenant resumed his corpse like pose. I couldn't tell if he was going into shock from the blood loss, or if he was just trying to hold still to reduce the pain and make it easier for the corpsman to bandage him.

On the other side of the clearing we entered the woods. Just then we got the word on the company radio that a squad from Mike Company's lead platoon had taken out the two snipers that had been pinning Lima Company down. They had approached through the woods, rather than on the trail, and caught the snipers by surprise.

I practically had to run to keep up with Captain StCroix, who was moving faster than the company as a whole in order to get up to where the action was. On the way we went past a bunker that had just been taken and a store of rice that the engineers were setting on fire.

Finally we caught up to the first platoon, which was held up now by a system of mutually supporting bunkers. StCroix talked to the platoon leader for a few seconds, checked his map, and then yelled over to me, "Find out if those choppers are on the way."

I went on the radio, then yelled back, "Hey, skipper, there's two gun ships on the way, ETA five minutes. We can relay messages to them through my radio."

StCroix answered, "Tell them that we'll set off two green smokes when we hear them coming. They can shoot at anything that moves north of the line between the smokes. Tell them if they see any bunkers along the line, blow them away." I passed the word.

StCroix got on the company radio and made sure two smokes were ready along the line of bunkers. When he could hear the whomp-whomp-whomp of the choppers getting close, StCroix gave the order to set off the smoke grenades. A few seconds later he yelled over to me, "Smoke is up."

I passed the word, "Smoke is up."

A few seconds later battalion responded. I told St. Croix, "Okay, skipper, they've got our smoke." I just barely got it out before the din of the 50 caliber machine guns on one of the gun ships made all voice communication impossible. I looked up through the tree branches, and for a few seconds I could see the bottom of the helicopter, and the orange flicker of the tracer rounds spitting from its guns.

Just before it went out of sight, it fired two rockets, which exploded about a hundred yards in front of us. They didn't fire again right away, so the rockets must have blown up the bunker, if that's what they were shooting at. For about a minute the two gun ships were moving to the north, getting further and further away. Then they turned around, still firing machine guns and an occasional rocket. As they got closer, I began to wonder if they were going to stop in time. I could only see where one of the smoke grenades had been, but by now the wind was diffusing the smoke, spreading it back toward us. I wondered if the other smoke was also being blown our way. I looked over at StCroix, but he didn't even glance back. When they were only a few hundred feet away, he yelled, "Tell them that's close enough."

I screamed into the handset, "Stop, stop, tell them they're too close."

A second later the choppers turned around and made one more pass to the north. By then they had exhausted all their rockets and most of their machine gun ammunition, so they headed back to the air base.

StCroix stood up then, and said, "Okay, lets see what we've got." The company moved slowly through the woods. They took several bunkers along the way, but none near us, until we came to a small clearing on a gentle slope. A huge tree lay across the low end of the meadow. Several Marines were behind the tree, one of them standing up yelling for a smoke grenade. I always carried a lot of smoke, in case I had to land a helicopter, so I yelled back, "I've got smoke and white phosphor. What do you want?"

"Phosphor," the marine yelled back.

I considered throwing the grenade myself, but hesitated, wondering if such an aggressive action outside my actual job description might give me bad luck. Then I flashed an image of my throw hitting a tree branch and the grenade burning a Marine, and that settled it. I threw it underhanded, still disarmed, to the Marine who'd asked for it. He caught it, pulled the pin, and winged it into the woods. A few seconds later there was a small fiery explosion and a thick cloud of white smoke began to rise through the woods.

Behind the cover of the smoke, another Marine scuttled down the hill.

Perhaps slowed by the burning phosphor, he was caught in the open when the smoke began to clear. A short burst of machine gun fire sounded from down the hill, and the Marine went down, calling for a corpsman.

The corpsman for that platoon was brand new, only three days in Vietnam. When he heard the Marine's cries, he started down the hill, not even waiting for cover fire. Just before he got to the wounded Marine, another burst of machine gun fire sounded and the Corpsman was killed.

Captain StCroix took up a position behind the dead tree, where the Marines were fighting from, and took command of the situation, preventing anyone else from going out to the wounded Marine. He yelled for the company radio operator to radio for an M-60 machine gun. I laid down on the ground about twenty feet behind StCroix, not wanting to give away the Captain's rank by being too close to him with the radio. This put me in the middle of the clearing, which I should have seen as too open, but at the moment I was just looking for a place within earshot of StCroix, even with the noise of the small arms fire, and the only good cover was behind the dead tree, which was too close to StCroix, and pretty full of Marines already. Perhaps I was influenced by the fact that Phil, the company radio operator, was also positioned near the middle of the clearing, probably for about the same reasons I was.

The machine gun crew arrived in about a minute, set up behind the dead tree - it was crowded there now - and began directing fire at the mouth of the bunker. Just as one of the Marines started to move around the tree trunk, ready to make his way down the slope, the gun jammed. The Marine quickly ducked back behind the tree, while the gunner worked frantically to clear the jam, and the rest of the Marines tried to keep the occupant of the bunker busy with short bursts from their M-16 rifles.

They were unsuccessful. The NVA in the bunker had a machine gun of his own and he began firing it in the direction of our M-60. I was caught in the open. I looked back and forth for cover, but I wasn't near anything I could crawl behind. To stand up and run for cover would surely hasten my death. There was nothing I could do but try to squeeze my body in, to somehow fit my full width behind my helmet, not even thinking of my face pressing against the ground as the rounds flew above me and on both sides of me, each so close that I was sure that the next round would get me.

The thought entered my mind that I was about to die, that the NVA in the bunker was trying to kill me - me personally, not just some Marine - and somehow, at the moment when I personalized it, I lost control of my mind. It only lasted for a few seconds, but while it lasted, I was completely overcome by fear, unable to do anything but cringe there, waiting to die. I had felt that powerless before only in my worst nightmares - the ones where I would be in great danger but unable to move or even cry out to save myself.

After a few seconds, the gunner had the M-60 going again, and we were back in control of the situation. The NVA gunner was unable to shoot at us any more. The Marine who had ducked behind the tree when the M-60 jammed started down towards the bunker again.

Sergeant Walsh, one of the men who was behind the tree, got up and ran back past me, a bleeding hole in his neck where a machine gun round had pierced him. It was his third purple heart and he was headed for the LZ to be medevaced out, and then home. I couldn't understand how a round could have hit him in the middle of the neck, without hitting something vital, but he was running at a good clip. Maybe it was a ricochet that had done the damage without going in too deep.

A minute later a call came in telling us to break it off and find a good place to settle in for the night. I told them that we were in the middle of taking a bunker, and had a wounded Marine to get out, and we'd pack it in once we took it.

I yelled down to StCroix, "Hey Skipper, they want us to break it off and find a place to set in for the night. I told them we'd leave as soon as we took this bunker."

StCroix yelled back, "OK."

While they were taking the bunker, I kept thinking about how I had lost it, been unable to do my job. That had never happened before. I felt like a coward. I tried to console myself with the thought that no one knew, since no calls had come in on the radio while I was incapacitated, and then with the thought that if a message had come in, or if the skipper had needed to send one, it probably would have broken the spell, and I probably would have done just fine, but I wasn't totally convinced. I kept remembering the panic, and wondering if I was really a coward. I kept telling myself that I wasn't, that I would have been okay if something had needed to be done, but I couldn't be one hundred percent sure. I reminded myself of the trackless trolley incident during the time when I waited to start my active duty, when I'd been a hero. I couldn't be a coward too, could I? The trolley incident would be my touchstone over the next few weeks, as my mind came back again and again to the machine gun fire, and, each time I came back to it, I wondered if I was a coward.

As soon as they took the bunker, and got the wounded Marine and dead Corpsman out, I gave them two smoke grenades to cover our withdrawal. We headed back through the woods the way we'd come in. As we walked back Phil came up beside me and said, "Man that machine gun fire was something else. I had a whole string of rounds hit on the ground in front of my arm, just a few inches away. I never felt anything like that before."

"No shit," I answered. "I don't ever want to see anything like that again." I wanted to say more, but I didn't. I think I could have said something to Phil, that maybe he had felt just as panicked as I had, but I was afraid someone else might overhear. I didn't want to make anyone nervous, wondering if I could do the job. They needed someone they could depend on to pass the word and get it right, especially when the shit was hitting the fan.

A few minutes later the man in front of me said, "Trip wire," and pointed to the ground. I spotted the thin metal wire running across the trail, stepped over it, waited there for the next man to come up, and pointed it out to him. He looked right at it when I pointed and said, "Trip wire." As I continued up the trail, I was so involved in my thoughts about cowardice that I didn't notice if he pointed it out to the man behind him or not, but a few seconds later I heard an explosion and felt a stinging on the whole right side of my face and neck. The man two behind me had tripped the wire, which, judging by the size of the explosion, had been attached to a booby-trapped 60mm mortar round.

Red came back to where I stood, stunned. "Are you okay, Steve?"

"Yeah, but they're calling for a corpsman further back."

Red stared at me for a second. "Man, you sure you're okay? The whole right side of your face is as red as a beet. Your neck too."

"I'll bet. It feels like some humongous hand has just slapped me a mighty slap. I feel okay though. I don't think my brain took any kind of a concussion, thanks to the helmet."

"Okay. I've got to go back and check on what's happening. The skipper wants to know and nothing's come in on the radio yet."

A few minutes later Red came back up the line and told me, "The corpsman's there now. The guy who tripped it got hit in the balls. Nobody else is hurt."

"Is he going to be okay?" I asked, wondering if maybe I was responsible. Maybe the guy behind me hadn't understood me, and he had just missed the trip wire by luck.

"Maybe," Red answered. "The corpsman said he's not going to die anyway. He told him he was going to be okay in the fatherhood department too, but he probably would have told him that no matter what, just to calm him down."

Later, as we were eating our C-rations, Red said, "Your face looks a little better now Steve, not so red."

"It feels better too," I said. "At first it stung so much I was afraid it got burnt, but now I think it was just the concussion. Except for this one spot on my neck that still feels funny, sort of itchy really. It feels like there's a little bump there."

"Let me see." He looked at it closely and then stepped back. "You have a small piece of shrapnel in your neck, maybe about the size of a coarse grain of sand. It's not bleeding anymore."

"No shit. My first purple heart. Two more of those and I'm out of here."

"That's doing it the hard way, isn't it?"

"Maybe," I answered. "Did you see Sergeant Walsh cut out during the fire fight. That was his third Purple Heart, and he wasn't waiting to get a fourth. As soon as our M-60 kicked back in, he went flying out of there looking for the medevac chopper. It looked like he was shot in the neck."

"Yeah, I saw him," Red said. "From the way he was running, he wasn't hurt bad, but that's still a hard way to get home. I just hope I'm lucky enough to just do my time and go home in one piece.

"Speaking of luck, did you hear about the arty forward observer from Lima Company?" Red asked, continuing without waiting for an answer. "This afternoon he and his radio operator were in a hole, and an artillery round landed in the hole with them, blew them both right out of the hole. Normally you would think a round coming after you in your hole was pretty bad luck, but the thing is, neither one of them was hurt, except they had their bells rung."

"No shit."

"Yeah, not a scratch on either one of them. No broken bones. Nothing. It blew up just right, and the concussion got to them before the shrapnel."

"That is what you call luck," I marveled. "I bet if you have that kind of luck you probably don't even need to worry about using it all up. That kind of luck has to be coming from an unlimited supply. Like a huge lake of good luck.

Whenever you need some you just reach down and grab a handful. You've got plenty, and after you've taken your handful, you look at the lake, and there's still just as much good luck left in it as there was before you took some."

"Yeah," Red joined in the fantasy, laughing as he spoke. "And if you really need a lot of luck, you just walk right in the lake, then dive in, surrounding yourself completely with it."

"Yeah, but not just a lake, it's a fucking ocean." I said, laughing, tickled by the thought of all that luck. "Like even if you just want a little bit of luck, you just sort of wade in, maybe up to your knees, but, next thing you know, these huge waves of good luck are crashing against you. It's just everywhere, even salting the air you breath, getting in your lungs, your hair, covering your skin with a fine mist of good luck. You lick your lips, and you can taste the good luck on them."

"Now that's more good luck than anybody's actually got," Red said.

"Yeah, I know."

Later that night, I had my radio tuned to the admin net rather than the tactical net. I was calling in the names of all the wounded from our company that the corpsman had given me. I was also trying to decide what to do about my own wound. I was worried that if I reported it, my family would be even more worried than they already were. They'd be notified that I was wounded in action, but they would have no idea how superficial the wound was, until they got a letter from me, which would take days to reach them.

I knew they must be worried sick anyway. Every time I got to someplace I thought was safe, I'd write them a letter to let them know, but it didn't seem to be working out. My first letter from Camp Carroll must have gotten to them just at the time when the news of the artillery attack there got to the papers at home.

I'd sent them a postcard on the back of a C-rations package, to let them know I was safe on top of Hill 881, not knowing until after I'd sent it that there were two hills 881, and the second one was still to be taken.

I knew that Cimarron was a big operation and would probably be in the news. If I sent them a letter saying I was out on operation Cimarron, that would probably end up being a worry for them, but if I reported my wound and didn't write until we got back it would be a couple of weeks before they found out that it was a minor wound.

I finally decided that the risk of worrying them unnecessarily outweighed the benefit of having my first Purple Heart. The odds of getting three minor wounds and getting out early, were pretty slim, whereas the possibility of causing unnecessary worry if I reported the wound were essentially one hundred percent.

Smitty was the radio operator receiving the messages on the other end of the admin net, so, when I was done, I started shooting the breeze with him. We weren't supposed to use the radios that way, but we kept it brief, so nobody ever said anything.

"Hey there was one more guy wounded."

"Give us the last one."

"I'm done with the list from the corpsman. This one's unofficial. I got hit in the neck with a small piece of shrapnel."

"No shit." Smitty must have been surprised. Although our normal conversations were liberally salted with obscenities, radio operators never swore on the radios.

"Yeah, but I don't want my family to find out, so I'm not going to report it. They'll just get all worried, and it's really nothing. Talk to you later. I'm switching back to the tac net now."

"Roger, see you on the tac net. Out."

We bombarded the bunker complex all night long, and into the early morning. Several tanks that were part of the operation, but that hadn't been close enough to help us the day before, were repositioned to spearhead the attack. We went in to take the rest of the bunkers, but the NVA had abandoned them during the night.

When I went by the last bunker that we had taken on the day before, I was surprised to see that the machine gun that had been firing at us was nearly an antique. It was so heavy that it was mounted on wheels so that it could be moved from place to place. Somebody said it was water-cooled. Still, it had done the job for a little while.

We moved through and blew up all the bunkers, dozens of them, and burned all the supplies we found. This had been a major medical and staging area for the NVA.

In the late morning we were eating our lunch before moving out to continue the sweep, when a call came in from the lieutenant in charge of the radio section.

"I heard you took some shrapnel yesterday."

"Yes, sir." I explained to him why I didn't want to document it.

"I want you to see the corpsman and get this documented. When you call it in, you can just include a comment on the form that the next of kin are not to be notified. Your family won't find out until you show them the medal, when you get back home."

"Yes, sir."

I went over to the corpsman and showed him the wound. He examined it and said, "I'm not going to write this up. There's not even a piece of shrapnel in it."

"I know, it was itching a lot last night when I was trying to get to sleep, and I kept scratching it. Finally the shrapnel came out in my fingernail, and it stopped itching. Red saw the piece of shrapnel in there yesterday."

"Let's go see the captain."

We went over to StCroix and the corpsman said, "This guy wants me to write up a wound on his neck that he says he got in the battle, but there's no shrapnel in it.

As StCroix examined my neck, I explained, "Skipper, there was a small piece of shrapnel in there yesterday, about the size of a coarse grain of sand, but black. It came out last night when I was scratching it. Red saw it in there yesterday. He's the one who told me that I'd actually been wounded."

StCroix turned to the corpsman. "Go ahead and write it up."

By the time we were finished with lunch, the corpsman gave me the documentation, and I called it in on the radio, being sure to specify that my next of kin were not to be notified.

The next day, in the late morning, we had a man killed, even though we had no contact with the enemy. One of the tanks that was attached to the operation had an accidental discharge of a cannon round. The round whizzed through the woods like a giant bullet, without hitting anything large enough to stop it, and decapitated a Marine. It was slowed just enough by the contact that it didn't explode when it finally hit the ground. The Marine was killed instantly.

At least that's what we think happened. Nobody was a hundred percent sure, and nobody really wanted to find out. StCroix got on the radio and had two animated but brief conversations, one with battalion and one with the tank commander, and then let it drop.

We continued to sweep the area for several days more, but had no further contact with the enemy, except that we found a few weapons. A Marine near me found one of them, a Chinese made wooden handled hand grenade. It was just laying on the ground, not booby trapped in any way. Some NVA soldier must have accidentally dropped it.

On the last full day of the operation, we were walking in a streambed, following behind Kilo Company, looking for a place to set in for the night. Kilo found a good place on a hill and radioed back to us that we should follow the riverbed for an additional three hundred meters and then look for a trail on our right that would take us up the hill. I passed the word to StCroix.

About five hundred meters later we still hadn't taken a trail to the right. I was getting pretty nervous wondering if I had gotten the word to StCroix correctly. Did I say it right? Did he hear it right? I didn't want us to end up someplace where no one was expecting us to be, because I had mumbled. That's how you end up in a firefight with other Marines.

Finally my doubts about whether I had successfully communicated were so strong that I had to make sure. I picked up my pace until I was beside StCroix and said, "Hey, skipper, the guy said it's supposed to be three hundred meters to the trail."

He answered angrily, "Don't second guess me."

I dropped back to my normal position in the line. I was angry that he had misunderstood my motivation, but in the Marine Corps enlisted men don't get into shouting matches with officers. A hundred meters later we found the trail.

My anger subsided in a few minutes, but all that evening while we were setting in, and even the next day as we returned to Camp Carroll, I wanted to let him know that I hadn't been questioning his judgment, but rather my own ability to get the word across. I never said anything.

A few minutes after we got in from the operation, Captain StCroix called me into his tent for a minute. "Steve, I want you to write a letter recommending Sergeant Walsh for the Bronze Star."

I was puzzled. It seemed to me that Walsh had just left as quickly as he could once he was wounded, which is what anybody would have done. Of course I didn't say that to StCroix. Still, he must have seen the confusion on my face, because he laid it out in more detail.

"Say that he was wounded in action and refused the help of others as he made his way back to be medevaced, not wanting to take other Marines away from the fire fight. That kind of thing."

I knew that it would only be trouble to say I didn't see it that way. I answered, "Aye, aye, sir." As I wrote the letter, it occurred to me that StCroix knew how to get things done in the administrative system of the Marine Corps, as well as in the jungle. A letter from the captain, who would be considered to have an interest in showing that he could inspire courage in his men, would not have the same weight as a spontaneous letter written by an enlisted Marine, who was grateful for the courage of a fellow Marine.

Within an hour I had written the "spontaneous" letter pretty much as dictated and given it to StCroix. I was a Corporal in the Marine Corps, and I wasn't about to confront a Captain. Even though I had no choice but to write the letter, it bothered me to be told to write about Walsh, instead of someone like King, who was killed in action while pretty much single-handedly breaking an impasse, and in the process getting a bunch of Marines medevaced sooner, rather than later.

The next day StCroix, who had less than two weeks to do in the Nam, was relieved by Captain Adams, who had just joined the battalion. If I'd known his replacement was coming so soon, I might have stalled on the letter, hoping it would slip through the cracks as StCroix passed command to Adams.

The next day I ran into Sharpie. "Hey, Sharpie, where you headed?" I called.

"Down to the COC. My first watch back with battalion is in three minutes."

I changed direction and walked down the road beside him. "So you decided to come in. How come?"

"How come? Because I have two weeks left to do in the Nam, three in the Marine Corps. I'm going to spend that time in the biggest, safest places I can. For now that's Camp Carroll. If I can wangle some kind of a detail to Dong

Ha, I'll go there. If I can wangle something in Da Nang from there, I will. Bigger is safer, and I want to be in the safest places I can be until I get out of here."

"Jesus, Sharpie, why you pissed at me? I was just asking."

"I'm mostly just pissed at Sergeant Miser. That drunk wasn't even going to bring me in. I had to go ask him, like it's some kind of a big fucking favor to get in out of the field when you're a short timer."

"Wow, I forgot you were that short."

"You ought to think about what you want to do too. Now that I woke him from his stupor, Miser might realize that you've done a full two months in the field and are eligible to rotate in if you want."

"Yeah, thanks."

We were standing outside the COC now, and it was time for Sharpie to go in for his watch. It occurred to me that I might not see him again before he left. I offered my hand. "Hey, listen, man, if I don't see you again before Mike goes back out in the field, good luck back in the states."

"Thanks, Steve," Sharpie shook my hand. "I'll see you before I go."

The conversation with Sharpie had gotten me thinking. When I saw Red later in the day, I asked him what he was going to do.

He answered, "I've been with Mike Company for almost four months now. I intend to stay as long as they let me. Sharpie's right that bigger is safer, but safety isn't everything. You gotta live too. If you stay back here at the base camp, next thing you know somebody will be asking you when was the last time you got a haircut, or when was the last time you polished your boots, or they'll be telling you you're using too much obscene language, or some other happy horseshit. Every time the base camp has more than ten days without incoming, they'll start treating you like shit.

"Out in the field they never treat you like shit. They know you have live rounds in your weapon, they know the shit could hit the fan at any time, and

189

they know that, if they piss you off too much, you could kill them and get away with it. That makes the field about the only place in the whole Marine Corps where an enlisted man can get treated like a human being. That makes it the right place to be, at least for me."

I thought about what Red said for a minute, then agreed with him. "I guess it is right for you. What I've got to decide is whether it's right for me."

The next day Sergeant Miser finally did come around and ask me if I wanted to come back to the radio section of H&S Company. I knew that I felt less safe with Adams, the new captain of Mike Company. How could someone new be anywhere near as good as StCroix? What if he turned out to be as bad as Carrington? But even though Adams was still a bit of an unknown quantity, what Red had said about the field was true. You just did your job, and nobody gave you any crap. I told Miser I wanted to stay in the field.

The following afternoon Mike Company left to be the reserve unit for an operation near Hue. We were trucked to the main base at Dong Ha, where we boarded amphibious landing craft. We rode inside them to the South China Sea, but I can't remember whether the trip was over land, or down the river. I just know that the troop bay doors opened, and there we were at the mouth of the river, near some sand dunes overlooking the ocean. We got out and heated our C-rations to the sound of the ocean lapping the beach. There was a sea breeze cooling the air, and the sand was soft to sit on. It was like being at a resort.

Sometimes, if things were too easy, I'd start to worry, waiting for the other shoe to drop. But on that operation there was no need. We arrived at our destination near Hue the next day, and just hung around beside the amtracks for a few days, waiting for the call that never came.

Gio Linh

When the amtracks returned us to Dong Ha, the trucks we boarded there didn't go back to Camp Carroll. Instead, they headed north to Gio Linh, a firebase just below the DMZ, on what was left of Highway 1 - right on it. Highway 1 is the main north/south road in Vietnam, but since nobody was allowed to use it to pass between North Vietnam and South Vietnam the gates to the fire base were always closed. In addition the road itself had been completely obliterated by the bunkers and trenches that were the base. If you had looked at the base from the air it probably would have looked like a low pile of red clay and washed out green sandbags, with the road sticking uselessly out of the north and south ends of it.

From the base, tank mounted cannon would shoot hundreds of rounds a day into the southern part of North Vietnam. We also received about a hundred artillery rounds a day, so we all lived and worked in underground bunkers, except of course for the artillery which had to be out in the open to fire. All the bunkers were connected by trenches, most of them about four feet deep, so that, as you moved from bunker to bunker to go on watch or to go to sleep, your helmeted head could look out over the tops of the bunkers and see a little daylight or moonlight.

Gio Linh had a lot of telephone lines connecting the bunkers. Since that was Red's department, he needed to spend a lot more time monitoring and repairing the landlines then he normally would when we were mobile, because the wires were often cut by incoming artillery rounds. In the field he would lighten our load by taking radio watches for us, but at Gio Linh he ended up on phone watch at the same time we were on radio watch. He had the same six on and six off watch schedule as me, so we spent most of our time together for the month we were there. With many people, a month of constant contact would be a problem, but with Red it was a pleasure. Before Gio Linh we had been coworker type friends, but during that month we became close friends.

It was probably our differences that made it possible to sustain all those hours of conversation. He was a country boy from rural Georgia, and I was a city boy from Somerville, Massachusetts, at the time one of the most densely populated cities in the world. Our life experiences couldn't have been more different if we'd been from two different planets.

In Georgia, on most days, he wouldn't meet a single person that he hadn't known all his life. In Somerville, I knew only a few of the hundreds of people that I came in contact with every day. His natural tendency was to be open and friendly, while mine was to be closed but civil.

Civil was a subject that came up often, the Civil War that is. Although he knew that all of the battles of the Civil War had already been fought, he still didn't believe that it was really over. He constantly brought up issues of states vs. federal rights that I had never even considered before I met him. Which led to the most central issue of all, the one where we had our biggest differences, segregation vs. integration. He believed in separate but equal, while I thought that integration would eventually insure equality.

But what was important was that, although Red had some strongly held beliefs that were different from mine, he always respected my right to hold different views. None of our discussions ever turned into fights, and I always felt free to tell him exactly what I thought. He welcomed my opinion, even when it was different from his, just as he welcomed the opportunity to perhaps change my view of things. This was good because I tended to be a little more dogmatic than he was, and it would have been a tough month if Red had been overly righteous as well.

Basically, Red was a kind man. I knew that from my first days with Mike Company, when someone had thrown a grenade at an incoming patrol, and he came to tell me that I was in the clear of any charges. All the stories and discussions during that month at Gio Linh confirmed that initial impression.

Sometimes the artillery units would leave the base to fire their missions from a different location, and, when they did, they would bring part of the infantry company with them for protection. One time it was my turn to go out with the artillery, and we ended up near the village of Gio Linh, which was just south of the base. It was one of the few inhabited villages left in the DMZ area. I didn't understand the point of moving the guns so close to the town, especially since the spot they chose was out in the open, but that's what we did.

Some of the people came over from the village to sell us bread and Coke. For some reason, even after the sale was made, some of the Vietnamese chose to stay with us for the rest of the day. A pretty young woman came over to where I had the radio set up and began to talk to me in broken English. She was the first woman with whom I had an actual conversation in the four plus months that I'd been in Vietnam. Talking to her was a pleasure, even though it made me realize how much I missed the company of women.

It was a beautiful day, and I was set up under some trees, so the heat wasn't too bad, and it just felt good to be there, rather than in an underground bunker. The woman had even brought her lunch with her, and when we started to cook our C-rations, she unpacked a bowl of rice and had a picnic with us.

By late afternoon the artillery had completed their fire missions, and we started packing up to go. Instead of assuming the best about her, for example that she was there just to be nice to the G.I.s, or even assuming an innocent ulterior motive, for example that she was there to practice her English language skills, I chose to assume that perhaps she was there looking to exchange money for sex. I'd had no indication of any such thing, at any moment during the day. She had been a perfect lady. Yet I repaid that woman's kindness in spending the day with us by asking her if she wanted "boom-boom." She refused and left immediately, and I immediately regretted that I didn't give her the benefit of the doubt.

On the way back we were walking on Highway 1, and a young Vietnamese man went jogging by on a trail beside the road. I only caught a glimpse of him as he ran, smoothly balancing a load of some sort on either end of a stick on his shoulder, but I was immediately suspicious, because he seemed to be of military age. Nobody else seemed to notice or care much, so I didn't do anything about it either, but, as we continued along, it struck me that the reason the young man had stood out was that, during the whole day, I hadn't seen a single man of military age near the village.

That's when it hit me. If I was lucky, I'd be home in six months, and able to talk to a girl anytime I wanted, but these people were stuck here leading this unnatural life for the duration. No wonder the young girl wanted to spend the day talking with us. Our visit to the village might well be her only chance to talk to a man her own age for a month at a time.

One day I went out on a squad sized patrol - sort of a novelty for me since I was a radio operator for the whole company, but they needed a radio operator, I wasn't on watch at the time, and I was tired of living like a mole, so I volunteered to go out. We went to a deserted village overlooking the DMZ.

All the houses were on both sides of a single street. They were made of clay bricks, with a skim coat of red clay added to smooth the walls. There were doorways and window holes, but no doors or windows in them. All the houses had dirt floors and thatched roofs, and many had a clay partition to divide the house into two rooms.

The town was spooky, a ghost town. I felt sad to see what had once been home to maybe a hundred people completely deserted. Some of the houses still had a few belongings in them, things the Vietnamese couldn't carry or didn't want when the village was evacuated, a huge pot here, a broken plate there. When I would see something in a house, I'd get the feeling that people still lived there, like everyone was just out somewhere.

As we walked down the street, I kept expecting people to pop out of the clay houses, but there was no one there. As sad as it was, it was pretty scary too. I kept expecting NVA to jump out from behind the empty doorways or pop up behind the window holes, but fortunately they weren't there either. If they had been, they would have had us all. That was the problem with a squad-sized patrol. There were only a dozen of us, and almost anything that could happen would be bad for most of us. The survivors would call in the big guns, so in the end it wouldn't go that well for the NVA either, but that was small consolation. We were just cannon-fodder, out there extending our sphere of influence by trying to draw enemy fire, to convince them that they had such superiority that they could afford to engage us. Pretty much the whole time we were out, I kept hoping nothing would happen. I was relieved when we got to the end of the row of houses. The deserted village had seemed like a particularly dangerous place.

The village was located on a hill, overlooking a wide, low plane, half of which was in South Vietnam, half in North Vietnam. The artillery forward observer who was with us pointed out a small bridge across a river that flowed through the middle of the plane. He said it was the Freedom Bridge. I remembered the documentary/propaganda film they'd shown us in boot camp about the partitioning of the country. I felt like I was looking at an historical monument, which, of course, I was. It made me feel better about being there, and about what the people of South Vietnam had to go through, to know that so many of them had chosen this path, rather than live under Communism.

The FO gave me the coordinates of a hill in North Vietnam that he wanted hit. By then I was becoming so superstitious about not ruining my luck, that I was having second thoughts about calling in the mission. Somehow the thought had gotten into my head that if I didn't actually kill anyone by my own hand, except if I had to, in self-defense, then maybe my luck would hold up and I would survive. But here there was no choice. The FO had a target he wanted hit, and it was my job to call in the coordinates he gave me. I decided that if it was my job, then I could to do it, and it would be OK. I just couldn't voluntarily do more than my job. I called in the artillery mission, and we moved on.

Our last stop was at a small Buddhist temple. I felt like an invader as we walked up the steps to check it out, like I was violating someone's religion. I wasn't sure if it was okay to wear shoes there, but even if shoes were okay, muddy jungle boots were probably a desecration. I was glad there was no one there to see us and be offended or enraged by our presence in their holy place.

It did feel like a holy place. It was so simple, just stairs on all four sides leading up to a platform, and over it all, the gentle arc of the roof. The only thing in the temple was a pedestal with an ebony statue of the Buddha sitting and meditating, unchanged by the war. It seemed to be showing the way to peace, to a serenity that made me want to join in the prayer or contemplation. Being there was the closest I'd come to praying for a long time.

I was tempted to place an offering in the wooden bowl that rested on the statue's lap, but decided that Charlie would probably be through there to pick it up long before a monk would. That thought broke the spell. I turned outward from the temple, using the height of the temple's platform as a vantage point to look out over the land. Being out there with only twelve men was no time to relax and get religion. Still, I felt like I was missing out on something when we left the temple and headed south, back to the base.

A few days later we got word that Captain Carrington had gotten zapped. They had taken him away from his administrative job, and sent him out with India Company, because India's commander was a short timer, and they didn't have anyone else to send.

Carrington didn't even last a full day with India. Supposedly a sniper got him, but Red and I both wondered if he got shot by one of his own men. I couldn't stand his arrogance when I had to work for him, but I still felt sort of bad that he got it. He didn't have a talent for field command, but he shouldn't have had to die for it, if that's what happened. Or maybe he did get killed by Charlie. Maybe he was trying a little too hard to make good this time, and he went when he should have stayed, or stayed when he should have gone. Maybe he was doing everything right, and his luck just ran out.

They sent India's original skipper back to the field. By the time they got another replacement for him, he must have been a basket case. I think he had only a few days left to do in country, when they finally got him out of the field.

About that time I got a letter from my brother Paul, who was studying at Harvard Divinity School. He wanted to know how I felt about using Napalm. He said it's not a very humane weapon. Here's the gist of the letter I sent back.

Dear Paul,

I got your letter today. Perhaps unfortunately, we have lots of time on our hands here at Gio Linh, so I can answer right away. I say unfortunately, because I'm sort of pissed at your letter, and it would probably be better if I didn't have time to answer for a few days. I think you've been hanging around your classmates from Harvard too long.

Although I have to admit that napalm doesn't seem to be a very humane weapon, you have to understand that things look a little different from here than they do from a college campus, or anywhere else back in the states.

From here it just seems to be about survival. If there's some weapon we have that will give us a little edge, then I'm all for it. I know that may seem dishonorable, but so be it. I guess it's about time that we got used to the idea that there's not much honor left in modern warfare. The weapons are too sophisticated compared with our puny ability to survive them.

Where is the honor when you line up a man's head in the sights of your rifle? Where is the challenge? The glory. The heroism. What incredible odds are overcome as you squeeze off the round that will obliterate his mind?

It bothers me to feel this way, to have my feelings override any higher principle, but I can't help being most interested in my own survival. The NVA will kill me in a minute, if they get the chance. I don't think I owe humane treatment to people who are trying to kill me. I really don't. I'll use any weapon at my disposal that will make it more likely that I'll survive, and they won't.

So much for honor. "Death before dishonor," they train us. Sure we have a kind of honor here. We try and stick together, and see it through, and get it done. We have that kind of honor, but we are not honorable men. We're just survivors. At least some of us will be. Some of us will lose our honor and our lives.

They talk about humane weapons. None of these weapons are particularly humane. They're not supposed to be. It's not humane to shoot someone, no matter what the caliber of the weapon. If we wanted to be humane about this whole thing, we could just line up all the people and weapons and figure out who would win each battle, without getting a bunch of people killed and maimed in the process. We could all fill out little questionnaires that would measure our morale and see who wanted to win the most. Plug it all into a huge equation - how many M-16s - how many AK-47s. We would have done this next. Yeah, well if you did that we'd do this. All these generals think they know what wins battles and what wins wars. They could just add it all up and see who has the most of what it takes, but they don't do it that way.

It's clear that we're not here to be humane, and neither are the NVA. A few days ago, about two miles from here, three Marines were burned in a trench by an NVA flame thrower. I know that doesn't make it right for us to burn them, but it makes it feel right from here.

I remember in boot camp I got a letter from our brother, John. He'd already been through Parris Island by then and knew what to expect. He told me, "Don't let them make an animal out of you." That letter helped me. I yelled "Kill. Kill. Kill." as loud as the rest of them, but I held something back through the fatigue and the brainwashing. I wasn't going to let them make an animal out of me. I'm starting to wonder if Vietnam has succeeded where Parris Island failed. It really feels okay to me that we use napalm.

I'm going to sign off now, Paul. Sorry if I was a little pissed in this letter, but I feel like you people aren't really trying to understand what it's like here. You seem to have a lot of empathy for the enemy, but not for your own troops.

Love,

Steve

The following week we had several days of particularly hot weather. Even the underground bunkers got heated up. On the last day of the heat wave, Red and I were on watch all night, and when we got off we went down into our living bunker. There was no air moving there - there never was - but now the stagnant air was both dank and warm.

I sat on my cot for a few minutes, hoping to cool down, but it was too humid. The sweat just beaded on my pores, until the individual drops began to grow together into little streams that dribbled down my neck and arms. Finally I jumped up off the cot and told Red I was going to try and find someplace outside to sleep. He came along.

We looked everywhere. The safest place would have been down in the trenches that connect the bunkers, but the pathways were just wide enough for a man to walk through. If someone were to lie down in the trench, the passage would be blocked.

There was a nice breeze on the bunker tops, but they would be in the direct sun most of the day. Once the sweat dried it wouldn't be cool. Besides, there'd be no protection from incoming on top of a bunker. If you ever got hit up there and survived it, they'd probably court martial you for not taking care of government property, or whatever the charge is for not being careful enough.

After making a circuit of the whole base looking for an out of the way cranny that was well protected, cool, and breezy, and that wouldn't be visited by an officer, we ended up back at the radio operators' bunker, where we'd started. It was the only safe place. We climbed back down into the hole. I sweated for a while, and finally fell asleep.

Looking back on what happened later, I wonder if I planted an idea in Red's mind that day, a rogue idea that would eventually grow strong enough to overrule all common sense. I also wonder if things would have been different if I'd stayed out with Mike company, rather than returning to the radio section of H&S company.

Cam Lo

After a month at Gio Linh, Mike Company moved to Cam Lo, where the battalion had just begun to set up a new base camp near the refugee village there. I think the walk back from Gio Linh was really what decided me to come in from the field. It was a very hot day, and they had a new rule that you had to wear your flak jacket and keep it zipped closed whenever you were outside the perimeter, so it was even harder than usual to keep from getting overheated.

We didn't even have to walk that far. The trucks bringing in the new company picked us up at the same time, but they did the transfer south of the base, so it wouldn't be so visible. Still, the walk was just far enough for me to get hot, and for my hip to start aching, as it always did from the weight of the radio plus my own gear. It was just far enough for me to remember what it was like humping the boonies on a bad day.

Instead of returning us to Camp Carroll, the trucks brought us to Cam Lo. A few minutes after I got there, I ran into Sergeant Miser. He asked me if I was ready to come in yet, and I told him I was, and that was that. They sent my replacement the next day. I spent the day getting him oriented, and then I gave him my cot and backpack frame, and moved my gear to the battalion radio section.

Almost everyone was new there. Sharpie was long gone. Of the guys that I thought of as old hands, the only ones left were Jackson and Miller, and they were both short timers, leaving the next day to spend their last few days in the relative safety of Dong Ha. I had about five months in-country, and the next day I would be the radio operator in the battalion radio section with the most combat experience, the old hand.

A couple of days later, we were setting up a new tent to be used as the radio supply tent, and I asked one of the new guys to do something. Instead of hopping right to it, he continued to talk, almost as if he hadn't even heard me. I grabbed him by the front of his shirt, shoved him back against the center pole of the tent, and lifted him up onto his toes. I said, "Look, asshole, don't think just because I asked nice that I don't want it fucking done. When I ask you to do something, that is an order. I want it done, and right fucking now. Got that?"

The incident had started out as some kind of theatrics, a training exercise for the edification of a newbie, but somehow before I was done speaking I was enraged. Maybe I was just tired that day. We had an expression – "All tired and pissed off" – that was a good description of how a combat Marine often feels, because we had to work at least part of almost every night. Another possibility is that, now that I was safely out of Gio Linh, I was reacting to the fact that we had been under daily artillery fire for a month. Explosive rage can be a symptom of PTSD. Whatever the cause, I had totally lost it over a relatively minor incident. I don't know what my face looked like at that moment, but if the fear on the new guys face was any indication of what was on mine, I think I must have looked angry enough to do anything.

Fortunately, because I don't know what would have happened if he hadn't submitted totally, he said, "Yes, I've got it."

I put him down and he immediately went to do what I'd asked him to do. I felt bad for letting my theatrics get out of hand, but I never did apologize. I never even thought of an apology as a possibility. I'd always wanted to be a Marine, and somewhere along the line I had become one, right down to being a much bigger jerk than was absolutely necessary. I wasn't proud of it.

A few days later I had the runs, but I didn't know it. You might say I found out by accident. I was on radio watch in the COC, breaking in a new man. A call came in from the refugee camp at Cam Lo village, about a kilometer from our base, saying they had contact on the perimeter. After the initial contact, nothing happened for about fifteen minutes. We called back to see how things were going, but we started having trouble with the radio. It needed a new battery.

I looked under the bench, where we usually kept a few spares, but there were none there. I asked the new man if he knew where we kept the spare batteries in our tent, but he didn't. Since the tent was only a hundred and fifty feet away, and since I expected to be gone for only two minutes, I decided to go myself.

I ran to the tent, stooped over the battery box, stacked five of the rectangular batteries up my left arm, reached in for two more to carry in my right hand, started to stand up, and shit all over myself.

My duty was to immediately run back to the COC, install the new battery, and sit in my own shit for the rest of the night, or at least until somebody competent came along to watch the radios for a few minutes. There was no doubt in my mind that that was the right thing to do.

Instead I put down the batteries and quickly took off the trousers, hopping on one foot and then the other to get them off over my boots, trying in the dark to not touch anything with the saturated center of the pants. I wiped myself with the soiled pants, and rolled them into a tight ball with the crotch in the middle so the sharp odor would escape more slowly, perhaps slowly enough to be dissipated without disturbing any of the sleeping radio operators. I found another pair of pants in my sea bag and put them on. I took the time to do all this, about three minutes, knowing that during that three minutes anything could be happening at the refugee village, knowing that maybe someone was getting killed right then because I left an inexperienced man on the radios alone. I was back at the COC with the batteries within five minutes of when I left, very glad to hear that nothing had happened at Cam Lo village while I was gone.

I thought about it during the rest of the watch. It just didn't make sense. Here I was, risking my life to help the people of South Vietnam, yet I wasn't willing to suffer embarrassment for the same cause. The more I thought about it the less sense it made. Finally I hit on the real difference. If I did die, I would expect to be honored for that. I would expect just the opposite for stinking up the COC. I could make no other sense of it.

About that time an incident occurred while I was on radio watch. The captain from some company in a battalion that was on the way to Con Thien was in the COC, talking to some of our officers. His company had ridden to Cam Lo by truck, and was about to walk the last few kilometers to Con Thien. He asked to use the radio, and I gave him the handset. He observed the normal radio procedures getting in touch with the commander at Con Thien, but once he was talking to him, it became apparent that they were old friends. He started to joke around, and all of a sudden he started to tell the commander that he was on the way there, and would be there in a few hours. I was appalled at this breach of security. Because radio transmissions can be monitored by anyone, you have to assume that the enemy is listening to every word you say. If they were listening, this officer had just given them advance warning of one of our troop movements, which could have devastating consequences. I wanted to take back the handset, but I was afraid of having a confrontation with an officer.

Fortunately, one of the officers from the COC had heard the loose conversation, and immediately came over and took the handset and gave it to me, along with a dirty look. I was relieved that the situation was resolved without my having to confront an officer, because I knew that was something that usually didn't work out very well for an enlisted man. I was also relieved later that day, when I heard that the company had made it to Con Thien without incident. I would have felt partially responsible if they had come under attack that afternoon.

It was at Cam Lo that someone stole my radio – not one of the radios I worked with, but my own personal radio that I used to listen to music from the armed forces station, when we could get reception. The theft was my own fault, in a way, because I'd had it sitting on a large rock outside the tent, and I'd forgotten to put it back in my sea bag when we all left for the mess tent at lunchtime. When we came back, it was gone.

It was a common model of radio, a Sony portable in a black leather carrying case. I'd bought it in a shop across from the main gate on Okinawa, which probably explains why there were so many of them around, and, though it hadn't been super expensive, I think around $30, it had been the single luxury purchase I'd allowed myself, and I couldn't afford to replace it. Besides, there was no place where I could buy another, and even if I could have bought one, mine had a lot of sentimental value because it had a hole in the leather where a piece of shrapnel had embedded after ripping through my sea bag on my sixth night in Vietnam. Thinking about that made me realize that my radio was unique. I'd be able to tell it apart from others of the same model. I decided to find it.

I began walking around the base, my eyes scanning back and forth looking for the radio. Although I didn't realize it, I must have looked like a thief myself. The first time I spotted a radio like mine, I told my story and asked for permission to look at it more closely. I verified that it didn't have a shrapnel hole, and proceeded on.

When I spotted the next radio, it didn't go as well. The Marine who owned the radio looked at me suspiciously as I eyeballed it. I approached and told my story. When I asked to examine his radio, he became angry. "What, are you accusing me of stealing your radio?"

"No, I just want to look at it is all." But of course, just looking was accusing him. Still I had to wonder why he was so angry. Could it be a ruse to prevent me from finding my radio in his possession? I walked over to the radio. Because the leather case was black, I had to bend down to get close enough to verify that it didn't have a shrapnel hole, but I didn't physically touch the radio. There was no shrapnel hole. He'd just been angry because he was. Still there were a lot of angry Marines. We joked and laughed, but we were always on edge, ready to explode at the slightest provocation. I could see that I might get myself into some serious trouble, if I kept up my search. Besides, I suddenly realized that I would only be able to see radios that were out in the open. What were the chances that a thief would put his booty out in plain view within an hour of stealing it?

The only possibility left was to report the theft to the higher ups. They had the right to inspect all our belongings at any time and would have a good chance of finding the radio, but, perhaps because of the amount of extra work involved, reports of theft were strongly discouraged. Their attitude would be that I had caused the problem by not properly securing the radio, and I was as much to blame as the thief. Even if they found the radio, it would be a problem for me. I had to accept that my radio was gone for good.

It was either at Cam Lo or later at the Rock Pile that they found a cobra. Although I remember the moment well, I can't remember enough of the surrounding physical or temporal details to categorically place it at one camp or the other. I do remember walking past the radio repair tent, and noticing that everyone was gathered outside the tent in a circle. It almost looked like one of the smoking circles from boot camp, but, instead of a red butt bucket in the middle of the circle, there was a black cobra. Most of his body was coiled under him, but his head was sticking up, and his hood was flared, as he threatened a Marine who cautiously approached him with a machete. When the Marine continued to advance, the cobra suddenly lowered his head and slithered back toward the tent. I was amazed at how quickly he could crawl, as were the Marines who didn't have machetes and were forced to run when the snake approached. In just a few seconds the snake had changed the circle into a horseshoe shape, as it slid past the Marines to hide in the pallets that formed the flooring for the tent.

I continued on my way, not envious of the men who would have to carefully pull up each pallet until they found the snake and killed it before it hurt someone.

While I was at Cam Lo, some general flew in to award the Purple Hearts for the battalion. We recipients all stood at attention in a single long row, and the general moved down the rank. He would stop in front of each Marine, and someone would hand him the medal. The General would then pass the medal to the Marine and ask, "Where did you get hit, Marine?" I could see out of the corner of my eye that, as each Marine answered, the general would look at the affected part of the Marine's body.

My presence at the ceremony was mandatory, but I was embarrassed to be there among the other awardees. Although the most seriously wounded Marines usually didn't return to the battalion, many of the men on either side of me had received serious wounds, and had suffered through weeks of pain before healing well enough to come back. My injury had been so slight, that I felt that somehow my presence diluted the magnitude of what they had been through. To make it worse, it had been about six weeks since I'd been hit, and the tiny wound was completely healed. I didn't have even a hint of a scar. I kept flashing this image of the general standing in front of me, craning his head back and forth, trying to find something on my neck that looked like an old wound.

When the general got to me, he handed me my Purple Heart. I took it in my left hand and saluted with my right. The general returned my salute, then asked, "Where did you get hit, Marine?"

I stood at perfect attention, eyes looking out to infinity, and sounded off,

"On operation Cimmeron, Sir."

The general hesitated for a moment - I wish that I could have looked directly at him to try and figure out what he was thinking - and then moved on to the next man.

A few days later we had a memorial service for all the guys who'd gotten killed since the battalion came in country. We were all lined up in formation, at parade rest, and they read all the names. It seemed a little strange because they broke it down by company, like it was some kind of a competition. You didn't die for your country, or to defend the people of South Vietnam. You died for the greater glory of Lima Company or Mike Company or H&S Company. All through the chaplain's prayer, which followed the reading of the names, I kept thinking it was sort of embarrassing to be part of H&S Company, because our list was relatively short compared with the line companies' lists. I was glad that I'd done three months with Mike Company.

When the bugler played taps though, I forgot all that. As we stood there with our heads bared and bowed, listening to the trumpet cry, I kept hoping the last sad note would play on, as if they wouldn't be totally lost to us as long as the bugler could sustain that last note, but he finally cut it off. In that silence the sense of loss was profound.

We were dismissed immediately. As we broke formation and walked away, nobody spoke to or even looked at anyone else. No one wanted to see anyone else's tears.

Con Thien

After H&S company had been at Cam Lo for about a month, the whole battalion moved to Con Thien. While we were there, we were taking in about 500 rounds of incoming a day, twice that on bad days, mostly artillery, with the occasional rocket thrown in. The base was desolation with roads, like a section of a city that's been demolished in preparation for urban renewal, empty streets separated by empty lots, only at Con Thien the ground never lay undisturbed long enough for the weeds that would normally populate vacant ground to germinate.

Yet, even without roots to anchor the soil, the low mounds scattered over the base didn't erode, even during this, the monsoon season, because the mounds were really the tops of bunkers, and thousands of plastic sandbags, hidden just below a damp dusting of exploded earth, held the soil in place. The mud of these vacant lots was covering a subterranean civilization of Marines.

We stayed underground as much as we could, leaving the bunker where we lived and slept, only to go on watch in the bunker where we worked. Sometimes, on the way to watch, I'd look out across the whole base, and I wouldn't see another person.

Other times, if a helicopter had just come in, there would be a large work party, like a colony of ants, trying to get the supplies underground quickly, but that was rare. There weren't very many helicopters because it was the monsoon season, and often the cloud cover was so thick and low that the chopper pilots couldn't get in safely. Sometimes the ceiling was high enough, but the incoming was so heavy that the helicopters couldn't land long enough to unload.

When we could get resupplied, the priorities were set. The most important thing to bring in was ammunition, then medical supplies, then food. We heard that some of the units were down to one C-ration a day on some days. We were lucky, because the people who had occupied our bunker before us had stocked up plenty of food while the weather was better. We had enough for two or three meals a day. Supposedly one C-ration a day is enough to sustain life, but your average nineteen or twenty year old can't feel satisfied on so little food, even with the sedentary lifestyle that was imposed by underground living.

One of the places I hated to go on that base was to the latrine. It was made of sheet metal and protected by sandbags on only three sides, with no overhead protection, so it was not a safe place to be. This became clear the first time I went there, because, as soon as I sat down, I looked at the wall a few feet in front of me and saw daylight through dozens of jagged shrapnel holes.

Not that I would have been tempted to stay long if it had been safe. The stench was awful. It had been weeks since the cut off fifty-five gallon drums which sat under the holes of the three seater, each drum holding about twenty gallons of human waste, had been cleaned. It was normal practice at other bases to burn out the drums of waste every day using diesel fuel. That was impossible at Con Thien, because the plume of black smoke from the incomplete combustion of the fuel would have made it easier for the NVA forward observers to direct their fire.

That first day, as I got up and started to button my utility trousers, a motion caught my eye. I looked down through the middle hole of the three seater at the drum below, and saw no sign of the deposit I had just made. The drum was full to the brim with a beige liquid that appeared to be boiling. I knew that was impossible - it was only about seventy degrees out. I looked closer and saw that what I had thought was a liquid was actually thousands of maggots, rolling over and over each other, teeming to get to the top or to the bottom - I have no idea which they preferred. Whichever it was, they were never able to stay there long before being pushed aside by the others.

From that first day until the day I left Con Thien, I never bothered to bring a book with me to the latrine. I knew when I went there, that I wouldn't be staying any longer than was absolutely necessary.

One of the biggest treats during our month at Con Thien was when one of the radio operators from the base camp managed to wangle a helicopter ride. He brought us much needed radio batteries, but, even more important, he snuck in a few goodies in the bottom of the box, not the least of which was a set of brand new utilities for each of us.

We had our only mail call for that whole month. Somebody got a package from home with that most delectable delicacy, a canned ham. We had a party, all dressed to the nines in our brand new jungle utilities. It felt so good to put them on. From the time I left the womb, I'd never spent so much time wet, as I had at Con Thien. That day was the first time in a full week of days and nights that I was completely dry.

By the time I was changed, the dank smell of the bunker was already being flavored by the sweet smoke from the singed ham slices, frying in a mess kit over a heat tab fire. While we waited for the piece de resistance, someone passed around hors d'oeuvres, crackers topped with cheese spread from a pressurized can.

The same guys who only hours before had been sitting around telling stories filled with yearning for home, were gathered around laughing and telling jokes. It was so much like a campfire, I kept expecting someone to disappear for a minute and come back with a miraculous bag of marshmallows. For a while, I didn't want to be anywhere else.

I felt so good when I went to bed that night, that I barely flinched when a centipede ran out from under the bed, as I sat down to take off my boots. I didn't even bother to try and kill it before it wriggled into a crack between two sandbags.

The next day I was almost killed. I was walking down the path, on my way to watch, when I heard a round coming in. As it whistled louder and louder, I realized this was going to be a close one. I had waited too long, and only had time to crouch down. I was pretty low, but I should have been lying down for this one. It was so close I thought it was going to land right on me. It seemed to be from a direct fire weapon, coming in at me, not down from above. Maybe that was why there was so little time to react.

Before it hit, I made it down to all fours. I closed my eyes and tried to draw myself in, to cover myself with my helmet and flak jacket. I must have looked like a turtle. Just when it seemed so loud that it had to hit me, I heard it land about 15 feet in front of me.

It took a measurable amount of time before I realized that it hadn't gone off. I stuck my head up and looked over at where I'd heard it land, and then around, as if I'd be able to see the next one coming.

I got up and took three steps, and looked down into the steaming hole. The round was hot enough to vaporize some of the water in the soil, but it hadn't gone off.

I turned around and looked out at the distant tree line to the south, where the round must have come from. I wanted to give them the finger, but I was afraid they'd be getting another round off any minute. Instead I walked to the command bunker, slow, surly, every step scoffing at their inability to kill me. I hoped they were watching, feeling like losers. The tree line was far enough away that they couldn't see how shaken I was.

All during watch I kept thinking about that round. If it had gone off at that range, it almost certainly would have killed me. I wondered what percentage of the rounds that landed were duds. I knew it was high by our standards, maybe fifteen or twenty percent, because the ground was so soft from all the rain. An artillery round has to be able to take fairly large accelerations without exploding, because one of the things that happens to it is that it gets shot out of a gun. No one would want an artillery round that would explode in the gun that was firing it. When there are very sudden changes in velocity, such as impact with the ground or other solid object, the round is supposed to explode. During the monsoon, many of the enemy's artillery rounds hit the ground so "softly" that they didn't explode. The one that was supposed to kill me was one of those. Still, I couldn't get the image of that shell hole out of my mind, especially the wisp of vapor floating at the top of the hole, as if the hot shell was alive and breathing moist air.

The last time I saw Red was about a week before we left Con Thien. It wasn't raining for a change, and I wasn't due on watch, and there weren't many rounds coming in, and it just seemed like a good opportunity to drop over to Mike Company for a visit. I exchanged pleasantries with a few of the guys and then found Red. We talked for a while, and then he showed me the sandbag hooch he'd built outside for himself. It was only one sandbag layer thick and had a top that was partially covered with sheet metal. I said, "Red, there's no real roof on this thing. What if a round comes in?"

"I know, but I can't stand the smell of the bunker. I can't sleep down there any more. I need the fresh air."

"Jesus, Red, you're taking an awful big chance."

"I know, I know. But I need to sleep too."

I wasn't comfortable in the openness of the hooch, and Red was nice enough to follow me back down into the bunker he hated, so we could finish our visit.

A few days before I left Con Thien I was on my way to my watch at the

COC when a corpsman stuck his head out of a bunker that was near the road and yelled for me to help him carry a wounded Marine down to the battalion aid station. I was almost late for watch, and I resented the delay. I didn't want to take any static from the guy I was relieving. I thought, 'Why don't you have one of his friends help you?' but immediately realized that if there was anybody else in the bunker, the corpsman wouldn't have been looking for a passerby. Then I felt guilty.

As we carried the Marine down the rain soaked road, I tried to come up with a set of circumstances to explain how the wounded Marine and the corpsman had come to be in the bunker alone. I probably should have just asked the corpsman, but I didn't, afraid that the question would betray my selfish thought at the moment of being asked for much needed help.

Before I could come up with a scenario, a round came whistling in and we quickly put down the stretcher to cover up before it hit. As I crouched down and waited for the impact, I saw the corpsman kneel down in the muddy road, quickly unzip his flak jacket, and cover the wounded man's torso with his own, hanging the flak jacket down on each side of the wounded Marine, to better protect him from any shrapnel that might come our way. This put his own body about 18 inches higher than it would have been otherwise, greatly increasing his chance of being hit. Fortunately, no shrapnel came our way, and he was unharmed. We picked up the stretcher and continued on.

As gray as the skies were outside, when we entered the Battalion Aid Station, it seemed dark. The only source of light was a Coleman lamp, but, in the room made of dirty sandbags, there were no reflecting surfaces, and the light was immediately absorbed. A surgeon was waiting for us, and, as the corpsman and I held the stretcher up, he slid the wounded Marine onto the long wooden table that would serve as the operating theater. That was my cue to leave, and as I walked out into the rain, the corpsman and surgeon were already working on the wounded Marine, trying to stabilize him until a medevac chopper could get in.

Later that day I was on watch in the COC bunker, when an incoming round exploded in the ventilation shaft. The shaft was made from sandbags, and connected into the bunker by way of an L shaped area that came up against a rectangular hole cut high up on the wall. Air could move freely up the shaft, but there was no straight line view of the outside world, so when the round exploded, no shrapnel came into the bunker.

The noise was another story. Even though most of the blast had gone back up the shaft, and there was no significant concussion or pressure build up in the bunker, the sound was thunderous, filling the enclosed space, and then subsiding, seeming all the louder because of the total silence that followed it for an instant, while my auditory nerves recovered from having all their synapses fired at once.

I immediately checked the radios. Not one of the three was working. All the wires that went from the radios out through the ventilation shaft to the antennas outside had been cut by shrapnel. There were three antennas under the bench where the radios sat, two ten footers and a two foot whip. Since the radio we used to communicate with the companies had to operate over the shortest distance, I attached the two footer to that radio, but I was unable to raise any of the companies. I managed to bend the two ten foot antennas around the corner of the ventilation shaft and out to the world. Once they were bent it was a little tough to get them to screw on the radios without double threading, but I was able to do it. I got radio checks with each company on one radio, and with the regiment on the other. That was a relief because those were the two tactical nets. The third radio was just the admin net, used for passing back and forth paperwork type information. I decided that the best chance of getting that up quickly was to try and get a hold of one of the antenna wires above where the shrapnel had cut it, and pull it through and reattach it to the radio. I stood on the bench that held the radios and inserted my head and shoulders as far into the opening as I could, trying to reach around the corner and up the shaft to feel for any dangling wires.

Just then the battalion commander came over. He was new to the battalion, and he appeared to be upset. Perhaps the blast had been his introduction to combat. He said in a stressed tone, "What's the status on the radios?"

I pulled my head back into the bunker. "Sir, we've got the tactical nets out to the companies and up to the regiment running. The only radio still out is just the admin net, and I'm working on that now."

The colonel screamed, "What's taking so long? You should have these radios up by now."

I gave him, "Aye, Aye, Sir," as if I were responding to an order to get the radios up, and contorted my upper body back into the ventilation shaft. When I came back out with the antenna wire a minute or so later, the colonel had returned to his usual station near the maps of the area. I connected the wire to the third radio, and we had communications on the admin net. A total of about four minutes had elapsed since the blast, and we'd gone from zero radios up to having all three running. I was relieved to have all our communications up, and proud that I'd gotten it done so fast, and angry at the colonel's implication that my outstanding performance was somehow sub par.

I stewed about it for the rest of my watch. It was clear to me that this guy was just scared because the round had been close, but he was a colonel, and I was a corporal, so I just had to sit there and take it. There was no alternative. If I made a big deal about it, I would only get myself in trouble for insubordination. I flashed an image of a Marine Corps recruiting poster I'd seen just before leaving the states, the young Marine, handsome in his dress blues, staring proudly out of the bill board. I guess I've never really expected advertising to be totally up front, but as I sat there in my soggy, mud splattered jungle utilities, having just swallowed my pride once again, I couldn't help feeling that the advertising was downright deceptive. I guess obedience doesn't sell, and dress blues do, so the dress blues go on the poster, even though they aren't standard issue, and obedience training isn't mentioned on the poster, even though it is the essence of being a Marine.

About that time a photographer and a reporter arrived. The kind of bombardment that we were under on a daily basis was news. Nobody seemed to care that much about the photographer, except to say that he was crazy to be there, and especially crazy to be taking pictures when he should be covering up.

But the reporter was the talk of the base. Who did she talk to? What did she say? Where did she sleep? Especially where did she sleep. Because what made it important wasn't that she was a reporter but that she was a she, a caucasian she. As I try to write about it, I realize that there's essentially nothing to say. A reporter came, stayed overnight, had a few conversations, and left on the next day. What's the big deal?

But it was a big deal, and that in and of itself is the big deal, because it speaks to the unnatural state in which we normally lived. In all those bases across the top of I Corps, the bases next to the DMZ, there were no females stationed. At the time of that reporter's arrival, I had not seen an American woman for nearly six months. When I heard that she was on the base somewhere, I looked for her anytime I was out, hoping to see her moving between bunkers. When I was on watch I kept looking at the entrance of the COC bunker, hoping to catch a glimpse of her, if she came by to talk to the operations officer. Whenever anyone talked about her, I listened for every detail. I was essentially lovesick at the thought of her proximity, even though I never did see her.

I was glad when we got out of Con Thien. We had to walk out, just as we'd walked out of Gio Linh two months before, but this time I was mentally prepared for the fact that I'd be out of shape after living underground for a month. When we got back to Cam Lo, instead of staying there, we boarded trucks for Dong Ha, the largest and safest base in the area. They even had amenities like an enlisted club, a PX, and a daily beer ration.

The day after we got back, while I waited in the chow line for breakfast, two reporters came up and started interviewing the Marine in front of me. After the first few questions, when they were looking for information of a mundane sort, like name, rank, and home address, they started putting words into the Marine's mouth. They asked only leading questions, that were best answered with yes/no type responses - questions like, "Would you say that it was pretty tough going up there?" and, "I bet you're glad to be out of there, huh?" They didn't ask any open ended questions. They had absolutely no interest in finding out what this Marine might really have to say about the experience of being under constant bombardment for a month. It was pretty clear that they already had their stories written, at least in their minds, and that they were only looking for a few quotes that would fit the existing story, without causing any rewriting.

Watching them use that Marine to give authenticity to what was sure to be a hack story made me angry. I think it must have shown on my face, because one of the reporters kept glancing at me and quickly looking away to his partner, perhaps to see if he noticed my anger. I'd like to think that part of the reason they left quickly was that they were a little afraid of the potentially war crazed Marine who kept staring at them, but I probably give myself too much credit. They probably just had all the authentic quotes they needed and wanted to be off to file their stories quickly and take the rest of the day off.

Although I couldn't have named it at the time, I suffered from a prolonged anxiety attack during that first week out of Con Thien. It was triggered when I got my built up mail, which included several issues of Time magazine. One of them had a picture of Con Thien on the cover. Somehow the fact that my recent experience was the cover story in Time magazine, brought it home to me, made me feel it more deeply than when I'd been living it. It didn't quite make sense, because we'd been in Time magazine several times before, and on the cover too. Over the months that I'd been in Vietnam, my battalion had participated in some of the heaviest fighting of the war to that point.

I had never heard of post traumatic stress syndrome - I'm not even sure if that phrase existed yet. But fortunately I knew about the shell shock that many World War I trench fighters suffered, so I sort of understood what was going on when I suddenly became afraid, even though I had little to be afraid of. The Dong Ha base was the safest place I'd been since the day I arrived in Vietnam. They probably only averaged a few incoming rounds a week, and those were spread over a huge base, larger than all the other DMZ bases combined. Although it was possible, it was very unlikely that I would be hurt while I was on the Dong Ha base.

Yet for nearly a week, whenever I wasn't busy doing something, I was apprehensive, and sometimes downright afraid. It was fortunate that we were in such a safe place, because that gave me the capability to look at the situation logically, and try to calm myself by consciously recognizing that I was safe. At the same time I recognized that it was the very safety of Dong Ha that was somehow allowing the fear to surface. While I'd been at Con Thien, in constant danger of being blown to smithereens, I'd consciously felt little fear. I was pretty sure that if I'd still been in danger, I wouldn't be feeling anxious. Still, I'm not sure what would have happened if I'd been in a dangerous situation during that week, if the fear would have gotten out of control and overwhelmed me. Fortunately, after about a week, the anxiety left.

A few days after we got back, I ran into a guy from the telephone group who knew Red and I were friends. He told me Red had been killed by an artillery round just two days before we left Con Thien, a direct hit on his hooch. When the guy told me, he seemed to be watching me for a reaction, not like 'I hope you're going to be able to take this' watching, but like a voyeur. I didn't want to give him the satisfaction of seeing my emotion. I answered, "Better him than me," and walked away.

I meant it too. Not that I wasn't sorry Red was dead, especially since I felt like it was partly my fault. I kept remembering the day at Gio Linh when I'd told him I wanted to find a place to sleep outside. I felt like I had planted a seed that kept growing in his mind until it crowded out his common sense. I wondered too if I might have tried harder to convince him at Con Thien of how foolhardy it was to sleep in his little hooch.

Still, my reaction worried me. The war was changing me. I was disconnecting from the people at home, writing less often, feeling like there were too many things they couldn't understand. Now I saw that I had disconnected from my fellow Marines too. If I could feel 'Better him than me' about Red, my closest friend in the Nam, than I was not the same person who'd wanted to go out and rescue Moorehouse, a relative stranger, during my first night of action, months before. I had become a Marine. Not the dress blues, billboard Marine, standing proudly a hundred feet in the sky, but a jungle utility, combat Marine, down in the dirt, smart enough to know when to move and when to duck, cold enough to act or wait as the situation warranted, not proud at all.

The Rock Pile

After our week of rest at Dong Ha, we moved to a base called the Rock Pile, named after a nearby steep rock formation which gave a commanding view of the area. During most of those last few months, we never took in more than a few artillery or sniper rounds a day, and most days we took in none. The NVA was licking its wounds and rearming itself, getting ready for what would become known as the TET offensive. Fortunately I was gone two months before TET, another bullet dodged.

Sometimes it was almost too quiet. Whenever we would have a period of more than a week with no incoming, the officers and staff NCOs would begin stressing things like haircuts and boot polishing. When it got like that, I began to look forward to the next incoming rounds, although always hoping that nobody would get hurt by them, especially me.

Half the casualties in this quiet time seemed to be friendly fire incidents. One that I remember most clearly happened to a new radio operator who had just joined our group. All the line companies were out in the field, so H&S Company was manning the perimeter. At dusk, this new guy, probably barely nineteen, a sweet, funny kid who'd been a welcome addition to the radio group, was moving just outside the perimeter of line bunkers, but inside the barbed wire. He had a Claymore mine in one hand, and the hell box and blasting cap in the other, looking for a good place to set the mine. The wire that ran from the hell box to the blasting cap was tangled, and he was getting the kinks out as he walked down the hill. The hell box fell out of his hand, and he stepped on it. Either he didn't have the safety on, or, more likely, the weight of his body was sufficient to push the trigger right through the safety. I heard a small explosion, like a fire cracker going off, and then this guy was running back up the hill to us, crying, holding one bleeding hand in the other. His thumb was blown off. Two of the guys walked him to the Battalion Aid Station, and we never saw him again.

One minute peace and quiet, the next minute boom, another man lost. Vietnam was a place where anything could happen. You never knew when the next catastrophe would strike, or whom; you just knew that it would be coming, and probably soon. Even in this relatively quiet time, the feeling that we were sitting on a bullseye, and Charlie was taking aim, a feeling I'd had since day one when we were floating down the Dong Ha River, never left me.

Around that time somebody got a package from home that included a bottle of scotch. As was the custom on those rare occasions when someone got booze from home, everyone who was off duty in the evening crowded together in the recipient's bunker for a party. This was particularly fortuitous, because it was my twenty-first birthday.

After a couple of hours of laughing in the circle of light from a Coleman lantern, I left, because I had to get up in a few hours for the midnight watch. As I climbed out of the bunker and the fresh air hit me, I suddenly realized that I was drunk. As I slowly made my way to my bunker, I was finding it difficult to apply the concentration needed to keep myself oriented in the dark. Finally, when I bumped into a bunker that I didn't think should be where it was, I was forced to just stand in one place for several minutes, barely able to keep myself upright.

I berated myself for being drunk. What if something happened right then, as it could at any moment. I could get myself killed, or, if called on for radio watch, I could get lots of people killed. I was ashamed of myself, because getting drunk or high was something that we just didn't do. Sure there were rumors that there was a laundry guy who was a good source of pot, but I didn't know anybody who used his services. Sure Sergeant Miser was drunk all the time, but he was a staff NCO, an administrator without any real responsibility for life and death stuff. Those of us who did the real work stayed sober.

Finally, after several minutes, my night vision began to kick in. I made my way to my bunker and fell asleep. Fortunately, it was a quiet night, and by the time someone woke me for my normal watch, I was sober again.

One day when I was on radio watch in the COC a long range recon Marine, his face blackened with camouflage paint, came in carrying a pack of the food he would eat for the next few days, a radio, spare batteries, the works. He was going out alone into the woods, and needed to coordinate his mission with the battalion, to know how to talk to us on the radio and to make sure that we didn't fire any artillery into the areas where he would be each day.

It didn't mean anything to me until a couple of nights later when I overheard him calling in on the artillery radios. He'd come across a unit of NVA and was asking for an artillery mission on the site, which was less than a hundred yards from him. His voice was barely audible because he was whispering the coordinates into his handset, and that was what made me finally understand. This guy was out there alone, in the middle of the night, in unfamiliar territory, in close proximity to the NVA, being the eyes and ears for my battalion.

I could trade war stories with just about anyone and not feel like I owed them a thing. I was doing my part. But there were guys out there doing more, lots more. Maybe I felt the relative difference in danger strongly right then, because it had been quiet for a while, but I was OK with that. I didn't want to trade places with the recon guy, to even things out by increasing my danger to the level of his. The danger was too real.

When I had just over a month left to do in-country, I got to go on R&R. I could have gone a month earlier, but decided to wait so that I wouldn't have much time left to do when I got back, and so that I could have an extra month to save up for it. With my combat pay and the fact that we didn't have to pay any income taxes while stationed in a combat zone, I had been taking home $212 a month. I had sent most of it home, but I had managed to save the $200 that I would need for the five day R&R trip. Although I would have loved to see Australia or Hawaii, or especially to go to Bangkok, the city reputed to have the most beautiful women in the world, I signed up to go to Taipei, Taiwan, because that was the least expensive R&R destination, the only one I could afford with only $200 to spend.

I was amazed by the efficiency of the R&R operation. I got a ride on an empty supply truck returning to Dong Ha, boarded a C-123 cargo plane to Da Nang, and got on a bus that went through a teeming civilian area to another part of the base where commercial flights landed. I presented my orders at the airlines desk - I think it might have been Flying Tiger Airlines, because I remember several airplanes on the tarmac with the tiger face painted on the sides - and was told that I would be on the next flight to Taipei, leaving in less than three hours.

I killed some time at a nearby self service coffee bar, run by a uniformed, female Red Cross worker. I tried to read my book, "Catch-22" of all things, but I actually spent most of my time just watching her as she moved among the tables. She was the first Caucasian woman I'd seen in Vietnam. Da Nang was certainly a different world from the DMZ area where I'd come from. I must have been looking at her too hungrily though, because, even though I was at the snack bar for over an hour, she never quite got to my table as she made her rounds, kibitzing with the other GI's.

When the plane landed at Taipei, we boarded a bus on the tarmac and, during the ride to the terminal building, we were assigned to hotels. When we got off the bus, representatives from the various hotels were there to greet us.

I'm not sure if they were independent guides working for commissions, or if they actually worked for the hotels. My guide, a man named Yung, took myself and another Marine named Ted to our hotel. I don't remember the name of the place, having needed to know the name for only the few minutes that it took to find Yung. He got us checked in, then took us to our rooms and told us to wait there. A few minutes later, he was back with the hotel's tailor, there to measure us for any clothes we would need. My own civilian clothes had been shredded by shrapnel on my sixth night in Vietnam, but, I'd borrowed civilian clothes from Lash, one of the Marines in the operations group who was my size, so I didn't need to buy any.

I unpacked my ditty bag, took off my green jungle utilities, took a quick shower, and, for the first time since I'd left Okinawa, put on civilian clothes. About fifteen minutes later, Yung came by with Ted and drove us to a night club, where a dozen women waited. No one else was there except the bartender. Yung chose a booth for us, got us a drink at the bar, and took our money for the drink. In a minute he was back with two of the women. I danced one dance with Katy who was a little older than I would have chosen for myself, probably in her mid twenties. Still, I didn't want to offend her, so I didn't ask Yung to get me someone my own age. At the end of the song, Ted and I guzzled our beer, and then the five of us headed back to the hotel. No wonder the bar was empty.

Yung left us at the hotel, where Ted and I split up. Katy named her price, $2 for an hour or $4 for 24 hours. I don't know if I was supposed to negotiate, but it didn't seem like much money to me. It probably seemed like a lot to Katy. At that time a factory worker in Taipei made $20 a month, if he could find a job. Nothing in Katy's manner indicated that the rate might be negotiable. I gave her $20 for the five days.

Katy took my $20 and brought me to the front desk, where she had to check in and show her prostitute's license and my room key. At that time the sex industry in Taiwan was legal and a major source of foreign currency, and it was highly regulated. Prostitutes had to see a doctor twice a month to make sure that they stayed healthy and didn't spread disease, and no decent hotel would admit a prostitute unless she showed proof that her license was current. At the same time, showing my room key protected her, since it provided an easy trail to follow if she ended up hurt or missing.

Back in the room, I took another quick shower - Katy demanded it even though I told her I'd taken a shower only an hour before - and then I was banished from the bathroom while Katy took a bath and made her preparations. I got into bed and waited, but after a few minutes, I decided that it was going to be a while, and found my book. When Katy finally came back from the bathroom, I was in mid sentence, so I read for a few seconds more to finish the paragraph before looking up to see her standing naked beside the bed.

Hands on her hips, she said, "So, you just want to lay there and read then."

I threw the book on the night table, and pulled back the sheets so that she could see that reading was not my primary interest at the moment. She noted my interest, but made me wait a few seconds before climbing in next to me, her body still warm and fragrant from the hot bath.

For the next four days, Katy and Yung ran my life, making all the decisions about where we would go, and what we would do. I was so used to being told where and when by the Marine Corps, that it didn't even seem odd to me. Somebody had to make the decisions. Besides, Katy knew how much money I had, and seemed to take personal responsibility for seeing that it lasted the whole five days. For example, one afternoon she took me souvenir shopping. I wanted to buy some silk for my mother, who liked to sew, and Katy helped me choose a few nice pieces of fabric. I offered to pay a little less than the asking price, and the vendor accepted. Then Katy said, "No, that's too much." She spoke heatedly in Chinese with the vendor, and I ended up paying less than half the price that I had negotiated myself.

The main expense was for meals. We ate all our meals out, and, naturally, I picked up the tab for both myself and Katy. If Yung drove us to an activity, Ted was usually present too, so Ted and I would split the cost of Yung's meal and admission. We seemed to have one group activity a day, but it was usually something inexpensive like a boat ride in the park.

One afternoon, Katy and I took a walk to her house, where she lived with her parents. I was a little surprised and apprehensive when I found out where we were going, but when we got there nobody else was home. We went to Katy's room so she could get some fresh clothes - she'd been washing hers by hand and hanging them over the tub each night - and so she could be among her own things. The hotel was the height of luxury for me, coming from living in holes in the ground, but it must have been just a sterile room for Katy.

For a while she sat on her bed and read through some letters from a fairly large bundle that she kept in a carved wooden box. They were letters from a GI who had been stationed on Taiwan. They'd fallen in love, but he couldn't get permission to marry her from his CO. He'd been transferred out at the end of his tour of duty, but he was supposed to come and marry her when he got out of the service. I was jealous.

On my last night in Taiwan, we went to Katy's house once again. She had three brothers who were fishermen, at sea for weeks at a time, and their boat had come in that day. None of them spoke English as well as Katy, but each one did his best with smiles, gestures and a few words to make me feel welcome. I imagine they knew why Katy and I were together that night, but they accepted me into their home with kindness. Even though most of the conversation was in Chinese, they seemed to take turns talking to me in halting English, so that I wouldn't feel left out of the party. To be polite I had a water glass of rice wine with each brother and by the end of the evening I was so drunk that Katy had to call a taxi to take us back to the hotel.

I fell into bed as soon as I finished undressing, too drunk for sex that night. Katy got me up the next morning, but there was no time for sex. Once I realized, I regretted drinking so much rice wine the night before. Even though I was somewhat satiated at the moment, I knew that I would be back in a state of constant horniness soon, and, because of my drunkenness the night before, it would happen a day sooner than was absolutely necessary.

When I got out of the shower, my bag was packed with my civilian clothes, and my jungle utilities were laid out on the bed. I put them on, and vacation was over. I was back in the Green Machine. Katy called a cab and got me to the air base just in time to check in for my flight back to Da Nang, a feat that I might not have managed on my own in my seriously hung over state. I kissed her goodbye and gave her all the rest of my money. There wasn't much left.

At Da Nang, it took a while to catch a flight back to Dong Ha. Going in that direction the planes were always filled with cargo, so there was only room for a few passengers on each plane. When my flight was due to leave, they were looking for volunteers to go on the next plane instead. I was tempted to volunteer. I'd heard about one guy who'd extended his R&R by three days in Da Nang, just by getting himself bumped off the plane time after time. The base was huge and it seemed so much safer there. Not totally safe like out of country R&R had been, but relatively safe compared with the smaller bases on the DMZ, where the artillery attacks were concentrated in a much smaller area, and where a determined ground attack could actually overrun a base. After being safe for five days, it was hard to go back. Plus, in Da Nang, my only job would be signing up for flights and volunteering to get bumped off of them, pretty easy work. It was actually thinking about the lack of work that got me to go back. I remembered that the guys back at the Rock Pile had been pulling extra radio watches for five days so that I could relax and drink and screw to my heart's content. I got on the plane back to Dong Ha and was at the Rock Pile by late afternoon, in time to stand my own watch that night.

Shortly after I returned from R&R, with less than a month to do in Vietnam, I went to see the First Sergeant at his office tent. I was beginning to think that I had a good chance of surviving, and I couldn't stand the thought of having to return to the stateside Marine Corps for three months. I wanted to stay in Vietnam until the end of my enlistment, then just fly home and be a civilian.

There was another reason I wanted to stay too, a nebulous thought that floated through my mind occasionally, but one that I feared so greatly that I couldn't latch onto it to give it words. Even though I yearned to go home every day, the thought of it always in the background, adding its melancholy flavor to nearly every moment, I was a little afraid to go home, afraid I wouldn't be able to fit in, that somehow the combat experience had made me so odd that normal people wouldn't want to be around me. I was afraid that my friends would fear me, fear that I could explode at any moment, killing everybody. I was afraid that they wouldn't like me any more. I was also afraid that their fear would be well founded. Maybe I was a walking time bomb. The idea that war veterans were inherently unstable was certainly one that pervaded our culture. The media frequently mentioned the veteran's status of anyone who committed a mass murder, but only if he was a veteran, implying a causal relationship.

When I explained to the First Sergeant what I wanted, using only the reason that I liked it better in Vietnam than on any of the bases where I'd been stationed in the States, he looked at me carefully for a few seconds before speaking. Then he explained that, in general, the Marine Corps didn't make a habit of sending men straight from combat into civilian life, without a transition period. Since it would have been counterproductive to piss off the First Sergeant, I didn't mention that the Marine Corps had sent Sharpie straight home a few months before, but, while I was sitting there thinking it, the First Sergeant began looking in a couple of manuals. After a few minutes he told me that he couldn't do it. I could extend my Vietnam tour of duty in six months increments, but to do that I would have to extend my Marine Corps enlistment, also in six months increments. Bottom line, I would still have three months to do in the stateside Marine Corps at the end of it all. I thanked the First Sergeant for his time.

It looked like I was going to be going home in a few weeks. That thought made me nervous. Just as, early in my tour of duty, accepting the likelihood of my death had helped to calm me, realizing that I had so little time left that it was conceivable that I could actually survive, especially now that things had gotten relatively quiet, made me anxious. I still laughed every day, just as hard as in the middle of my tour, but now my laugh sometimes had a forced quality to it. I was uptight, counting down each day on my mental short timer's calendar. The fear and anticipation mixed together in just the right proportion to lengthen time, making each day seem interminable.

Home

They sent me back to Dong Ha on Christmas eve. My flight wasn't until December 26, but they sent me back a couple of days early, in case Charlie might have something planned for the holidays. It was the loneliest Christmas of my life, separated from my buddies at the Rock Pile, but not back to my family yet, just waiting, waiting.

Finally December 26 arrived. I walked over to the air strip and handed in my orders to proceed home for thirty days leave and then to proceed to Quantico, Virginia. Just as on my R&R I caught an empty C-123 down to Da Nang right away. The only real difference was my emotion. For the R&R trip I'd been excited. For the trip home I was a nervous wreck. All I could think about was the often told story of the guy who was on his flight home, when a sniper round came through the bottom of the plane and killed him. Logically I knew that it might not even be a true story, or that it might have happened once or twice, but that it wasn't likely to happen right now, to me, on my plane. I knew that it didn't make any real sense to be afraid, because most of the time when you were, nothing happened anyway, and, at a time when you weren't particularly afraid, something could get you from out of nowhere. It was all pretty random. But all my logical thought had no effect on my emotion. I was a basket case.

I can't even remember if the flight to Okinawa, the first leg of the journey home, was a commercial flight or military. I suspect military, because I don't remember riding to the commercial side of the base, but I also don't remember showing my orders, boarding the plane, or doing anything else that I must have done before sitting in my seat on the plane that was to take me home. But I do remember sitting there on the plane at the end of the runway, looking out the window, and realizing that we were going to take off headed inland. As we accelerated down the runway, I saw a Marine on the other side of the aisle slide his hands under his butt. It seemed like a good idea, so, as the plane lifted off, I did the same. Then the guy next to me slid his hands under his butt. It seemed like a lot of people were thinking about the story where a sniper gets you at the last minute.

As the plane climbed we began a wide banking turn. I wished we were higher. Our flight path was taking us over a lot of land. Was it all under our control? Was any of it? Still, it was beautiful. At one point in the turn, the plane was positioned in exactly the right spot, and I saw a flash of sun reflecting off a body of water that was surrounded by the lush green land. It was like Vietnam winked goodbye to us. A few seconds later I could see the white beach of the coastline coming into view, with the ocean and safety beyond it, then the plane straightened and I couldn't see anything but sky past the wing. In about a minute, the captain came on the PA to announce that we were over international waters. I joined the spontaneous cheer that filled the cabin. It was low at first, almost a growl, caused by the release of partly held breath. Then on the next breath it swelled to fill the cabin, drowning out the throb of the engines for a few seconds. We had left Vietnam, the place where anything could happen, and were back in the world. I took my hands off my ass and leaned my seat back. I'd made it through. I was actually going home.

The trip took a little over two days, including a half day of time zone differences. There was an overnight on Okinawa, where I learned that most of the uniforms in my long term storage sea bag had been destroyed by mold. Fortunately, I had a uniform to wear home that hadn't been destroyed by mold in Okinawa or shrapnel in Vietnam. It was a summer uniform, and it was December, but I needed to be in uniform so I could fly military standby for the last leg of my trip, a commercial flight from Los Angeles to Washington, D.C. The cost saving would give me spending money for my thirty days of leave.

In the evening of my second day after leaving Vietnam, I arrived in uniform at the airport in Washington, D.C. I got into the cab at the front of the line and gave the cabbie my mother's address. I rode in silence for a few minutes, but then my excitement bubbled over. "Hey, man, I just got home from Vietnam today."

The cabbie glanced at me in his rear view mirror and said, "Yeah, fine."

I checked the name on his license to see if maybe there could be some kind of a language problem, then I tried again. "I'm going to see my mother for the first time in over a year."

"Yeah, fine."

I detected no trace of a foreign accent. This guy could understand me perfectly. Then I suddenly understood. He was probably one of the millions of Americans I'd been reading about who opposed the war and thought that the military was to blame for it. I'd expected that he would share my excitement, and thank me enthusiastically for my contribution, but I was disappointed.

A few minutes later we arrived at my mother's house. Normally I thank a person who provides me with a service, but I didn't thank the taxi driver. I gave him a normal tip - he still had to make a living - but I was angry, and I didn't thank him, neither one of us getting the thanks we deserved for the service we'd performed.

I put my sea bag on my shoulder and bounded up the stairs to the front door. I rang the bell, opened the storm door, and dropped my sea bag on the porch. My mother flung the door open, and we hugged. This was how a homecoming was supposed to be.

As I hugged my mother, reality pierced my expectation of what it would be like to see her again. This would be a common event over the next months, as my dream of coming home to my old life was fulfilled, but not exactly as I dreamed it. As I stood there in my first homecoming embrace, I realized how thin my mother had become. The stress of my being in combat had sometimes made it difficult for her to eat. On the day I got home, she weighed less than a hundred pounds. I'd known that my being in Vietnam would be tough on her, but, fortunately, I didn't find out just how hard it had been until I got home. Over the next six months she would return to her normal weight.

The first of my last three months in the stateside Marine Corps went by quickly, because I was on leave. The last two months were molasses. I was stationed at Quantico, Virginia, providing radio communications for the various officer training companies, when they would go out on long field marches. I can see now that it was pretty good duty, but, at the time, I was just wishing away the days, counting down to my discharge.

Finally the day came, March 28, 1968. I reported to the office to get my final orders. The officer there was a little perturbed because I'd used more than 60 days leave, which was all you were supposed to get on a two year enlistment. I explained that I hadn't put in for any leave, that the Marine Corps had just automatically given me leave at the end of my initial training, and then long leaves before and after going to Vietnam. I'd just been doing what I was told. He looked at the record and was apparently satisfied that I hadn't deliberately tried to shorten my enlistment by requesting excess leave for individual reasons. He told me that he was going to have to dock my final paycheck for the excess leave time, which may be what put him in a bad mood, since it probably meant extra paperwork for him.

He gave me my pay, the money for my flight to Boston, and my orders. I was to report to my reserve unit at the Fargo Building in Boston anytime in the next five days. Even though he'd been a jerk, not unusual for an officer, I gave him a smart salute. He still seemed to be in a bad mood, and I wasn't going to blow it at the last minute with a charge of insubordination. I did a sharp about face and marched out the door, a free man.

Somehow it took the whole five days for the one day trip to the Fargo Building. It was less than a mile from South Station, where I'd started my journey to Parris Island on the first day of my enlistment, and across the street from the old army base, where I'd had my draft physical. I turned in my orders at the office of my reserve unit, which apparently had a few permanent personnel who were there full time. They took my green ID badge and replaced it with a pink reservist's ID badge. When I was just about ready to go, the officer in charge came out of his office to talk to me.

He explained that I was now a member of the active reserve, and would be for the next four years. I could be called up for duty anytime the Marine Corps needed me during that four year period. My status was the same as someone who signed up for the active reserves in the first place, but only did six months of active duty. The only real difference was that someone who did only six months of active duty was required to attend reserve meetings one weekend a month and to do two weeks of active duty in the summer, while I was not.

At the end of his canned explanation the officer took on a friendly tone. "You know, we could use a guy like you, with combat experience as a radio operator, in a more active role in this unit. If you wanted to attend meetings, we could sign you up for that. It would be extra income every month, for just a little extra work, like having a little part time job on the side. We have a meeting this weekend. Why don't you stop by on Saturday morning to meet the guys? No commitment. It's a real good group. You'll like them."

It was flattering to hear that I had a skill that was needed in the unit, and the guy seemed pretty nice, even though he was an officer. Although I was a little wary, I meant it when I said, "OK, sir. I'll stop by on Saturday."

But when I walked up Summer Street, away from the spiel, I thought about what those weekends would really be like, the boredom of maintaining the equipment, the stress while they inspected everything - always managing to find something wrong, however trivial, just so they could justify their own existence - and the subordination to those of superior rank, whether they actually deserved respect or not.

Then my body voted. My abdomen knotted in a cramp that was designed to exercise veto power. What was I doing, letting a little sweet talk convince me to stop by. As soon as they got me there, they'd be on me with nice until I signed up to attend meetings, then they'd just be on me period, for the next four years.

I took deep breaths until the cramp eased, and then went on my way. I didn't stop by that Saturday or any other Saturday. I became a former Marine.

Epilogue

It was about a year after I got out of the Marine Corps. I was working the graveyard shift at the South Postal Annex in Boston, and going to school at the downtown Boston campus of the University of Massachusetts, only a few minutes bike ride from work. Tufts hadn't seemed to have that "Welcome home vets" spirit. They had wanted me to pay for a whole semester on my own before they would even consider reinstating my scholarship, with no guarantee that they would give me any financial aid then. I didn't want to put off getting back to school for the extra year it would take me to save that much money, especially since, if Tufts didn't come through, I might end up having to quit after a semester. The University of Massachusetts at Boston was the answer.

I was much more careful about getting enough sleep than I had been before the Marine Corps. I scheduled all my classes as early in the day as I could, so I was done by noon and usually home and in bed by one in the afternoon. I used every minute between classes to study, and avoided the student cafeteria completely, fearing that if I went there at all, I would soon be laughing it up and wasting as much time as I had at Tufts. I had no free time during the school year, but I was doing well, with no sign of fatigue buildup. A somewhat altered version of my plan was working. I was going to succeed this time.

In those polarized days, there were Hawks and Doves, and I was definitely a Hawk. I didn't understand what the protest against the Vietnam War was about, and resented the fact that I had not received a hero's welcome when I returned from Vietnam. I thought that the protest endangered our troops by giving the North Vietnamese hope that we would eventually pull out. I still felt as I had when I was on the DMZ, that winning every battle that the North Vietnamese brought to us was not enough. We owed it to the South Vietnamese and to the Americans who were fighting there to win the war, that is, to invade North Vietnam on the ground and finish it, even if that meant the Chinese would invade from the north, as they had in Korea. I didn't want everything that I and my fellow Marines had been through to be wasted.

One day a large manila envelope arrived from the Somerville draft board office. The draft board didn't send it, but that's where it was from. My father told me the envelope was there, even though it was addressed to Phil, my youngest brother, who was draft eligible. Phil wasn't home at the time, and even though we never opened each other's mail, I opened that envelope. It contained Phil's draft records, along with a letter stating that they had been stolen as a protest against the war.

I sat at the kitchen table for nearly half an hour, my eyes staring at the documents, my mind ten thousand miles away. The situation seemed to be that Phil had signed up for the draft and had a legitimate draft card in his wallet. If he ever got stopped, he was legal. Yet, in my hands, I held what appeared to be the records that could remind the local draft board of his existence.

Without telling my father what I was about to do, I took our largest cast iron frying pan out of the pantry. At the stove I crumpled up the first document from the envelope and lit a match to it. When I saw how much smoke there was, I started to run into the bathroom with the paper still burning in the pan. I saw the ball of hot, smoking ash dancing in the air current caused by my motion, and, afraid that the embers might fly out of the pan and start a fire in the house, I slowed to a walk.

I closed the bathroom door, set the pan down on top of the sink, and opened the window. This was better than the kitchen anyway. Instead of putting the ashes in the trash, where the FBI could find them and use them to incriminate me, I could flush them down the toilet, where they would disappear into the Somerville sewer system, unrecoverable. I guess I had an unrealistic view of what resources the government had at its disposal to enforce the draft laws.

One by one I burned each sheet of documentation completely. When there were scraps of unburned paper left, I placed them in the middle of the next sheet before crumpling it up and setting a match to it. I was working as fast as I could, listening for the FBI's knock on the front door, wanting to be finished. Finally all that was left was the envelope that the documents had arrived in. When I burned that, there was a lot more smoke. I fanned the air to thin it out before it went out the window, hoping nobody outside would notice it and report a fire. Finally the envelope too was just a ball of ash. I dumped it into the toilet and flushed three times, carefully inspecting the toilet bowl to make sure that there were no incriminating traces left. I brought the frying pan out to the kitchen sink, washed it thoroughly, and put it back in the pantry.

My youngest brother was safe from the draft. The evidence of the felony that made it so was destroyed. I could be a Hawk as long as it was someone else's brother who would go to the war.

Afterword

I'm guessing that, if you made it this far in the book, you thought it was a good use of your time to read it. If you can think of anyone else who might benefit from reading this book, please be sure to tell them about it. I think it's a good book, but there is no huge PR budget to get the word out. I'm depending on you, the reader, to do that.

Made in the USA
Charleston, SC
11 December 2011